# The Magic of the Scented Flowers

# The Magic of the Scented Flowers

Unfolding the healing power
of *The Scented Flowers*
of *Sinjin-Ka* in crafting an
elegant and magical life

## Martin Hart

**ASAT Press**
*Topsfield, Massachusetts*

Published by ASAT Press

Designed by creativepublishingdesign.com

Copyright © Martin Hart 2020

All rights reserved. No part of this publication may be reproduced, stored in a retrieval system, or transmitted in any form or by any means, electric, mechanical, photocopying, recording or otherwise, without the prior permission of the copyright owner.

For press and media related inquiries, contact: Martin Hart, asat@asat.org

Paperback / Softcover ISBN: 978-0-9895518-3-0

eBook ISBN: 978-0-9895518-4-7

Library of Congress Control Number: 2020908945

Copies are available at special rates for bulk orders. Contact the sales team at ASAT Press, asat@asat.org

I wrote this book for me.

*May he exercise the strength and wisdom
to become more from the practice and living of it.*

# Dedication

For Lazaris and Rho
*My friends and guiding light upon my journey
Coming Home*

# Table of Contents

### Introduction

### Cultivating *The Scented Flowers*
#### Working the Magic and Healing of *'The Scented Flowers of Sinjin-Ka'*

One Story Oracle ..................................................................................10
Three Story Oracle ................................................................................11
Writing Your Own Interpretation .........................................................12
Freewriting .............................................................................................12
Working With Your Healing Community ............................................14
Working With Your Spiritual Family ....................................................16
The Meditation ......................................................................................17
Using the Cross-Reference Chart .........................................................19

### The Oracle of *The Scented Flowers*
#### The Commentaries

01: The Fool and the Apple .................................................................23
02: Not Enough Enough .....................................................................26
03: Where the Animals Went to Die ..................................................29
04: The Disciple and the Idiot ............................................................32
05: A Gift from a Squished Squirrel ..................................................35
06: The Doll Maker's Helper ...............................................................37
07: The Witch of the Darkened Wood ..............................................40
08: Standing Before the Judge ..........................................................43
09: The Love of Winning ....................................................................45
10: Gobi's Tiny Seeds ..........................................................................48
11: The Testing of Amit Don ..............................................................52

| 12: | The Man Who Walked Backward | 55 |
| 13: | The Saint Who Could Not Be Harmed | 58 |
| 14: | What Danila Learned of Love | 61 |
| 15: | How the Master Found Enlightenment | 65 |
| 16: | The Man Who Said, "Thank You" | 68 |
| 17: | Nilla's Dearest Friend | 71 |
| 18: | A Lesson on Believing You're Special | 74 |
| 19: | The River | 76 |
| 20: | The Tale of the Chuckling Saint | 79 |
| 21: | Two Healings | 82 |
| 22: | The Path Maker | 85 |
| 23: | Mohan at the Gate of Bliss | 87 |
| 24: | Rumesh Pays Respect | 90 |
| 25: | The Saint Who Loved Science | 92 |
| 26: | The Two Lovers Who Never Met | 95 |
| 27: | The Answer is Always, "Yes" | 97 |
| 28: | In the Fire of the Muse | 99 |
| 29: | What a Rare and Special Child! | 102 |
| 30: | The Secret Teaching | 105 |
| 31: | Kotia and the Bawdy Woman | 107 |
| 32: | Bindu at the End of the World | 109 |
| 33: | Martyr's Many Lifetimes | 112 |
| 34: | Three Old Women | 114 |
| 35: | Gopol Talks to God | 117 |
| 36: | The Actor Assumes His Role | 119 |
| 37: | The Greatest Gift | 122 |
| 38: | Thirty Days in the Infinite | 125 |
| 39: | Sundeep and the Simple life | 128 |
| 40: | The King of Beasts | 130 |
| 41: | A Legitimate Profession | 132 |
| 42: | A Tale of Two Villages | 134 |
| 43: | The Captain and the Sea | 137 |
| 44: | An Abandoned Garden | 140 |

| | | |
|---|---|---|
| 45: | The Purpose of Life | 142 |
| 46: | The Passing of the Torch | 145 |
| 47: | The Poet's Skill at Fishing | 148 |
| 48: | Rathgar Gets His Name | 151 |
| 49: | The Counting of the Stars | 154 |
| 50: | The Way of the Dreamer | 156 |
| 51: | The Laughing Fool of Binduvan | 159 |
| 52: | The Thousand Coats of Suma Ti | 161 |
| 53: | In the Valley of the Singing Stones | 163 |
| 54: | Just Imagine | 165 |
| 55: | A Marriage Made in Heaven | 168 |
| 56: | The Eternal Companion | 170 |
| 57: | Manju Among the Saints | 173 |
| 58: | The Selfishly Generous Woman | 175 |
| 59: | The Master's Perfect Imperfection | 178 |
| 60: | King or Seeker | 180 |
| 61: | Where the Two Worlds Meet | 182 |
| 62: | My Life Has Never Been So Bad | 184 |
| 63: | Mother Seagull and the Ocean | 187 |
| 64: | The Man Who Talked With Trees | 189 |
| 65: | Mukta and the Magic Purse | 192 |
| 66: | Sinji's One and Only Tale | 196 |
| 67: | A Simple Tale of Hope | 199 |
| 68: | Coming Home | 201 |
| 69: | Sumitra and Her Friends | 204 |
| 70: | The Sweet Old Couple | 206 |
| 71: | A Most Unconventional Master | 209 |
| 72: | The Secret of Sima Sen | 211 |
| 73: | The Sweet Taste of Vindication | 214 |
| 74: | What Kamila Learned from a Chipmunk | 217 |
| 75: | Galen's Glimpse of Hell | 220 |
| 76: | Being Real | 223 |
| 77: | Grandmother Seeta's Words of Wisdom | 226 |

78: Holiest of Holies ............................................................................ 228
79: Entering the Hall of Eternal Bliss .................................................. 231
80: The Gathering ................................................................................ 233
81: Tandori Had Two Teachers ............................................................ 236
82: The Child Who Could .................................................................... 239
83: Amil and the Most Beautiful Flower ............................................ 242
84: The Woman Who Had Everything ................................................ 244
85: The Demon Within ........................................................................ 247
86: The Artist and the Fisherman ...................................................... 252
87: The Compassionate Thing to Do .................................................. 255
88: Knowing .......................................................................................... 258
89: Some Things Are Just Worth Saving ............................................ 260
90: The Ministers of Kushtan .............................................................. 263
91: A Gift of Laughter .......................................................................... 265

# Appendix One
Working With Your Many Selves

# Appendix Two
Questions and Answers

# Appendix Three
Cross-Reference Chart

# Appendix Four
Glossary

# About the Author

# Introduction

I wrote this book as a companion to **The Scented Flowers of Sinjin-Ka** (*ASAT Press*), a collection of ninety-one short tales. I wrote it for the reader who, having been touched by the book's magic and teachings, would like to take the magic and teachings to another level, a healing level.

This book is not for everyone. Why? Not everyone relates to the stories. Not everyone senses their magic. Not everyone journeys its magical path. I would never suggest this path is better, but I will suggest it's different. If the magical tales in *The Scented Flowers of Sinjin-Ka* speak to you, if you wish to take their teachings further, then this book may be for you. This book could be a powerful addition to your healing and growing work, and a companion on your unique journey of self-awakening, self-discovery, and Coming Home.

I did not set out to write *The Scented Flowers of Sinjin-Ka*. I was working on another book at the time. But during the summer of 2014, the first of the stories appeared. Over the next thirty days, the ninety-one tales sprang up, often at mind-numbing speed. I would awaken in the middle of the night and start working on a rough draft for a new story. I often interrupted daily activities to jot notes or record passages. On several occasions, while driving, I had to pull over to the curb to write down ideas for fear I'd forget them. On the thirtieth day, the last of the tales came through; no more appeared after that.

All in all, it was an exciting time and a scary time, a fun time, and a crazy time. But it was, above all else, a magical time. I also learned to pace myself, a gift I truly cherish. And I also improved my parallel parking.

But what was I going to do with these stories? What's next for them? It wasn't until a few months later that I came up with the idea of incorporating them into my counseling and group work. Why not? They'd be an interesting conversation starter.

I'd begin sessions by asking clients or students to close their eyes and pick a number from one to ninety-one. Then I'd ask them to read the story corresponding to the number.

Well, ka-boom!

The results were mind-boggling! The synchronicity was astonishing! It turned out that the stories, each randomly selected, related precisely to an issue needing attention in the person's life at the current time. The readings led to amazing sessions. Each story read, along with the subsequent discussion, led to breakthroughs and healings at profound levels, and each tale provided valuable insights for future processing. The whole experience was not only fun; It was magical.

Every story in *The Scented Flowers of Sinjin-Ka* teaches a valuable lesson, and every tale addresses a topic that, when worked with, will further the reader's self-understanding, advance the reader's self-development, and contribute to the reader's self-healing. The stories are road-maps for a journey of immeasurable growth and awakening. With this in mind, and with their successful use with clients and students, I began writing commentaries on each tale.

I wanted the commentaries to serve as a starting point for self-discovery, self-understanding, and self-healing. I wanted the commentaries to open the reader to synchronicities and magic on the journey he or she is currently on. And I wanted the commentaries to be another way to channel the guidance and wisdom of the reader's Higher Self for even greater awakenings and change. And I also felt that the stories and commentaries, when working together, would allow both the left and right brain equal participation in the healing process.

So this book, **The Magic of the Scented Flowers** came to be. It's written to be an oracle of self-exploration. Its objective is to serve as a means for deeper, more profound healing. And it will, if used wisely, provide a way for the reader to process his or her healing and growing independently. And, of course, it's written to be fun and magical.

*The Magic of the Scented Flowers* is, in a sense, the workbook for *The Scented Flowers of Sinjin-Ka*. Combined, they'll serve as an excellent guide on your unique journey of growth and discovery. Approaching this work with honesty and humility will open you to insights and revelations that can, and will, help awaken the 'more' of you.

These are books of stories. These are books of healing. These are books of magic. They're books of your story, your healing, and your magic if you'll allow them to be so.

You're about to embark on a new phase of your journey. Let it be magical, mystical, enchanting, and fun. Be willing to explore the mysterious unknown that lies before you. On the other side is the *'you'* you've always sought to become and so very much more. On the other side, your Future Self and your Truer Self wait with arms wide open.

Enjoy!

# Cultivating
# 'The Scented Flowers'

### Working the Magic and Healing of
### *'The Scented Flowers of Sinjin-Ka'*

Thousands of years ago, people sought the counsel of oracles. They believed these hermit messengers of the gods could help them navigate the rigors of daily life. While their messages were often vague and confusing, people found solace in their guidance and direction.

*"Will my daughter marry a wealthy man?"*
*"Will the weather be favorable to my crops?"*
*"Will I find the love I seek?"*
*"Will the gods please change my child's behavior?"*

In time the form changed from half-crazed oracles in musty caves with weird sounding disembodied voices to a somewhat less dramatic approach. People now sought the counsel of the gods through sacred objects and divinely inspired tales. Oracles became cards, bones, coins, stones, tea leaves, and the recitation of sacred stories. From tarot card readings to Viking runes, from the I Ching to bone castings, from tea leaf scrying to recitations of epic songs, people pursued ever-elusive divine guidance. All life's wisdom and answers were pursued with great hope and zeal.

*"Will my daughter marry a wealthy man?"*
*"Will the weather be favorable to my crops?"*
*"Will I find the love I seek?"*
*"Will the gods please change my child's behavior?"*

In time the form changed once again, this time back to the person to person approach. Today's seekers now travel to musty office caves seeking the counsel of licensed experts with weird sounding disembodied voices. They seek out therapist oracles that channel the vague and often confusing messages of the gods of psychology.

*"If my daughter doesn't marry a wealthy man, I'll be devastated!"*
*"With the Market the way it is, I'm terrified of losing my portfolio!"*
*"Oh God, how will I ever get over my breakup with Bob?"*
*"My kid is driving me insane!"*

Now, instead of going back to our hovel and sacrificing a goat to appease the gods, instead of casting chicken bones all over our newly polished kitchen floor, instead of blowing rum in our spouse's face, we journey to our local pharmacy to appease the bottom line of the gods of the pharmaceutical industry.

People always have and always will seek the counsel of both seen and unseen forces whether they're oracles in a cave, or therapists in an office, be it through coins, stones, bones, tea leaves, cards, or by way of stories with life-enhancing messages. People are seekers. We always have been and always will be; it's what makes us so wonderful.

But times have changed again. This time significantly. Our pursuits are much different now. Now we're seeking the truth of 'who' and 'what' we are. Now we're exploring unknown places known only by our future self. And we're pursuing higher callings as we hear more clearly our destiny's whispers. Life is urging us to listen to these whispers and to answer these calls. It's asking us to seek guidance from a world each uniquely creates, and from that more real world within us. Our future is calling us. Our future is calling us to become more, and our destiny whispers for us to Come Home. And our life asks us now to become the oracle we so desperately sought in lifetimes past.

*"Who and what am I really?"*
*"Can my life truly be a dance with the Divine?"*
*"Can I live a life of elegance, magic, abundance, and fun?"*
*"Can I really be the author of my reality?"*
*"Can I consciously create my dreams, my hopes, and my desires?"*
*"Can I co-create a new world with God/Goddess/All That Is?"*

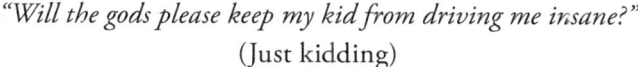

*"Will the gods please keep my kid from driving me insane?"*
(Just kidding)

This book can serve as an oracle's companion without the musty cave and cluttered office vibe, without the need for coins, stones, tea leaves, bones, or cards. It can provide insight into the workings of our reality creation and provide counsel on our journey of greater self-awareness and understanding. But most of all, it can help awaken the ancient oracle within each of us. Each of us is an oracle, and each of us is a storyteller. And each life is a story in constant need of editing and re-writing; each story is a quest to become a masterpiece.

Since this work is a collection of commentaries on each of the tales contained in *The Scented Flowers of Sinjin-Ka* (ASAT Press), you may want to have both books for the magical work ahead of you.

The following are a few suggestions on how to work with the books. Choose the ones that resonate with you. You don't need to do all of them. In time you may discover other ways of working. That would be great. It's always better if you allow the work to become your own.

Let these books be magical. Allow the mystery to be at play throughout your processing. There's immense power in magic and mystery. Avail yourself of it.

When working with the books, pay attention to what comes up in you. You'll experience resistance along the way. This resistance is natural, and a sign your work is touching deep chords in you. Be attentive to your feelings and check-in regularly with the various parts of yourself (See Appendix One for guidance). Also, don't push yourself. Learn to pace. You don't have to do or accomplish everything right away.

Growth is an on-going process. Be patient. You've got an eternity and a day to achieve it.

Growth is a spiraling process that involves patience and much attention.

Growth is a process that ebbs and flows. There must be times of pause (integration), and there must be times of action (expansion).

Growth is a process that requires being gentle and forgiving with yourself and requires the courage to admit the truth.

Growth requires that you come from a place of strength. Avoid self-pity and desperation when doing your work of processing and healing.

Growth asks for trust, not blind trust, but trust born of certainty and faith in your process and guidance.

In time your growth will require the willingness and courage to lean on that which is more than yourself: Your Future Self, Higher Self, Soul and Spirit, and God/Goddess/All That Is. You can only reach so far on your own, after which you'll need help. You'll need to be lifted.

You're loved and supported beyond all measure. Let that love and support have meaning and value for you. And ask yourself, *"Am I strong enough to ask for help? Am I stronger still to allow it?"*

Now go and work your magic. And have fun doing so.

## One Story Oracle

*To invite magic, allow the process to be magical*

An easy way to work with this book is to invite your Higher Self to participate with you. Ask your Higher Self to help you choose which of the stories best aligns with what needs attention at the current time. I always begin every session with a client by asking, *"So, what's up?"* So ask this of your Higher Self and be open to the response.

There are any numbers of ways to receive impute from your Higher Self. The simplest is to close your eyes and imagine a number from one to ninety-one. The first number that pops into your head is the story to explore. Another way is to open the book, and without looking, point to a page. The story on that page is the one you should work with.

Now go to your copy of *The Scented Flowers of Sinjin-Ka* and read the story twice. When done, go to *The Magic of the Scented Flowers* and read the '*Suggested Areas of Attention*' followed by the

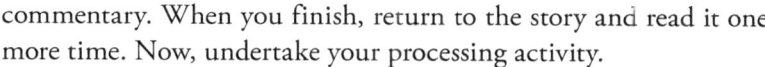

commentary. When you finish, return to the story and read it one more time. Now, undertake your processing activity.

While reading, be open to whatever comes up in you. Maybe feelings will surface, or a word or a phrase will catch your attention. As you sit quietly for a little while, perhaps a gestalt will occur; that sudden realization of what needs attention. Trust the process. Don't give it over to your negative ego, or your fear, or your need to control. The number you receive is the correct one. It's the story you should be working with now. At other times other numbers will appear. Those stories will be the right ones for that time.

People have tried testing the process by closing their eyes several times to see if they get the same number; this is their ego at play here. What they're looking for is proof, not guidance. They're looking to validate their need to say, *"I told you so."* They're not looking for help. Your Higher Self will never participate in your ego's games. To do so would give validity to them. Approach this work honestly. Allow it to be mystical and magical. After a time, you'll come to trust the process and your Higher Self.

Another way to select a number is to use an app that makes random number selections. There are many random number generating apps available for smarts phones. Some are good; some not so. Choose an app that's simple to use. Avoid apps with unnecessary bells and whistles. Also, be sure to select an app that allows you to program random numbers from one to ninety-one.

Your Higher Self will use any means to help you. You may want to go into a meditation and ask your Higher Self directly for a number. Although your negative ego always lies to you, your Higher Self never will.

## Three Story Oracle

This suggestion is a variation of the *One Story Oracle*. Select three numbers instead of one. Working with three stories, along with their commentaries, can broaden your perspective of the issue at hand. But don't use more than three stories; doing so can muddy up the process and lead to confusion. Like the three-card spread in tarot card readings, the three-story approach can provide intriguing possibilities with more in-depth insight.

Look for common elements in the three stories. What ties the stories together? What similarities do they have that relate to the situation currently up for you?

Do the processing of all three stories and commentaries at the same time. Don't take a break. Continuity is essential here.

## Writing Your Own Interpretation

Why not write your own commentaries on the stories? Use your unique insight and voice. It will make your magic and healing process more personal. Since we're all different and approach everything from unique perspectives, writing your own commentaries can be both personally insightful and rewarding. But when you do, make sure your negative ego is not involved in the process. Seek always the input and guidance of your Higher Self. Ask your Higher Self to participate with you during the writing. And of course, be honest with yourself.

Since you're not sharing these commentaries with others, don't concern yourself with grammar and punctuation. Let the whole process flow freely.

## Freewriting

A remarkable technique for self-processing and self-healing is an approach called 'Freewriting.'

In her book, *The Artist's Way* (Jeremy P. Tarcher/Putnam Press), author and artist Julia Cameron outlines a unique method for awakening creativity called, *'The Morning Pages.'* Her exercises have the

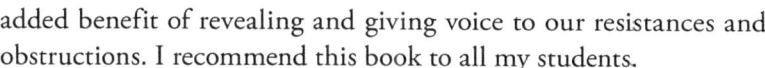

added benefit of revealing and giving voice to our resistances and obstructions. I recommend this book to all my students.

The various parts of yourself reside in the domain of your Unconscious (Read Appendix One). They express their hurts, fears, resistances, and concerns consciously through the feelings you're having, and in the outer reality you're experiencing.

> *"Whatever resides within the domain of your Unconscious will, in time, become conscious in the form of fate."* –Lazaris

Everything you observe is an out-picturing of your inner reality. Instead of limiting the voices of your lesser selves to your outer experiences, which is never a good idea, why not give them another avenue of expression. You can accomplish this through the process of Freewriting.

The exercise is simple. Each morning before beginning your day, write no more and no less than three pages of whatever comes up. Don't write about something; just write down whatever randomly appears on the paper. At first, the writing may be slow due to your mind wanting to control the process, but after about two or three days, it'll stop interfering, and the writing will flow more easily. A subconscious and unconscious dialogue will start taking place. Over time you'll get the sense that you're having a conversation with yourself. You are.

Let the writing flow. Don't concern yourself with grammar, legibility, or spelling. Since no one's going to read this, let it come out in whatever way it does.

Freewriting will give your lesser selves, as well as those more real, a more elegant means of getting your attention. But be careful not to control the process. Let the writing flow without interference.

Again don't concern yourself with grammar, legibility, and spelling. Let this activity be free-hand. Never type it on a computer. The act of writing by hand connects the neurophysiology of the process directly with the brain; typing does not.

Freewriting is not journal keeping or diary writing. And you're not writing an autobiography here. Let it be a unique activity. What you write should never be shared with others, even if they're your friends, your therapist, your spouse or partner, or members of your Healing Community or Spiritual Family. When you finish writing, make sure to hide the notebook. Your writing is for you and you alone.

## Working With Your Healing Community

Another way to unfold the magic and healing power of *The Scented Flowers* is to work in partnership with other travelers on this unique path. You can set up a 'spiritual community' or a 'healing community,' whatever you wish to call it. This suggestion involves getting together regularly with a few friends to go over and discuss relevant stories and commentaries. This approach utilizes constructive and honest feedback to provide each member with greater insight and understanding to advance his or her processing.

Of course, the most important consideration when forming this community is the people you invite to join it. You should trust that each member will take the work seriously and will approach it with honesty and integrity. And they should have the willingness and ability to give feedback in a constructive, helpful, and tactful manner. The objective for members is not only in their own progress but the progress of each member of the group. No jealousy, competition, or grandstanding should be allowed.

The people you select should possess an honest frankness that comes from a place of love and friendship. A good friend is one who'll tell you the truth, whether you want to hear it or not. A good friend will not buy into or enable your games and distractions. A good friend will be a cheerleader in your growing and changing, not a competitor. As rare as they may be, such people would be excellent choices for your community.

## The Magic of the Scented Flowers

Not all friends and family members would work well here; this does not mean you don't love and respect them; it just means they would not be a good fit for this kind of work. You may love and trust your spouse or partner dearly, but having him or her in this kind of group may not be a good idea for both of you. Your relationship with your spouse or partner is a different kind of relationship, not better or worse, just different. It may or may not be the kind of relationship that best serves this particular process. Respect the relationship for what it is, and don't try to squeeze it into a place it shouldn't be.

The selection of your community is essential. Give it much thought and consideration. We recommend you choose no more than seven members. The ideal number would be between two and five.

When you have your group selected, decide among yourselves a schedule for your gatherings. You could meet once a week, once a month, or whatever best works for all of you. The important thing is regularity, not a random occurrence, or whenever the mood strikes you.

This gathering can be fun, but don't let it become frivolous. Remember, the point is growth and healing; this work must be taken seriously, and everyone should be on the same page. Avoid it becoming a social gathering to play, snack, and chat. I conducted a class once at a private home in California. 80% of the time was devoted to eating and socializing; the other 20% went to the class. I would recommend the other way around. But we're talking California here. Whatcha' gonna do?

Again structure your gatherings in a way that best works for all of you. With that said, I would like to offer a few suggestions.

1) One member selects a number from one to ninety-one. The person then reads the story out loud, followed by the commentary. Now discuss among yourselves how the story and commentary relate to the person's current situation. When finished, move onto the next member.

2) Members will have different takes on a person's particular situation, and this can provide varied perspectives with the potential for

richer understanding and insight. Honest frankness and tact will be needed here.

3) Each person in the group should have an equal opportunity to read and explore. No one should dominate the time, and no one should be omitted from participating, whether by lack of time or personal choice. If a member of the community consistently ops out of selecting a number, preferring only to give advice, maybe that individual should consider withdrawing from the group. This approach works best when all members participate, none dominate, and all speak truth with harm to none.

Working with a spiritual or healing community can be an elevating experience in your growing and healing. Have fun, but stay away from the alcohol until after the meeting is over. This will be very difficult to do if you live in California.

## Working With Your Spiritual Family

Another way to work with community is by incorporating a 'spiritual family' into your process. Where the Healing Community is composed of seen friends, your Spiritual Family is composed of those unseen. This work is done meditatively, of course.

You can select the members for this group, you can invite them to select you, or you can do both. But keep the number between two and five; no more than seven.

Your spiritual family may include Ancient One Grandmothers and Grandfathers, those crones and hermits of times long past. They may consist of friends and teachers from ancient spiritual traditions of lifetimes past. You may wish to invite someone currently living or passed that you much admire and respect. Perhaps you'd like your Higher Self and Soul in personified forms to become part of your spiritual family. As in any suggestion we put forth, allow the process to be magical. But again, keep the number between two and five; no more than seven. More than that will make the process too unwieldy and cumbersome.

When you gather with your spiritual family, be respectful of each member present. Don't dominate the proceeding, and don't dictate how things should be. Negotiate among yourselves the work to be done. Work as a team with members contributing their unique insights and magic to the process. Function as a team always. And it's also recommended that you meet together regularly.

The synergy of all your various magic's working together will produce remarkably powerful results. The whole process will be wonderfully magical and mystical. Have fun with this.

## The Meditation

1. Gently close your eyes. Allow yourself to become quiet and still in whatever way is comfortable for you. When you feel calmer, slowly count down from seven to one. With each number, feel a shift and change taking place mentally and physically.

2. On the count of one slowly open your mental eyes. Imagine yourself in your 'Safe Place.' Your Safe Place should be outdoors in nature away from the hustle and frenzy of daily activity. Let it be beautiful, enchanting, loving, and filled with blessed solitude.

This Safe Place is yours and yours alone; no one can disturb you here, no one can enter this place uninvited. This place in nature may be a creation of your imagination, a place you'd like to use from a movie or a picture, or a place of beauty and safety you remember from your past. The important thing is that you feel safe, protected, and at peace in this haven in nature.

In every meditation, return to this same place, and in each meditation, take time to explore more of its space; explore more of its detail. *"Love pays attention to detail."*

3. After you've spent time allowing your senses of sight, sound, touch, taste, and hearing drink in this place, invite your Higher Self, in personified form, to join you. Sit together for a little while. Feel your Higher Self's presence and love. Talk of your desire to meet with

your Spiritual Family. Talk about why you'd like to meet them; speak of the issue at hand. *"There's magic in the telling."*

4. After you finish expressing your desire, walk by yourself to the edge of your Safe Place, and step across.

Walk the changing terrain for many miles, perhaps for many days, until you come to a beautiful, enchanting, and magical place. This sanctuary will be a place in nature where magicians for thousands of years have gathered. Perhaps standing stones will be there, or a sacred grove of trees. Maybe this place will be on a mountain top, or in a lovely valley surrounded by majestic snow-covered peaks. Let your imagination be at play here.

5. Now call your spiritual family to join you. They'll come one by one, or in groups, or both. Perhaps they magically appear, or maybe they come from around some trees or standing stones. Let it be what it is. Now choose which part of step six you'd like to work.

6a. When all are present, sit in a circle. Ask them to suggest a story to explore. At first, they may sit quietly; they may talk among themselves, and they may ask you questions. Allow what happens to happen. After a time, someone from the group will give you a number, maybe two or three. It will be a number from one to ninety-one.

6b. If you've been working with a particular story or issue, and would like more guidance with your processing and healing, or would like greater insight into your resistances and apprehensions, ask for their help with this. Again they may sit quietly at first; they may talk among themselves, and they may ask you questions. Allow what happens to happen. After a time, one or more will counsel you. You may receive this counsel verbally, telepathically through mental pictures or images, or through feelings or memories from your past. It will come in a way you'd be more receptive and less resistant. Stop trying to make it happen. Let the magic flow.

7. With the work completed, thank your spiritual family. Now close your mental eyes. Slowly count from one to five. On the count

of five, open your physical eyes and return to your room. Your meditation is now complete; the magic is now undertaken.

If you'd like, you may find it valuable to write down your experience.

Again I emphasize strongly, let the whole process be magical. Why? Because it is magical.

## Using the Cross-Reference Chart

If you already have an idea of what you'd like to work on, go directly to '*Appendix Three: Cross-Reference Chart.*' Select from the list the topic that best covers the issue. If it's 'shame,' go to the section on shame and work with the stories and commentaries listed there. You may find that you can winnow it down to one, two, or three stories. If you have difficulty finding the exact listing, try finding the closest listing to what you're looking for. Maybe get input from your Higher Self, or your Healing Community, or your Spiritual Family.

*Now let the magic begin! Have fun!*
*Enjoy!*

# The Oracle of
# *The Scented Flowers*

The Commentaries

# 1

# The Fool and the Apple

## Suggested Areas of Attention

* Let go of your investment in struggle, pain, and hardship. Stop trying to make your life work. Be open to allowing it to flow and fulfill synchronously. Choose elegance and ease in the living of your life.
* Pay attention to the beliefs and attitudes, thoughts and feelings, and choices and decisions you make and hold that restrict your happiness and the hearing of your destiny's call.
* Be aware of your fear of magic and your need for control. Choose magic over control. The two cannot co-exist.
* Let go of the sweet intoxication of martyrhood and your addiction to conflict and crisis.
* Step away from consensus thinking. You'll never be happy or genuinely fulfilled there. You'll never be at home there.

There are two ways to fulfill a desire: consciously and unconsciously. Choose 'consciously.' It's more fun, and you'll awaken more of your authorship.

There are two approaches to fulfilling a desire: through effort or elegance. Choose 'elegance.' It's more fun, and you'll allow more of your magic to flow.

Elegance and harmonious living result when one lives life consciously and in alignment with the rhythms and patterns of All That Is.

In Nature, only humans value hard work and toil. We elevate effort to a noble status while relegating elegance and synchronous living to the domain of fools and holy men. We hold Promethean and Sisyphean struggles and martyrhood as exemplifying grand and heroic pursuits while subjugating a life lived in ease and effortlessness to the realms of the filthy rich, the half-wits, and the lazy.

*"O' How noble the struggling hero!"* proclaims consensus thinking with pride and admiration.

But it's the 'Wise Fool' who knows the secrets of living, not the struggling martyred hero. It's the Wise Fool who knows the secret magic of play, grace, and fun, who is adrift in the fluidity of all existence, and who knows that life's an illusion and that we can have as much of illusion as we like. And it's the Wise Fool who lives such a magical life. And it's the Wise Fool who plays in the Fields of the Divine.

Be a Wise Fool, dear one. Choose it as your life's ambition. Open to the ever-flowing synchronicities abounding in such a choice. Be a magician in the living of your life. Always dance the dance of the Wise Fool. It's a fool's dance, it's an ancient dance, and it's an eternal dance with God/Goddess/All That Is. It can be your dance if you're brave and wise and foolish enough to dance it.

To become the Wise Fool you're destined to be, be conscious of your resistance to synchronous living. Own and release your need to struggle and toil.

To become the Wise Fool you're destined to be, identify your valuing of a martyred life, and choose a higher path.

To become the Wise Fool you're destined to be, allow your desires to manifest. Be conscious of your resistance to such successes. Be willing to release it.

To become the Wise Fool you're destined to be, face your fear of magic, and let go of your need to control.

To become the Wise Fool you're destined to be, always be in pursuit of the 'more of you' by challenging your limiting beliefs and attitudes, thoughts and feelings, and choices and decisions.

To become the Wise Fool you're destined to be, step away from the false safety and constricting boundaries of consensus thinking. Make your path and travel it. Don't follow the path of others.

If you do these things, you'll find the freedom you've sought for all your many lifetimes. Eventually, dear one, there'll come a time when you'll find yourself on no path at all. Then you'll be Home. Imagine that, dear one! You'll be Home! Wherever you are, whatever you do, you'll be Home.

Being 'Home' is not a place but a state of being. It's where you co-create with God/Goddess/ All That Is worlds yet unimagined. It's where existence exists in freedom, and existence exists in Oneness. It's where you once were, and where you'll be once again. And it's in such a state real living begins. It's also where you can manifest apples from a mango tree.

> God /Goddess/All That Is are waiting for you there.
> Are you fool enough to make the journey?

# 2

# Not Enough Enough

## Suggested Areas of Attention

* Start healing the shame you carry, this shame born of your own making or passed to you by others.
* Stop believing you're undeserving and that you're not enough.
* Attend to your lack of confidence as well as your need for attention.
* Recognize, acknowledge, forgive, and release your self-limiting beliefs and attitudes.
* Take the pressure off yourself. Lighten up and enjoy your life!

Shame is the belief you're flawed, defective, or broken.

Everyone, to a greater or lesser degree, holds the resonance of shame. We came to this belief in waves, beginning in childhood and continuing throughout our adolescence and into our adult years. We were either taught we were broke or defective, were wronged into it by being put into situations we couldn't emotionally handle or came to it through the ravages of abuse.

The destructive nature of shame is devastating. It distorts, impedes, and stifles loving relationships and denies the realization of our more real self. Shame denies us a sense of genuine fulfillment from successes and accomplishments. Shame holds us back from our life's pursuit of 'becoming more.'

You're not broken or defective you just believe you are. In harboring this lie, you attract realities to either prove you're not or to prove you are.

This hidden belief underlies other destructive beliefs we hold, like the belief we're undeserving, the false notion that we're incapable of love, fulfillment, success, and the erroneous belief that we can't be happy because we're not worthy of it.

> *"I can't do it!"*
> *"I'm not good enough!"*
> *"I don't have enough!"*
> *"I need extra help!"*

Some compensate by adopting the even more destructive counter belief that they're somehow special; that they're either better or worse than others. Some seek attention or wallow in the doldrums of self-pity.

> *"I'll never have what others have!"*
> *"Good things never happen to me."*
> *"I need extra attention!"*
> *"Poor me!" "Poor me!" "Poor Me!"*

You don't need to prove you're enough by accomplishing what others accomplish or by having what others have. There's no need to prove anything. If you feel you lack what you need to craft an extraordinary life, just ask for what is missing. What you need will be given; help will be provided.

You'll succeed in the pursuit of your destiny. Pretending you're not enough only hampers the succeeding. You can answer the call of your future in this lifetime or another. It's your choice; your destiny's patient. You will, however, ultimately succeed.

Take the pressure off yourself. Lighten up! Enjoy! Move at your own pace, not the pacing of others. Growth is not a race. In the meantime, process the lies you tell yourself and heal and release the shame that haunts you still.

You're enough! You have the means to achieve whatever you desire in life as long as it's your desire and not the desire of others, and indeed not the aspirations the consensus says you need to be happy. Your dreams and visions are limited only by you. You have all you need to awaken your magnificence. And that's the only accomplishment that matters, isn't it?

> Yes, you can even build a magnificent palace
> with only a tiny feather,
> if you really believe you need that feather.

# 3

# Where the Animals Went to Die

## Suggested Areas of Attention

* Accept the power and beauty of your loving.
* Allow yourself the time and space to grieve what needs grieving.
* Own and release your need to control to keep love safe.
* Forgive, and release your delusions of insignificance.
* Address your fear of letting go.
* Allow your freedom to strengthen you.

*Oh, the magnificence of the human heart!*
*Oh, the magnificence of your heart!*

Yes, you read correctly, *"Your heart."*

The Divine of You always provides opportunities for the unique majesty of your love to shine through. Some opportunities bring pain and hurt; others light and joy. But the Divine of You never brings more than you're capable of handling. Your love is strong enough to hold the hurts and pains, and tender enough to nurture the sadness and loss. You're stronger than you yet realize. Be strong enough to be the love you're capable of being. Be tender enough to be the love you're destined to become.

Love grows stronger when you're willing to let it go; it weakens when you're not. Your need for control is born of the desire to keep love safe; the greater the control, the greater the fear of its loss. Attend to this need for control. Understand why you're engaging in it and forgive yourself for such behavior.

Now dive deep within yourself and feel the dread, the hurt, the loneliness, the despair, the anger, the fear, and the pain of love's loss you hide there. Feel your feelings deeply. Beyond your pain and dread, beyond your loneliness and hurt, beyond your anger, despair, and fear, your love resides imprisoned. Free it. When you do, it will free you.

Love is never lost to you when you let it soar free and wild. God and Goddess set you free to journey on a quest to discover a grander loving, a conscious loving. You're not lost to them. Their gift of freedom allows your love to deepen over lifetimes. They know you'll return Home.

You're learning the depth and breathe of their love for you, a love that becomes more without ever having been less. You're learning that God/Goddess/All That Is, and your Higher Self and Soul, are with you always. And you're learning that you're indeed loved and loving and that you're safe in allowing it and safe in giving it. You're in this life to learn to love more; to learn to love divinely.

No, you're not wrong or bad for your love's many setbacks, losses, failures, or disappointments. You're not flawed or defective. This belief is the shame you feel. Let it go. Let the old image you hold of being unlovable die. It's not you; it's not your heart. It's a lie you tell yourself to control the pain of love's loss. Tell yourself this lie no more.

You're learning to love more, dear one. It's your grace to do so. It's your very nature to do so.

Love has both dark and light faces. To grow love, you'll need to accept both. They'll bring you Home if you allow yourself to honor them within you.

*Dear one, your love is so much stronger than you know.
Let it carry you Home.*

# 4

# The Disciple and the Idiot

## Suggested Areas of Attention

* Stop judging yourself and others. Let go of this investment in judgment. Why is it so necessary to hold onto it?
* Acknowledge, own, and release your arrogance and your need to feel special.
* Be open to the beauty and majesty of innocence. Awaken the beauty and majesty of your innocence.
* Discover and awaken the 'Wise Fool' within you. There's so much it has to show you.
* Receive the gift of freedom the Wise Fool gladly offers.
* Let go of your need to hold on to fear. Let go of your need to control.
* Acknowledge, own, and heal your fear of separation. It's at the root of all your other fears.

Delight in the Wise Fool; politely retreat from the foolish.

The Wise Fool understands that life is a play of light and dark, and laughs with glee at its limitless expressions and possibilities.

The Wise Fool takes joy in the dance of love but compassionately retreats from those enamored with themselves.

The Wise Fool is the weaver of truth who joyfully weaves truth into knowing.

The Wise Fool, from a place of innocence, joins in the play of life with laughter and with fun.

The Wise Fool offers wisdom with grace and humility.

The Wise Fool is an empathic lover.

The Wise Fool embraces death while being lovingly mournful of the dead.

The Wise Fool is eternally free.

The foolish, on the other hand, are enamored with themselves.

The foolish will parrot the thoughts of others since they have none of their own to offer.

The foolish fear what they don't understand; they retreat in panic from what they can't control.

The foolish look for simple answers since the pursuit of complexity involves too much effort.

The foolish fear death almost as much as they fear life.

The foolish are self-imprisoned by dogma, blame, and judgment.

Since the true, the good, and the beautiful are much too revealing; the foolish will not pursue such things.

Pay attention to your investment in judgment. And pay attention to the trap of arrogance with its need for specialness.

Judgment has as its primary purpose, the desire to separate oneself from the object of judgment. Judging in and of itself is not a bad thing. If someone holds that mashed potatoes are better than au gratin, that judgment is entirely acceptable since it expresses a preference. If someone judges racism as hateful and destructive, that judgment is expressing a moral viewpoint and, as such, is also entirely acceptable. But if one judges as a means to separate from people they dislike, or hate, or fear, judgment becomes a destructive force and should be attended to and healed.

Arrogance is the false belief that one is better or less than others. Like judgment, it'll always deprive the one holding it from fully knowing and appreciating others. Although the purpose of arrogance and judgment is to separate oneself from others, they, in truth, separate the holder from his or her self.

Self-awareness cannot result from such destructive attitudes, and self-awareness is how we grow to become more; how we grow to become a Wise Fool.

Delight in the Wise Fool. Discover this Sacred One within you. Why? Because skipping stones on a ripple-less sea is so much fun!

# 5

# A Gift from a Squished Squirrel

## Suggested Areas of Attention

* Let go of the guilt you're carrying. Feel the emotions that lie hidden there.
* It's time to let die what needs dying; it's time to birth what needs birthing. It's time to grieve and celebrate those times of passage.
* Be open to the opportunities for healing and growth that are always available to you. Be strong enough to acknowledge those opportunities, and stronger still to use them.
* Accept the gifts and love of others. Be humble enough to accept them, and gracious enough to grow from them.

Guilt is a non-emotion; it's an artificial man-made thing. It has only a dark constricting side.

Every genuine human emotion has both dark and light aspects. Hatred, for example, is a human emotion. Its negative side is an intense and passionate dislike for some person or group of people; its positive side is an intense and passionate dislike for a destructive personal or societal behavior, attitude, or belief. Its value lies as a motivator of change. For example, *"I hate it when I lie to myself and others. I'm going to stop doing this."*

Guilt is a non-emotion as it only has a dark constricting side. It comes from self-judgment over having an emotion you believe you've no right to feel. As long as you're in guilt, you won't feel the emotion that needs to be released.

When you find yourself in guilt, stop what you're doing and choose to let it go. When you genuinely and thoroughly let go of the guilt and allow the real emotion to surface, you can begin the healing process. Feel deeply and thoroughly the newly surfaced emotion, then ask to have it lifted. It will lift if you'll let it go. This process will end the guilt that plagues you.

At some level, everyone and everything chooses to die; to 'move on' in the more real sense. One may not be aware of the choice, but the choice was made none-the-less.

There must be a means for dying. Some ways are elegant, some less so. Some may involve an illness such as cancer or heart disease, some many involve an accident, and some will use other ways. But regardless of the means, a choice was made at some level. The squirrel *'crossing over'* needed a means. The cart provided it quickly and painlessly.

The beauty and majesty of this ageless ritual of passage lie within the gift this ritual provides; the blessed gift of healing. Sometimes this gift is accepted; sometimes it's not. By accepting the gift, one honors the giver, and by utilizing the gift, one grows and heals. All of life's passages bring the wonderful gift of healing.

Let go of the guilt and self-blame you're holding. Let go of your hiding and denial; feel your grief and pain deeply. Feel your anger and despair deeply. Feel the hurt and fear deeply. In doing so, you accept this beautiful and majestic gift of healing. In doing so, you honor the one who gave it; you honor the gift of their passage.

*Oh, the splendid beauty of life and death!*
*Oh, the wondrous symmetry!*

# 6

# The Doll Maker's Helper

## Suggested Areas of Attention

* Claim your self-worth; own your value.
* Drop the mistaken belief in the earn/reward cycle.
* Recognize, acknowledge, forgive, and release all self-limiting beliefs.
* Process through your hopes and desires. Weed out those that do not lead you to the more of you; accept, acknowledge, and give attention to those that do.

Self-esteem is earned; self-worth is not. Your worth had already been given to you by God and Goddess, and it's priceless. You never have to earn your worth; you only have to claim it.

What you do in life is only a part of who you are. It's not 'who' you are. Of course, value what you do in life, but value more the 'you' you are and more so the 'you' you're becoming.

You'll never fully realize how truly valued you are, but you can grow to appreciate more of it. You matter more than you know. Accept this, own this, live this.

Live a life of mattering without giving it to your negative ego. In living such a life, you'll come to know how truly loved and valued you are, not just for what you do in life but for the value of your being in it.

We grow up believing that receiving involves earning. Likewise, we believe that if we do not receive, we failed at earning. This belief is wrong. All of our institutions and societal structures foster this earn/reward fallacy: schools, religions, family, work, athletics, friendships, etc. We go through life believing that if we earn, we're rewarded; if we do not earn, we're punished. Our growth, our future, who we're becoming, requires we break with this destructive belief.

You are valued, you have worth, you are loved, and what you need is always provided. What stands in your way of receiving is your mistaken belief that you must first earn it. Recognize this error. Forgive yourself for holding tenaciously to it. Let it go. Now exercise the courage to receive and allow.

If you don't receive what you desire, process the desiring. Ask yourself;

*"Is this what I truly desire, or is this a desire given to me by others?"*

*"Is this what I truly desire, or is this a desire born of unrealized dreams held by lesser developed parts of me?"*

*"Is this what I truly desire, or is this some standard of proof I use to test the love of God/Goddess/All That Is?"*

*"Is this what I truly desire, or is this what I believe I should desire?"*

*"Is this a desire from my unfulfilled past, or is this a desire from my awakening future?"*

*"Do I desire this for what it will get me, or do I desire this for where it will lead me?"*

If you don't receive what you desire, it's never because you're not worthy or you're undeserving of it. Better things await you; things of higher value, things providing greater fulfillment and happiness, and things better positioned to lead you to your real aspirations. Have patience, dear one. You'll receive your heart's desires, your genuine heart's desires.

*You are loved, dear one.*

*Are you gracious enough to receive it?*
*Are you courageous enough to allow it?*

# 7

# The Witch of the Darkened Wood

## Suggested Areas of Attention

* Pursue the fullness of healing that lies beyond the limits of curing. Discover the healing and guidance of the Ancient One within you.
* Don't let fear paralyze you or keep you from your happiness.
* Let go of control. Your faith and trust are lacking. Allow magic to happen. Allow magic to lift and heal you.
* Dare to ask for help. You don't need to carry the weight of the world on your shoulders.
* There's no death sentence until you sign it, despite what others tell you.
* Heal the shame you're tenaciously holding.
* Know and release your resistance to gratitude. Know and release your resistance to love and healing and nurturing.
* Pursue what lies beyond the safety of logic and reason. Stop hiding inside your head.

Seek the counsel of the Ancient Ones. Seek the guidance and protection of those Ancient Grandmothers and Grandfathers of traditions long forgotten.

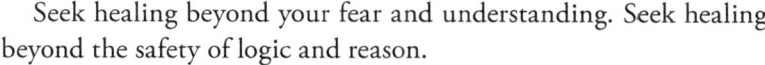

Seek healing beyond your fear and understanding. Seek healing beyond the safety of logic and reason.

Seek the healing from a love that's more. Seek the healing of the Ancient Ones.

Seek the healing of these blessed crones and hermits from times long past. They wait at the edge of your belief just beyond what you hold to be true. They wait at the edge of your imagination just beyond your vision. They live in a place more real than you and reside where love's more grand. They're there. Seek them out. Ask for their help.

The most powerful healing magic is the easiest to do. Yet this healing magic is the one most people find the hardest and the scariest. It's the kind of magic most avoid and least understands. It's the magic of 'asking for help.'

Many will not ask for help because they let their shame, their false belief they're flawed, defective, or broken, rule them. Many will not ask for help because of their reluctance to feel gratitude due to some foolish notion that gratitude involves indebtedness. Many will not ask for help because they believe their specialness entitles them to whatever it is they want. And of those who ask, most will not allow the receiving.

Ask for help, but ask from a place of grounding. Support is offered but not received when asked from a place of self-pity and desperation. Self-pity and desperation are tools used by shame. They create static that cancels out the receiving of love and healing.

The belief in your entitlement also prevents the healing magic of the Ancients. If it did not, such healing would lock you into the false notion in your specialness. You must step out of entitlement and specialness to let in the healing of the Ancients.

Ask for help from the Ancient Ones. But in so doing, gather the courage to be willing to receive that help without your ego's strings and conditions. And most of all, beyond the asking and the willingness to receive, attend to whatever impedances you hold that prevents you from allowing the healing to happen.

Are you using your condition to get attention?
Are you reluctant to give up your personal and private war
with God and Goddess?
Are you reluctant to forgive yourself or them for a wrong you
falsely believed occurred?
Are you afraid to give up control?

Seek the counsel of the Ancient Ones. Be willing to enter the Darkened Wood of your fears and resistances. Don't run from fear; go deeply into it. Have faith and trust in your process, dear one. By going through to the other side, you'll discover help and guidance waiting there. Ask for help, be willing to receive it, and allow the miracles to happen.

*Miracles abound. Magic is afoot.*
*The Ancient Ones are calling you beyond the Darkened Wood.*

*Do you have the courage to answer their call?*

# 8

# Standing Before the Judge

## Suggested Areas of Attention

* Stop your self-judgment. You're not guilty of anything. Dare to forgive yourself and others. Set yourself and others free.
* Acknowledge, own, and release the shame you're still carrying.
* Accept the authorship of your life. Stop giving it away to old wounds and hurts.
* Stop trying to earn your self-worth. Claim it and move on.

You have within you an archetypal voice of self-judgment and a propensity for unhappiness. This part of you, born of shame, holds the mistaken belief that you're flawed, defective, or broken; that you're undeserving of being happy, successful, fulfilled, or loved. You created this judge to validate your negative self-image and to prevent yourself from being hurt if you should, heaven forbid, allow yourself such happiness, success, fulfillment, and love. It condemns and imprisons you to keep you safe from failure and disappointment. It's a break you apply to keep you safe from vulnerability. And it's a part of you that never fails to do your bidding.

You're not wrong or bad for having created this judge. It was for the child you once were a means to keep yourself safe and unharmed from the devastating ravages of disappointments and pains you believed was due you.

But now you're being called to cast off this belief and stand tall and free in your innocence. You're being called to be the author of your life, not a defendant in an endless trial of self-judgment. You're being called to pay attention to your inner judgments, to give them a different voice within you, and to choose different outcomes. You have such power. You have such a voice.

Forgive yourself for holding onto shame. There's no blame here. Forgive yourself and exercise the will and courage to ask your Higher Self to lift it from you. The answer will always be, *"Yes."*

Bit by bit, step by step, allow the happiness, success, fulfillment, and love to flow into your reality. It will come if you'll only receive and accept it.

Turn your self-judgment into self-permission, your self-admonishments into self-acceptance, and convert the archetypal judge into your archetypal liberator. You'll accomplish this through forgiveness, having the courage to ask for help, and attending to those parts of you still clinging to their shame and belief in not being good enough. You're the author of your life. You're not some defendant in a never-ending trial of denied dreams and self-judgments.

Your archetypal judge will always obey your wishes. Stand tall, stand free, stand forgiven, and proclaim yourself worthy.

> *You're the one who says, "Yes."*
> *You have such power.*

# 9

# The Love of Winning

## Suggested Areas of Attention

* What does 'competition' mean to you? You compete with no one. Choose only to be the winner at the living of your life.
* Look to your greed and attend to your belief in scarcity.
* Stop listening to the false promises of your negative ego. Heed the guidance of your Higher Self instead.
* Always pursue win/win outcomes.
* Stop trying to earn the right to be loved and valued.

During the early days of the ancient Greek games, athletes had great respect and appreciation for their fellow competitors. They understood competition to be a means of self-challenge to bring out one's personal best. And they knew that their fellow competitors helped them achieve it. Today's athletes approach competition as a means to destroy or humiliate competitors in some ill-guided attempt to puff up their self-image to project a sense of specialness or superiority.

The consensus likewise views competition as a means of providing the ego's need for *'better than.'* Personal challenge has now become the collective ego's need for tribal gratification. The pursuit of excellence has now become the collective ego's pursuit of bragging rights. In our world today, there's little emphasis on personal challenge and the pursuit of excellence. 'Winning' becomes the god to whom the consensus pays homage.

Pay attention to your competitive nature. Are you attempting to defeat an opponent, or are you engaging with an opponent as a means to challenge yourself? Your intention here will determine whether you're choosing to become more or choosing to settle for less. One's intention is everything. Be vigilant of your ego's promise of specialness. Heed your Higher Self's call to be more.

Pay attention to your greed with its belief in scarcity. Not to do so will rob you of freedom and any personal sense of bounty. If you believe there are only a limited number of slices of the pie of life and that you must fight to get your share, end this belief. This belief is your ego talking. If there are only a fixed number of slices, make another pie. You have an unlimited supply of dough and apples at your disposal.

When you perceive limitations around you, you're projecting a limited sense of yourself. You create your reality, no one else. Instead of projecting limitations, start creating opportunities. Instead of believing in scarcity, start awakening to your true nature to create without limits.

To accomplish this, distinguish between the voice of your negative ego and the voice of your Higher Self. Your negative ego projects limitations; your Higher Self promises and delivers unlimited abundance and opportunity. Your negative ego lies to you; your Higher Self tells you the truth.

When engaging with others, always pursue win/win outcomes. Avoid compromise since compromise involves both sides losing; with win/win outcomes, both parties gain. Win/win outcomes take more attention and determination, but you're up to the challenge. Your pursuit will lead to success if you keep at it. One's intention is everything, remember?

Pursue challenge; avoid competition.

Pursue excellence; avoid the accepted mediocrity of the consensus.

Become more by awakening the more of you. Avoid trying to be more by making others less.

Win at the living of life. That's the only winning worth pursuing.

When you're winning at the living of life, there can be no loss to anyone or anything. Life becomes a win/win situation.

*This is the love of winning.*

## 10

# Gobi's Tiny Seeds

### Suggested Areas of Attention

* Open yourself to the incredible power of hope. Challenge your old beliefs and distortions about it. Be hopeful; be full of hope. Stop giving in to your fear.
* Now is the time to work your magic, now is the time to dream your dreams of hope, and now is the time to take action. Get into the game!
* Be the magician you're meant to be. Let the magic happen. Stop controlling.
* Release your love, hope, and compassion into your world. Stop hiding them. Stop hiding from them.

The world is much in need of hope, dear one. The world is sorely lacking in creativity and innovation. People are not dialoguing with one another; they've become so lost in dogmatic thinking. The world is much in need of hope, dear one. The world is much in need of magic. The world is much in need of love: your love, your hope, your magic.

Hope is a powerful resonance. Hope, when sincerely held, is ripe with magic and rich with wonder and miracles. Hope is the ultimate healer. Hope can lift one to heights beyond imagination. Hope can liberate one from the shackles of the impossible and the improbable. Hope can spur one to change. Hope can spark creativity and lift it to the heights of innovation.

But to harness the power of hope, you must first change your current relationship to it. You must challenge your old distorted beliefs and fears around it.

Many believe that hope is the desperate act of desperate people; this is not what hope is. Many view hope as futile, weak, and valueless; this is not what hope is. Many see hope as a setup for potential disappointment and dashed dreams; this is not what hope is. Many view hope as wishful thinking; this is not what hope is.

What is hope for you? What is your relationship to it? If it's dark, lighten it; if it's light, brighten it. If you resist it, know and feel your resistance and release it. Ask for help here. It will come if you're willing to receive it.

When you elevate the power of hope within you and allow it's resonance to propel you, work your magic, and heal your world. Be Gobi.

## Meditation

1. You may wish to bring hope to a region of conflict in your world. Or you may choose to awaken hope where blockages are impeding progress. Choose where in the world there's a need for hope, healing, creativity, innovation, dialogue, and magic.

2. Now gently close your eyes. Allow yourself to become quiet and still in whatever way you feel most comfortable. When you feel calmer, slowly count down from seven to one. With each number, feel yourself shifting and changing both mentally and physically.

3. On the count of one slowly open your mental eyes. Imagine yourself in your Safe Place. Your Safe Place should be in nature away from the hustle and frenzy of daily activity. Let it be beautiful, enchanting, loving, or filled with blessed solitude. This Safe Place

is yours and yours alone. No one can disturb you here. No one can enter this place uninvited.

This place in nature may be a creation of your imagination, a place you'd like to use from a movie or a picture, or a place you remember from your past. The important thing is that you feel safe, protected, and at peace in this haven in nature.

Return to the same place in each meditation you do. In every meditation, take a little time to explore more of this place; explore each detail. *"Love pays attention to detail."* Spend a bit of time opening your senses of sight, sound, touch, taste, and hearing to make this place more real for you.

4. Now, like Gobi, close your mental eyes and dream. Imagine your hopes and desires for peace in some region of conflict unfolding, or imagine breakthroughs for those researchers struggling to find a cure or those politicians locked in the throes of bitterness, division, and hatred or those scientists blocked in their creativity and innovative pursuits. See this troubled region changing and healing. See the researchers discovering cures. See the politicians working together to find solutions. See the scientists awakening to new and innovative ideas. Add your love and compassion to your dreams and desires. Add your hope.

With your mental eyes still closed, imagine your hopes and desires, filled with your love and compassion, forming tiny seeds within your hand.

5. Your Higher Self will cocoon you now in a sphere of light. Surrounded in this radiant sphere, it will take you to that troubled place, to that place where hope is lacking.

Sense yourself, within your cocoon of light, lifting gently off the ground and floating beyond time and space. When you arrive at your location, your cocoon will float gently to the ground and fade away, leaving you amid this troubled region of conflict, or among the struggling scientists and researchers, or the arguing politicians.

Now open your mental eyes and sense this place around you. Know that you're safe, that your Higher Self is by your side, and that no one can see you.

6. Here plant the seeds you carry. Plant your seeds of hope filled with your love and compassion. Perhaps you plant them by that old woman quivering with fear and despair, or by those politicians filled with hatred and lacking in vision. Maybe you plant them near that scientist desperately seeking solutions, or by that doctor looking for a cure to end the suffering, or by that helpless mother clinging desperately to her dying child. Plant your seeds of hope, dear one. Plant your seeds of hope and magic.

7. When you finish, close your mental eyes and slowly count from one to five. On the count of five, open your physical eyes and return to your room. Your meditation is now complete; the magic is now undertaken.

You're a magician, dear one. Work your magic. Release hope into your world. In time your seeds will grow and blossom.

You do make a difference, dear one. I hope you come to realize this.

*Be Gobi. Be you.*

# 11

# The Testing of Amit Don

## Suggested Areas of Attention

* Stop being so hard on yourself. Learn to have fun and enjoy your life. There's nothing you need to do, nothing you need to accomplish. Have fun. Be at play in crafting a life of your preference.
* Take responsibility, not guilt, in the living of your life.
* There are lessons to be learned in life, but no tests are ever given. Accept the challenges of life's lessons. Reject the notion of tests.

    You're not being tested, dear one. Stop the foolish belief that you are and start enjoying the life you're living. Respond elegantly to its challenges and opportunities. Pursue a life more real, a reality that calls you to become more with grace and dignity. Take responsibility, not guilt for the life you're living. Whatever happens is a result of what you're either creating or allowing. You're the author of your reality; you and you alone.

    Projecting mother and father onto God and Goddess is denying the gifts of freedom and choice they've given you. By projecting mommy and daddy onto them, you relinquish your power to make conscious choices, be they wise or foolish. In trying to remain a child, you're expecting others to make choices for you. By taking responsibility for your life, you can respond to the choices you're making and choose differently. You can learn the power of choice and avail yourself of its magic. You can become a master at the crafting of life. And, if you so choose, you can lift your mastery to the level of artistry. Responsibility is freedom. Taking responsibility is the work of a spiritual adult.

You're not being tested, dear one. Yes, there are lessons to be learned in life, but no tests are given or required. Learning is at your own pace, and through the various means you choose. Some of the ways you're choosing are much too hard and difficult, and others are poignant and beautiful. You're learning the craft of authorship, dear one. You'll fail at times, and other times you'll succeed; this is how we learn. So stop being so hard on yourself. Learn to be patient and forgiving toward yourself and lighten up a bit.

There are two lessons we're all destined to learn:

(1) To consciously create our reality.

(2) To have fun while doing so.

There are other lessons we choose to learn, as well. These lessons vary from individual to individual. Call them "electives" if you wish. Some elect to learn more about love by experiencing all of its dark and light expressions. Some choose to heal shame, or martyr, or rage, or anger, etc. Some elect to learn forgiveness or any of the myriad resonances and conditions we engage in our pursuit of becoming more. These lessons are chosen prior to the unfolding of each lifetime. Failure to learn these lessons is not important; we have other lifetimes to continue our learning. There's no judgment here; there's no grade given. You should know this, however. You'll succeed in learning all the lessons you've chosen to learn. You're destined to do so. You cannot fail.

So lighten up, dear one! Enjoy! Stop being so hard on yourself! God and Goddess are never hard on you. They've promised never to leave you and to support and love you forever. And they'll keep their promise to you.

So, no matter how foolish or dark your choices may be, you're not alone and will always be helped if you ask for it. Of course, you must be willing to allow the receiving of it. And in those elegant, magical, and lighter choices you make, there'll be so many who will dance and celebrate with you and cheer you on.

You're Higher Self, your Soul and Spirit, and God/Goddess/All That Is always celebrate your learning and growing.

*Enjoy!*

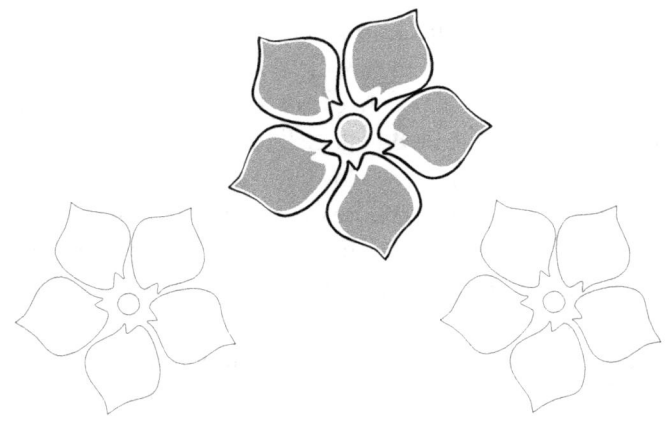

## 12

# The Man
# Who Walked Backward

### Suggested Areas of Attention

* Don't avoid what you're becoming by always trying to fix what was. Listen and respond to your future's call. Your healing lies in where you're going, not in where you've been.
* Respond to the fears of your past by feeling them deeply. Respond to the fears of your lesser selves in response to your future's call.
* Make new maps. Stop following the boring well-traveled paths of others.
* Stop nobilizing your present actions by blaming past hurts and disappointments.

What we're becoming is more powerful than where we've been, yet consensus thinking believes the opposite. It thinks our past created the person we are today and determines what we're becoming tomorrow. It considers it necessary to fix the past to create a better future.

The consensus also thinks that pursuing futures is little more than an act of fantasy, wishful thinking, human potential workshop hype, and the pastime of daydreamers and the young.

These beliefs are not only wrong; they're limiting to our growth and fulfillment. They deny the full power of choice in creating what we're becoming. When we give belief and attention to these erroneous perspectives, we trap ourselves in our past and become deaf to our future's call. We spend our time and energy trying to fix what was while ignoring the pull of what we're growing to be. We neglect the higher resonance that lies in our future.

Lazaris, in describing the real relationship of past, present, and future puts it this way;

> *"The future creates the present on the backdrop of the past."*

What we're becoming is real; our past is not unless we choose to make it so. We make the past real by giving our attention to it and by allowing its beliefs, patterns, and experiences to have meaning and significance for us today. Many spend their entire life dredging around in the muck and mire of events long gone. They're oblivious to the opportunities and healing that await them in their future.

Change the direction of your life. Look to the future. Be guided by what you're becoming. No, don't live in the future, stay in the present, but put more weight on the 'you' you're meant to be. Give it more value and meaning. Always dream and pursue grander futures. Grander futures are where real power will be found and awakened in you. The power you'll awaken while becoming your future self will lift and propel you toward greater and brighter horizons, and more magnificent future selves.

Stop trying to fix your past. Quit using it as a way to hide from your fear of unknown futures. And stop excusing your present actions by blaming past circumstances and events. The past is over; it's not real anymore. For example, claiming that you can't love anymore due to past hurts is a lame excuse; it's an act of cowardice. It's an attempt to nobilize your present actions by blaming past hurts and disappointments. It's a lie you repeat over and over to hide from the rigors of loving. Be courageous and move forward. If the past comes up to block your way, as it will surely do, then attend to the resistance with commitment and forgiveness and keep moving forward.

You're on a great adventure, dear one. Be an adventurer, not a historian. Make new maps. Stop taking the well-traveled routes of others. Claim the 'you' you're destined to become with confidence, trust, will, and courage. Use your will to keep moving. It's upon the journey to your future that you'll discover the fullness of living.

Know that you're not alone here. Your Higher Self walks beside you, your Soul walks beside you, and so many unseen friends journey with you. And God and Goddess and All That Is walk with you and guide you always. And dear one, your Future Self is calling with arms outstretched, and with your permission, will walk beside you and offer guidance. How can you possibly fail?

## 13

# The Saint Who Could Not Be Harmed

### Suggested Areas of Attention

* Accept the authorship of your reality. Stop giving it to your fears and the belief in your vulnerability. You have nothing to fear, and you're not vulnerable.
* Process through and release the destructive resonances you're employing and allowing in your life.
* Identify and replace your old negative self-image.
* Let go of the erroneous belief in punishment and divine retribution.
* Pursue the truth of 'who' and 'what' you are; accept the love, guidance, and protection such pursuits will unfold for you.

*"Nothing in life can harm you
unless you allow it so."*

You're the author of your reality. Everything in it you either create or allow, with no exceptions. No one's punishing you; you're not paying off karmic debts.

Retribution is a man-made concept. It's not a part of God/Goddess/All That Is. As such, it's not real. Nothing is threatening you unless you create it so. God and Goddess do not determine the play of your life; you do. Don't blame them for how your life's unfolding. Don't blame fate; don't blame yourself. Just own your reality and change it.

Life plays out negatively or positively as a result of choices and decisions, beliefs and attitudes, and thoughts and feelings you hold and make. These resonances attract the stuff of your reality. And the 'stuff' of your reality is shaped in alignment with your self-image. If you cling to the image of a 'loser,' you lose in the living of your life. If you hold the image of being 'unlovable,' your life will lack the love you sincerely seek. If you have the image of 'victim,' your life will prove you right. Change the choices and decisions you make, change the thoughts and feelings you hold, and change the beliefs and attitudes you cling to, and your life miraculously changes. When you let go of your old negative self-image and adopt a new, more elevated one, everything becomes different.

*"Nothing changes until you do."*

No one's punishing you, dear one. Nothing in life is there to harm you. Nothing in life can hurt you unless you create or allow it to do so. Re-claim the authorship of your life. Don't give it to others, or fate, or your negative ego to create for you. Take responsibility for your life without guilt and blame. Forgive the choices and decisions you've made, and the beliefs and attitudes you've carried from the past. Lift your thoughts and feelings to align with the 'you' you're destined to become, and choose a self-image opposite the one you currently hold.

Now go forward into your life invincible. Go forth knowing and allowing the truth that you're indeed loved and protected. Craft your future as a winner, and engage that future as one loved and loving. Be confident and assured that all you undertake in the crafting of this life is supported and nurtured.

Oh, there'll always be dark times, for this is the way it must be in the living of life. The dark times' temper and make your reality more dimensional and challenging. Dark and light times are never punishments or rewards; don't hold them as such. No, you're not punished, dear one; and no, you're not rewarded. But you are promised love and support, freedom, and protection. And, dear one, above all, you're gifted with free choice.

Don't succumb to the belief in conflict, hold instead to the value of challenge. Don't pray to God and Goddess to save you. There's nothing from which you need saving. Ask instead for help in seeing more of the truth of what you're creating or allowing. When you discover the truth, then with courage, authority, and commitment, make different choices and ask that the old lies and templates be corrected; your wish will be honored and granted; your desire supported and nurtured.

Also, realize that death is never a punishment or a failure but instead a beautiful part of living. It's another doorway through which you travel on your endless journey of becoming more.

*"Nothing in life, including death,*
*is there to harm you unless you allow it so."*

## 14

# What Danila Learned of Love

### Suggested Areas of Attention

* What do you believe about love? Does love get you something, or does love lead you somewhere? Let go of a love that 'gets you' and choose a love that 'leads you.' This love will lead you Home.
* Honor the ebbing and flowing of love.
* Seek always to learn and understand more of the one you love. It will keep love alive and fresh. Let the one you love always amaze you.
* Respect others by letting go of the need to control or manipulate them.
* Practice loving daily. Practice giving without conditions and practice this daily.
* When you commit to loving another, let your commitment be forever, whether in the relationship or not.
* Hurt is the only thing that can destroy love. Be careful not to do it.

'Experts' lecture us that to be happy, *"all we need to do is to love more."* But they never tell us how to do it. Why, because they don't know. They expect us to know. For them, just saying the words is enough, or they think that just feeling love is more than sufficient; this is simplistic nonsense. Don't they think we've all tried to love more!

We're all born with the capacity to love, but we're not born knowing how to do it. We're taught love from our parents and the influences of the cultural perspectives of the time. Our parents learned love from their parents and their cultural views of their time. Some learned that love was something ugly and distorted; some learned it was beautiful and authentic. Some learned that love was something painful and hurtful; some learned it was all-embracing and nurturing.

Love, for some, was taught through the overpowering influence of martyrhood, for others through acts of violence. Love, for some, was expressed through conflict and division, for some abandonment, betrayal, humiliation, or rejection. Love, for many, was said to be found in the nobility of sacrifice and pain. Yet, for a few, the love learned reflected its real nature. As varied as our teachers were so to the many versions of love they taught.

Religions firmly hold that love expresses itself through sacrifice, suffering, and martyr. Often societal beliefs view love as some romantic fantasy like the ones portrayed in Hollywood fiction.

What did you learn of love? Ask yourself these questions:

"What was I taught of love?"
"What do I believe love to be?"
"What influenced these beliefs?"
"Who were my teachers?"
"Is this the love I live today?"
"Is this the love I teach to others?"
"Is my version of love expanding or contracting me?"
"Is my version of love leading to the more of me, or keeping me imprisoned in the less?"

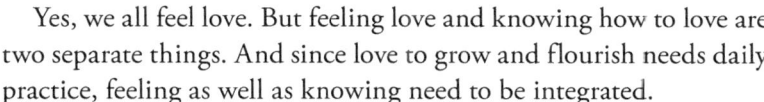

Yes, we all feel love. But feeling love and knowing how to love are two separate things. And since love to grow and flourish needs daily practice, feeling as well as knowing need to be integrated.

First, know that love is not a destination but a journey. We discover more and more of love along a road that has no end.

Love, like the sea, ebbs and flows. There'll be times when love requires flowing and times when love requires integration through its ebbing. There'll be times when love needs action and times when it needs pause and reflection. Ebbing and flowing are both crucial in the living and practicing of love.

Love requires that we practice giving daily, giving without strings attached.

Love requires that we respect the choices of others by letting go of the need to control or manipulate those choices regardless of what we believe is in their best interest.

Love requires that we always seek to know more of the one to whom we're practicing our loving. Never take the other for granted; doing so deadens the love.

Love requires commitment. Commit always even though you may be parted for reasons painful or hurting.

Love requires that we allow its freedom. By letting love free, we'll never be free of its presence.

Learn love from the Ancient One within you. Love's truth lays hidden deep within you on the other side of your pains, hurts, heartbreaks, disappointments, and distortions. Although you'll need to learn love anew, you have an abundance of resources available if you but ask and pay attention. Your Higher Self is an excellent teacher and is always at the ready. Just ask and pay attention to your Higher Self's responses.

Be conscious of your old distorted views of love; let them go. Discover and practice the more real love your future will awaken within you, and learn and grow the love that your more real self knows and is willing to ignite in you.

Love is always becoming more without ever having been less; seek to understand this. And be open to a different loving, but only if you dare to live it.

Love's Grand Adventure awaits you.

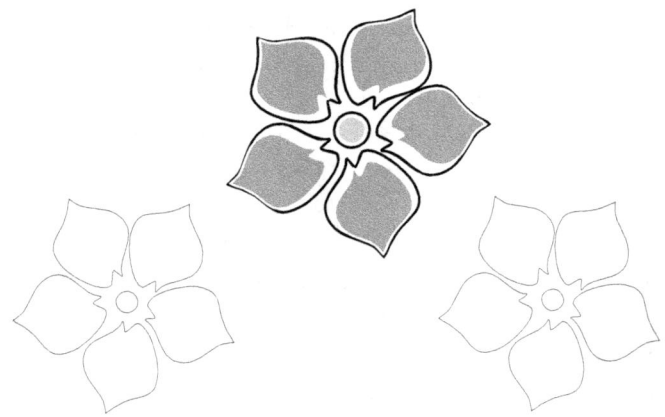

## 15

# How the Master Found Enlightenment

### Suggested Areas of Attention

* Make *'becoming more'* a priority.
* Avoid taking short cuts in the living and growing of your life.
* Recognize and heal the trap of perfectionism in you.
* Don't listen to the lies that *'specialness'* promises you. Free yourself from its prison.
* Pursue the challenges of growing and becoming more; avoid the need for conflicts and struggle.

When talking about taking short-cuts in the pursuit of growth, Lazaris often says, *"Taking short-cuts cuts one short."* Listen to the whispers here?

Are you growing tired of your growing? Are you wondering when this 'personal growth' thing will ever come to an end? Do you think to yourself, *"How long will it take me to finally become perfect?"* The answer is simple. *Your growth is forever, and you'll never be perfect.*

Perfectionism is the negative ego's vain pursuit of specialness. Specialness promises a cure for low self-esteem and a balm for the pain of self-loathing. It never delivers on its promises. Also, the pursuit of specialness often involves the search for quick-fixes.

The belief in one's specialness is an insurmountable obstacle to allowing the realization of one's uniqueness and in awakening the fullness of one's self. We must reject the lure of specialness whenever it emerges, and it must be forgiven and released as a part of our growing and becoming; there are no exceptions.

When you find yourself pursuing quick-fixes and short-cuts in your growing and becoming, stop what you're doing and make a different choice. Growth is an ever-evolving spiraling process, and it never ends. There are no short-cuts or quick-fixes in growing and becoming. Think for a moment. *If we were ever to become perfect, where do we go from there?* The eternal boredom of such a state would be complete hell.

Everything is growing and evolving to become more. Everything! There's no limit in the idea of 'more.' Even God and Goddess and All That Is are not perfect, although, at the same time, they're not imperfect. They, too, are continually growing and becoming more without ever having been less. Love is like that. It always becomes more without ever having been less. We should view our growth as a marvelous and grand adventure. And when you discard the desire for perfectionism and specialness, and when you stop pursuing short-cuts and quick-fixes, it will be.

Listen to the whispers here. Reject the voices that urge you to take a faster route. There is no 'faster' route. There's only the route you're on.

Listen to the voice that tells you your growth is much too hard and demanding; this voice is your resistance. Attend to it as such and continue to pursue the endless adventure along the path you travel.

Lighten up! Have fun! There's no cosmic law that says growth must be hard and painful. Although growth will be demanding, and although growth will have its dark and light times, you're strong enough to keep the journey adventurous, alive, vibrant, and fulfilling. Pursue the challenges of growing and becoming; avoid the need for conflicts and struggle.

Pursue the adventure. Heed and attend to the voices of your resistances. Pursue the Light upon your journey and don't run from the dark but into it. On the other side, your destiny, your destination, awaits; on the other side, your growing and becoming assume a higher octave. Your journey forward gets really interesting and fun on the other side. Mystery and magic wait for you on the other side.

## 16

# The Man Who Said, "Thank You"

## Suggested Areas of Attention

* Explore and harness the incredible power of gratitude.
* Always look to life's bigger picture because the little picture is never what you think it is.
* Stop wallowing in your misfortunes. With gratitude, you can free yourself from your troubles by allowing them to become opportunities, which in truth they are.
* Happiness resides in gratitude; gratitude resides in joy. Discover gratitude as if for the first time. It's there you'll find the happiness and joy you seek.
* Stop playing the victim and start living your life with confidence and certainty. Trust in your process and travel your path with grace and elegance.

Gratitude is so much more than just thankfulness and appreciation. It's a resonance that opens us to happiness and joy. It's an energy that inspires us to create and inspires in us the willingness to be created.

Gratitude is a generating energy that generates futures that shine resplendent in our goodness, truth, and beauty, and it's a virtue that lifts all our actions to achieve such futures.

Gratitude opens us to a willingness to be loved and loving, and it provides us with the gift of being understanding.

Gratitude inspires one to be a good and virtuous person. And gratitude, being a generating energy, provides more reasons to be grateful. It generates boundless opportunities complete with remarkable synchronicities that allow those opportunities to flow with grace, elegance, and magic.

Gratitude is a powerful doorway through which the love and miracles of your Higher Self, your Soul and Spirit, and God/Goddess/All That Is flow elegantly to you. It's also a doorway through which your love and compassion flow to them, and to the world you so beautifully cherish.

Gratitude is essential in the claiming of your authority and a principle force in igniting a generosity born of self-acceptance and self-worth.

Gratitude awakens the thrill of living and motivates one to pursue adventures that make our living so much more exciting and fun.

Cultivate sincere gratitude. It'll be a powerful ally in your pursuit of healing and growth.

When you cultivate gratitude, you open yourself to perceiving life's bigger picture. You won't get bogged down in its nuisances. When you look to life's bigger picture, you strengthen your understanding and appreciation. It becomes easier to let in the love that freely flows to you, and it becomes easier to flow that love back into your world. When you look to life's bigger picture, you awaken love and wisdom in you, and you become a conduit for the love and wisdom of God/Goddess/All That Is.

Stop wallowing in the misfortunes of life; they're temporary. Love, beauty, healing, and gratitude are not. Face the adversities of life with solid confidence, trust, and faith. Draw upon your presence, courage, and grace and keep moving forward. Misfortunes cannot stop your progress unless you allow them to. With grace, troubles become obstacles easily overcome, failures become opportunities for grander successes, and tragedies become minor speed-bumps.

You are loved, dear one; you have powerful allies. You cannot fail in your quest to become more. Isn't that worth your gratitude?

*Ah, gratitude!*

*The more you feel it*
*the more reasons you have to feel it.*

# 17

# Nilla's Dearest Friend

## Suggested Areas of Attention

* Feel the emotions you're hiding, but feel those emotions cleanly.
* Invade your privacy and go deeper into those secret places within you.
* Stop feeding your rage with your attention and denial. Recognize, acknowledge, and transform it. Ask for help in doing so.

Anger is a natural human emotion. As such, it needs to be expressed cleanly. *'Cleanly'* means to honestly feel the emotion without using it to punish, hurt, or harbor. Anger can be quickly released when handled cleanly.

For example, if someone backs into your car, it's perfectly natural to feel and express anger. And it's ok to express anger to the offending driver. However, it's not ok to use it to hurt, punish, or harbor for further use. Let your intention be on releasing your anger, not on dumping it onto another. When anger comes up, feel it fully. Feel it, express it if need be, then choose to let it go; doing this 'cleanly' handles the emotion.

Constructive Emotion: Any emotion dark or light that you feel and then release (for the darker emotions) and that you feel and then integrate (for the lighter ones.)

Destructive Emotion: Any emotion, dark or light, that you'll not allow yourself to feel; that you shove down within you.

When you choose to hold on to anger, you're choosing to harbor it in you. Harboring an emotion is the choice to keep it alive within you so you can use it over and over again to blame, to punish, and to fuel your righteous indignation. When people claim, *"I'm getting in touch with my anger because I'm feeling it all the time,"* they're not getting in touch with their anger, they're harboring it, and they're recycling it. And worst of all they're lying to you and themselves. Anger, at its most destructive resonance, is rage. Harboring anger grows and strengthens it. Over time, anger becomes rage.

Rage can express itself as loud and overtly aggressive, or it can be silent and hidden, appearing as passive aggression or persistent fatigue. Rage, either loud or quiet, will eventually devour its host if left unattended.

Feeding rage makes it grow ever more powerful and deadly. Rage feeds off the attention you give it. Understand that simply ignoring it is giving it attention. By pretending it doesn't exist, you hide it deeper within you. And your denial feeds it. The stronger your rage becomes, the more you risk being devoured by it. Rage is like a wild beast; when ignored and left unattended, it will over time kill you. Cancer is an example of this.

Face your 'Rage Beast" meditatively (See Appendix One). Have the courage to enter its lair. In the dark and stench of its abode, you'll find it. If not, it'll find you.

Now standing before your Rage Beast, feel its wrath. Face its hate and torment. As you choose to go into it more deeply, you'll come to a place where you'll feel a strange intoxication. You'll feel a sense that you indeed like this rage. You may even consider it a friend. You may even admit that it makes you feel good. Great, you're now very close to its healing. When you can honestly admit that a part of you likes your rage, you can make a different choice, an empowered choice to change it.

It's important to note that we do not release rage, we transform it.

Rage is an archetypal emotion. Like love, it has two sides, dark and light. The dark side of rage is *'enrage;'* the light side is *'outrage.'* The energy is the same, only directed differently to a darker or lighter value.

Be outraged at man's inhumanity to man, be outraged by the suffering in the world, and be outraged for lying to yourself. Be outraged at your choice to take the easier path instead of the path best reflecting your truth and principles. Rage can significantly fuel your will, and it's a strong will that motivates one to take action to change. Will drives love, will initiates magic, and will elevates your healing.

Face the rage you hide so deeply. Acknowledge its attraction and intoxication. Ask for help from your Higher Self to transform it. Ask for help in elevating it from *'enrage'* to *'outrage.'* When you do, what love will flow, what magic will happen, and what healing you'll achieve! In so doing, your rage beast can and will become a powerful ally on your incredible journey of becoming more. It can warn you when you're about to fall into its trap.

> Be outraged at your reluctance to make such a choice,
> or to take such an action.

## 18

# A Lesson on Believing You're Special

### Suggested Areas of Attention

* Let go of the belief that you're special; because you're not. Discover, instead, your uniqueness; because you are.
* Become more self-aware. Your growth and expansion require this.
* Always monitor and challenge the many voices and lies your negative ego tells.
* Recognize, acknowledge, forgive, and release the shame you hold.

    The belief in *'specialness'* is a trap set by your negative ego. It's your ego's lie that you're either 'more than' or 'less than' others. It's a belief born of your feelings of shame and fed by the attention you give it.

    As a child, you discovered 'specialness' by observing it in those around you. Or you were taught 'specialness' by those seeking to find their specialness through you. Or you adopted it as a means to combat the pain and hurt of shame with its false belief that you're flawed, defective, or broken.

You weren't wrong in adopting this belief. It was how you survived as a child. But now, as an adult, it'll imprison you unless you heal it. The trap of 'specialness" will blind you to the discovery of your more real self. It'll rob you of the gift of self-awareness. And it'll deny you your magnificent uniqueness. As long as you hold to the lie of specialness, you cannot know what's real and what's unique about you. You'll remain in self-delusion and self-ignorance until jolted out of it.

No, you're not special; no one is. But you're wonderfully unique; everyone is.

Drop the belief that you're special. Catch yourself when you slip into it from time to time. Acknowledge the 'why' and 'how' of your need for believing it. Forgive yourself and let it go. Choose to pursue the more real of you, the more unique of you.

Remember, you're not wrong or bad for believing your special; you're just making a mistake. Thinking that you're wrong or bad is shaming yourself once again. And shame is not what you want to make real anymore.

Mistakes can be corrected. So correct yourself and move on. Drop the specialness. Pursue your uniqueness.

*Enter the Hall of Self-Awareness.*
*You have such amazing things to discover there!*

# 19

# The River

## Suggested Areas of Attention

* Put more trust in the relationship than in the individuals comprising it. Trust the synergy.
* Trust when trust is warranted; never trust blindly.
* Look to your relationship to *'that which is more than you.'* Look to your spirituality; value it; prioritize it. In time, your spirituality will become your only priority. Always work to make your spirituality more.
* What is your relationship with love? How do you define it for yourself?
* Value the temporal, but pursue the eternal more.

1 + 1 = 3

You (1) + another (1) + the relationship, the synergy (1) = 3

Synergy is that which is greater than the sum of its parts. A relationship, being a synergy, is likewise greater than the sum of the two or more engaging in it. Synergy is an independent energy standing

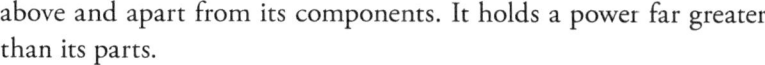

above and apart from its components. It holds a power far greater than its parts.

Love, being a synergy, is a transcendent force more potent than those engaging in it.

You may not trust fully the person you love, but ask yourself, *"Do I trust the relationship?"* If your answer is *"No,"* don't put your trust in it. If your answer is *"Yes,"* then trust it. Lean on the relationship; it will support you. The relationship transcends both of you.

As poets are fond of saying, *"love is eternal,"* that's true, but the synergy of love is where the eternal lies not in the participants in the loving. Always seek the "eternal" of love; always pursue its synergy. You'll discover your majesty, your magnificence, and your more real self in the lofty heights of the synergy of love. It's in the transcendence of love you'll discover yourself.

On your journey Coming Home, the synergy of love will carry you all the way. Along your journey Coming Home, there'll be dark times and times of light. By trusting the synergy of love, you'll find support during the darkest times, and during the frightening realness of the times of light.

Spirituality is *'one's relationship to that which is more than one's self.'* It's the nature of the relationship that defines your spirituality. Some spiritualities are dark and violent, some light and liberating. It's what you bring to the relationship that sets it for you.

The relationship God/Goddess/All That Is have with you is beyond all labels and defining. It's transcendent. It's more than you'll ever come to know or experience fully. Their relationship to you, their love for you, is always becoming more without ever having been less. Such a paradox is unfathomable. Don't try to figure it out. Instead, place your trust in their relationship with you. The resonance of God/Goddess/ All That Is, being higher than yours, will elevate you. It will lift you to realms unfathomable and beyond. And know this, dear one, the synergy, the resonance the emerges from the relationship between you and God/Goddess/All That Is, is higher than both you and God/Goddess/All That is. The synergy of your spirituality lifts both you and them to even grander heights. Wow!

How exciting such a journey is! How much love and loving wait for you in such unfathomable places and beyond!

You're a drop of rain on a journey to an endless sea, dear one. Along this journey, you may come to discover that, in truth, you are the endless sea.

*You are the love you seek.*

# 20

# The Tale of the Chuckling Saint

## Suggested Areas of Attention

* Stop allowing your negative ego to interpret your reality. You, and only you, should do this.
* Claim your worth, accept your value, and stop trying to earn them. It's only self-esteem that's earned.
* Let magical synchronicities flow uninterrupted by your ego. Your magic is a gift you give yourself and a gift you give to your world. It's also a gift from the Divine. It's a gift that's available to everyone; it doesn't make you special.
* Shame asks for proof of your value. Heal shame, and you'll see your value glowing radiantly all about you.
* Let your life be light and fun. You're taking it much too seriously.

Don't give your life over to the false promises of your negative ego. Listen instead to the wise counsel of your Higher Self.

Your negative ego always lies to you. Your Higher Self always tells you the truth.

Your negative ego will always lead you down the path of pain and enslavement. Your Higher Self always leads to Light and freedom.

Your negative ego promises the illusion of specialness. Your Higher Self offers the realness of self-awareness and the awakening of your more real self.

Your negative ego delivers only sadness and death. Your Higher Self offers joy and never-ending awakening. It's your Higher Self who guides you into the waiting arms of God/Goddess/All That Is.

Choose between the two, dear one. Make sure you choose wisely. Your future will unfold with misery or with elegance, depending on your choice.

Stop trying to prove your worth and value. There's no need to do so. You already possess the fullness of your worth and value. You just need to claim it. Stop trying to prove yourself. Stop trying to correct past blames and judgments made by yourself and others so very long ago. What point is there in such folly? Accept that you're enough and move on.

Care not for the projections and opinions of others. What value do they have to you? What weight are you still giving to them? Free yourself from the judgments and shame of others. It's a burden they must attend to, not you.

Lighten the weight you place on living. Your life was never meant to be as hard or as heavy as your making it. Start prioritizing fun and those things that awaken laughter and joy in you. Stop taking yourself so seriously.

Your life is a play. You can make it a tragedy or a comedy, a drama or a love story, a melodrama or a tale of magic and enchantment. You choose. Why not choose fun, love, magic, and enchantment? Such a choice is, well, more fun, more loving, more magical, and more enchanting. I'm just suggesting.

Keep your magic close to you; don't give it to the foolish. What value is magic to those who trap themselves in the false safety of logic and reason, and hide in fear of that which they cannot control or understand? What worth is magic to those who will not dream or pursue the more of their living? It's your ego's fantasy that seeks the praise and affirmation of others. If you seek such praise and affirmation, then know, dear one, there's work to be done to heal your shame and in accepting your valued self.

A mango waits for you on the highest branch. Are you going to waste your time scheming and plotting the many strategies to force it to the ground? Are you going to labor and effort to climb the gnarly branches to obtain it? Are you going take no action but instead wallow in self-pity believing you're not loved, or not deserving of its juicy goodness? Or are you going to float effortlessly to the top and claim the sweetness awaiting you there? It's your call.

# 21

# Two Healings

## Suggested Areas of Attention

* Respond to the messages that come to you be they shouts or whispers. Address the whispers before they turn to shouts.
* Choose to heal with elegance and dignity.
* Be open to allowing more of your courage, dignity, and grace to shine in your life.
* Always look for the more of you.
* Seek healing more than fixing.
* Pursue and be pursued by beauty.
* Fear waits at all the many crossroads of change and passage. Fear is your Threshold Guardian. Accept this. Don't run from fear; embrace it, and transcend it. You're so much more powerful than your fear. When in fear, accept the love that always embraces you. When you do, fear transforms into a brilliant light guiding you beyond the change and passage into the arms of your realness.

It's time to attend to your healing, whether it's physical, emotional, or mental, whether it's in your relationships or your spiritual growth.

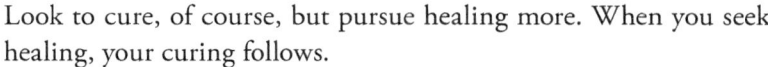

Look to cure, of course, but pursue healing more. When you seek healing, your curing follows.

Healing is not about preventing death, though sadly, many healers believe this. People get a false notion, either directly or indirectly, that death results from failure; this is not true.

Healing is more than getting better. Healing is about awakening more of who you are. It's about attending to the root causes of disconnection with one's more real self. It's about transcending a condition, not merely fixing it. If that transcending involves curing, fine. If that transcending means moving on with elegance and grace through the gentle act of dying, that too is fine. Both choices are acts of healing. Healing is so much more than curing. A healed person is one who rises beyond the limitations of the condition to a state of 'becoming more.'

Death is not a measure of failure; living is not proof of success. The awakening of one's dignity, grace, elegance, and becoming is where one discovers the fruits of healing. Connection to one's goodness, truth, and beauty is where one discovers the promise of healing. Healing is found in the process, not in the result.

Look within yourself for what needs healing. Shun attempts to fix it. Choose instead to heal; to recognize its presence, to acknowledge its impact on you, to forgive yourself for its existence and for not heeding its whispers or shouts, and choose to address it with elegance and dignity.

Whatever requires healing always sends a message; the more serious the need, the more urgent the message. All illness begins in the unconscious. It will eventually become conscious in the form of a condition or a crisis. It's the way your unconscious communicates with you. Addressing the message as a whisper prevents your unconscious from having to deliver it as a shout.

Since all messages are from your unconscious, not from someone else's, the message is for you and you alone to interpret. And since the language of the unconscious is myth, metaphor, archetype, or symbol, it's there you'll find its meaning.

Some examples:
* A speeding accident or a speeding ticket (each a metaphor) could be a shout to 'slow down' in the living of your life. It may be a message to take time to process and integrate. *"You're going too fast, slow down!"* or *"Be more vigilant, if not your life's going to crash!"*
* A heart condition (a symbol) could be a shout to attend to issues around love, especially around allowing more love into your life. It can involve any matter concerning your emotional heart.
* Cancer (a metaphor) is often a shout to address the rage that's eating away at you.

Beauty is a source of majestic healing. To activate healing, pursue beauty. Let it seduce you, enveloped you, lift you. Let beauty carry you into transcendence. Within beauty, you'll find healing and so much more. Isn't it time now to attend to your healing? Isn't it time to welcome beauty into your life?

Attend to your healing. Do so with honesty, courage, dignity, and grace. Ask for help, and you'll receive it. But will you allow the support? That's a question you must ask of yourself.

A grander you, a more awakened you, always waits on the other side of healing, whether it's in this life or another.

*The 'Grander You' is found in the sweet seduction of beauty in this life and the next.*

## 22

# The Path Maker

## Suggested Areas of Attention

* Get off the path others have chosen for you and make your own; craft a new, more personal way.
* Dare to step away from consensus thinking.
* Choose between your investment in *'struggle'* and the elegant satisfaction found in *'challenge.'* Choose between the constricting nature of *'conflict'* and the elevating thrill of *'adventure.'*
* Avoid effort. Pursue the passion and sense of accomplishment inherent in 'efforting.'
* Welcome the challenges and adventures you'll discover on your path to Coming Home.
* No law says life has to be as hard as your making it. If there is, it's a fool's law.

Don't settle for a road well-traveled. Don't settle for a road less traveled. Make your own road instead. There's where the adventure lies.

There are an infinite number of paths for you to follow on your journey Home. But there's only one path for you; the one you're on.

It's time to step outside the consensus; it's time to honor your uniqueness. Stop trying to play safe by fitting in. No one in the consensus ever accomplishes greatness. No one playing safe ever becomes exceptional.

Be the first to witness the stunning vistas you'll discover upon your uncharted path. In time others will follow. But only you, the first to travel this unknown terrain, will have experienced wonders the others will never know.

The others who journey along the path you make will find the going easier. You'll find the going hardest. But would you have it any other way? You're a path maker, an adventurer, a dream maker. It's your nature to discover unknown places. It's your nature to found, not find, virgin futures.

Stand up, stand out, and step forth. Be the Path Maker. The way will not be easy. But it doesn't have to be difficult unless you create it so.

Along your journey, replace old habits of struggle with the desire to be challenged. Replace old beliefs in the value of effort with elevating and rewarding acts of 'efforting.' Replace past investments in conflict with the spirited wonders found in adventure. You'll journey to places within yourself that for lifetimes you've refused to go. You'll discover light places, brilliant places within yourself that are even more frightening, for they'll reveal the truth and magnificence of you.

Seek these places. They're the terrain of your becoming. And along the way, accept that you're always loved, always protected, and always guided. You're not alone, dear one. You'll never be alone upon your journey Coming Home.

*Be a Path Maker. Make a new path.*

*In so doing you'll awaken and inspire others
to pursue their own path Home.*

## 23

# Mohan at the Gate of Bliss

### Suggested Areas of Attention

* Isn't it time to forgive yourself? Isn't it time to forgive others to whom you cling so tenaciously?
* Lean on that love much grander than yours; it's there for you to lean on.
* Make different choices now. Choose to pursue the more of you. Choose to attend to your lesser selves with love, understanding, acceptance, forgiveness, and healing. Respond to the call of the 'more.' It's your call Home.
* Forgiveness turns the light on at the beginning of your journey; it turns the light off at the journey's end.

Forgiveness is a powerful energy. When you truly forgive, when you genuinely let go of harbored anger, pains and hurts, you'll be able to live once again. Perhaps you'll find yourself living for the first time.

When you truly forgive yourself and others, when you genuinely break the cords that bind you, you'll free yourself from your prison of blame and be able to pursue your grand adventure of becoming more. You'll be able to find the happiness you seek. Forgiveness is what your life's about, dear one; it's what it was always about. It's why you're here.

Your lack of forgiveness will always bind you to the past. It will deny you futures, deny dreams realized, deny visions of better tomorrows, and deny hope, blessed and miraculous hope. And you cannot ultimately heal while stubbornly holding to your blame of self and others.

Forgiveness does not require that you forgive the acts that hurt you. To do so would send a devastating message to those offended parts of you that their hurt and pain were of little consequence. No, don't forgive the acts. You don't need to do so to free yourself. Forgive the offender instead. Forgive the *'why'* of their actions. Forgive why they did what they did. Be understanding of their pain, and fear, and loneliness. Be understanding of their weakness and ignorance and rage. The key is to be understanding.

And when forgiving yourself, dear one, likewise don't make light of your actions made in truth or imagined, but forgive the lesser developed 'you' who chose the lesser way. Forgive yourself, love yourself, understand yourself, and don't abandon your younger selves to their pain, and hurt, and loneliness; this is a gracious act of self-love, dear one; this is your destiny's way.

Yes, forgive the *'why'* of the offense, not the offense itself.

Know that such things as karma and retribution are lies and myths released into your world by the negative ego. Karma and retribution are your ego's way of keeping you imprisoned in your need for vengeance. Your Higher Self, your Soul and Spirit, and God/Goddess/All That Is do not hold such falsehoods as karma and retribution. They always maintain what's real, not the lies you tell yourself, or what you believe yourself to be. They hold sacred the truth of you and will never waver from it. And when you're ready, and when you're willing, and when you will allow it, they'll awaken that truth in you. Such is the way of forgiveness.

You're loved, dear one. You've always been, you always are, and you'll always be. Lean on that love by forgiving yourself and others, and by letting go of the past. It's time now. The call is to do so.

*Let it end! Let it go! Be free!*

*Enter your Gate of Bliss, dear one.*
*You're ready now. You're so very, very ready.*

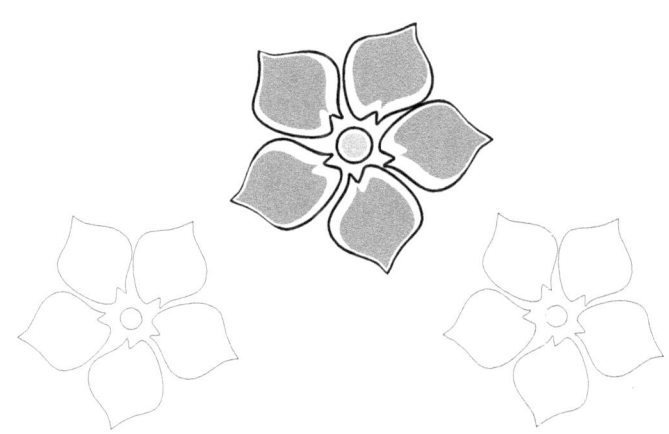

# 24

# Rumesh Pays Respect

## Suggested Areas of Attention

* Display honestly held respect; avoid the shallowness of hollow rituals.
* Challenge your routines. Discover the freedom found in spontaneity.
* Open to the love you'll discover in letting go.
* Grieve the passing of the old; celebrate the arrival of the new.
* What needs to die in you? What are you desperately trying to keep alive?
* What needs birth in you? What are you desperately trying to deaden?

Ritual can be a powerful working of magic. But when ritual becomes routine, it loses power; it loses the ability to elevate our life and manifest our desires. In the same way, when love becomes habitual, we run the risk of either losing it or greatly diminishing its impact upon us. Respecting others, as well as loving others, is never to take them for granted by allowing the relationship to become routine. Never let respect and love become a hollow ritual.

When our life stagnates into a routine or habit, we run the risk of living a dull and predictable existence with little joy or happiness. Our life becomes devoid of richness and depth. When love and life

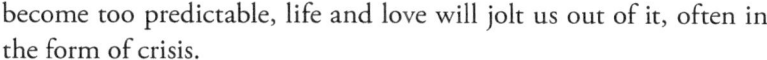

become too predictable, life and love will jolt us out of it, often in the form of crisis.

Be wary of a lifeless spirituality.

Even though one can awaken spirituality through ritual, spirituality is not ritual. Our spirituality needs shaking up now and then to keep it alive and vibrant.

We're on a magnificent journey. Upon that journey are times when we must pause and rest, and times when we must rise and move. Our path will not allow us to sit too long or move too much. A crisis will force us to pause; a crisis will kick us into action. There are more elegant ways to travel through life than to employ a crisis as a traffic cop or a punt-kicker.

Be wary of routines.

If you drive the same way to work day after day, year after year, try something different. Drive to work a different way now and again. Shake your life up a little. If you don't, your life may do it for you. Don't take love, or life, or your spirituality, or anything for that matter for granted. Shake it up from time to time. Pay attention to it.

To keep love, be willing to let it go. The more you set it free, the more it remains with you. When a loved one passes, or when any phase of your life comes to an end, let go. Celebrate that loved one; honor that passing phase. In so doing, you'll forever retain the 'real' in that relationship, and will forever maintain the realness of that passing phase. Letting go also makes space for the new to arrive.

Love is never lost, dear one. Its form can change, but it's never lost. By respecting the love you have, and by avoiding hollow rituals, love will shower you with its omnipresence.

There's never loss only gain, dear one.<br>
Celebrate this Law of Nature.

## 25

# The Saint Who Loved Science

### Suggested Areas of Attention

* Avoid complacency. Never stop searching and reaching.
* Ask yourself, *"What is my current relationship to that which is more than me?"* Be truthful in your answer.
* Deepen your spirituality by giving it more attention and value in your life.
* Always pursue your goodness, truth, and beauty. You'll see it reflected in the goodness, truth, and beauty all about you.
* Avoid dogma, and consensus beliefs and ideology.
* Reach beyond into the Unknown without relinquishing your hold on logic and reason. Keep searching, dear one. Keep reaching. Never stop the search. Never cease from reaching.

Religion lost spirituality the moment it believed it found God. It's in science that you'll discover spirituality because science is always looking.

Science does not always acknowledge that God is what it's pursuing. But, in truth, it is. Science is much more comfortable using terms like *"God Particle."* But that doesn't matter. Spirituality is awakened and enlivened by the search, not in the ego's claim of arrival. And science, in its pursuit of mystery, touches spirituality's power and magic.

What makes humans so remarkable is that they're always pursuing that which is more than themselves; be it the search for alien life, or the search for meaning in material things, or the search for God in the mysteries of scientific inquiry, or through the countless other pursuits they engage. Humans always reach out to find the 'more.' And when humans fail from time to time, as such quests require, they pick themselves up, dust themselves off, and start their pursuit again. They never give up. Lifetime after lifetime, they keep searching.

Keep searching, dear one. Always seek the 'more.' But most importantly, always seek the more of you. The pursuit of the truth of you will always lead to higher truths. The never-ending quest to discover your lost Holy Grail will lead to an awakened life beyond what you can yet imagine. This ever-unfolding truth of you is what will set you free.

But be warned. Don't get lost in dogma, or consensus beliefs and ideology. You can find spirituality in religion, but you'll never find religion in spirituality.

Blaze a new path in your pursuit. Awaken the explorer in you. There'll be times when your search will advance you; there'll be times when you slide back; this is all part of the grand adventure, this is the 'Explorer's Path.' Realize that your spirituality is your spirituality uniquely; no one else's. Your relationship to God and Goddess and All That's Is is your relationship uniquely; no one else's. Even if you believe you have no relationship at all.

Also, know that logic and reason will only take you so far in your pursuit. In time you'll reach a pinnacle. There you'll be asked to leap into the unknown beyond logic and reason. When you come to that pinnacle, you'll be ready. Process your fear, attend to the voices of your past, handle and forgive your resistances, then leap. Let go of the safety of logic and reason, but don't abandon them either. Let go of the security of the familiar. Let go of the side of the pool and start swimming in unknown waters. It's in the Unknown truths reveal themselves. It's in the Unknown mystery is found. The Unknown is where you'll discover yourself. The Unknown is where you'll dance with God/Goddess/All That Is. The Unknown is where you will, in time, 'Know.'

*Keep searching; this is how you'll be discovered.*

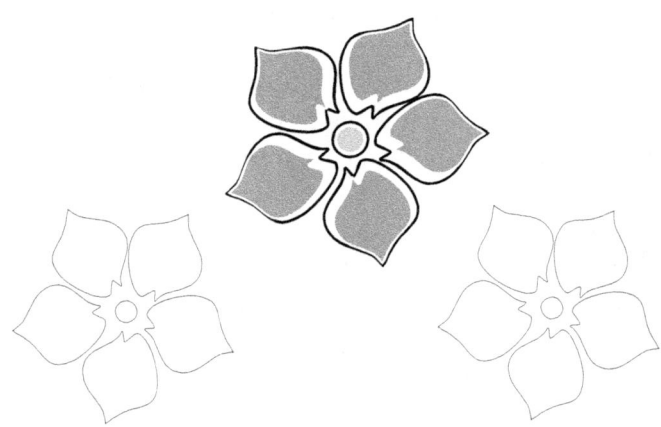

# 26

# The Two Lovers Who Never Met

## Suggested Areas of Attention

* Practice love every day.
* Be open to your oneness; ask for a life that expresses it.
* Stop trying to find your lost love in others; it's in yourself you'll find it.
* Grow to love your lesser parts of self. When you can love the least of you then, and only then, will you come to love the whole.
* Reclaim the love you believe you lost; it's not lost its hiding. Release the love you lock away inside you; it's not dead, it's imprisoned.

You're the love you seek. You stand upon the shoreline gazing out at an endless sea searching, searching ever searching for the return of your savior. You've waited and waited and waited for lifetimes. Search and wait no longer. The one you yearn for has arrived, and dear one, it's you.

Within you hidden and often imprisoned, a radiant love shines brightly, a love that for countless lifetimes you've sought desperately to discover in others. If you continue to search for your lost and hidden love outside yourself, you'll keep searching for lifetimes more.

You cannot find your lost and hidden love outside you; your world only reflects what you project upon it. But know that all you love in others, and all you love in your world, you'll find heightened within yourself if you'd only take the time to look.

When you discover the love you are, when you stop hiding it and free it from its prison, then and only then will you fully know and accept the love of others without the strings your wounded self attaches. When you truly and fully own the love you are, then dear one, you'll no longer define yourself by the love of others. When you no longer need others to fill the emptiness of your own denied love, then you free others of having to be your savior, a task they cannot fulfill.

A time will come when you will no longer need the love of others. You'll realize it overflows abundantly from you already. When you no longer need the love of others, you'll find love from others beyond measure. You'll be awash in their love. You'll be at one with their love.

Then, dear heart, you'll discover the oneness of everything; you'll discover your oneness with everything. Then, dear one, you'll dance in the Oneness with God and Goddess and forever shine in the oneness of All That Is.

> *"And when all he loves about her he finds within himself,*
> *and when she no longer needs him,*
> *then, and only then,*
> *will these two lovers meet."*

# 27

# The Answer is Always, "Yes"

## Suggested Areas of Attention

* Remember your covenant with God and Goddess. Choose to Come Home. From this choice, your life will take a different direction.
* Take responsibility, not guilt, for the choices and decisions you make and the life you're creating and allowing.
* Learn to distinguish between your negative ego's lies and the voice of your Higher Self, who always tells the truth.

Goddess will never say *"No"* to any request you make. It's because of her love and covenant with you.

When you chose to separate from her, a covenant was made between you. In that covenant, Goddess promised never to abandon you, never to stop loving you, and to honor your freedom and choices at all times. The promise you made to her was that you'd eventually Come Home. Although you forgot your covenant with her, she never forgot her covenant with you.

Free Will and Determinism

You have free will and free choice in the direction of your life. You have free will to grow and change in your way and in your time. What is determined is that you'll someday remember your promise to Come Home, and you'll choose to keep that promise.

Goddess will never interfere with your choices and will never violate your freedom. To do so would break her covenant with you. But more so, it would interfere with your destiny of learning and growing in your divine pursuit of loving more.

Goddess will always say *"Yes"* to all that you request, but will never say *"Yes"* to the requests of your negative ego. She'll remain patient and wait by your side while you learn and grow to discern and choose more wisely.

Your negative ego desires you harm and, as such, will always lie to you. Learn to separate your negative ego's lies from the voice of your Higher Self, who always tells you the truth. Ask yourself, *"Is what I'm asking born of my negative ego or reflective of my Higher Self?"* Choose wisely.

Coming Home is not a destination but a destiny. It's a state of recognition. A recognition of the Divine of You, a recognition that you're indeed one with God/Goddess/All That Is, and a recognition that you're completely free, completely loved, and wholly loving. But more than recognition, it's a state of being.

Choose to end your private war with God/Goddess/All That Is. Stop projecting mother and father onto them. They're not your mother and father. Be an adult, but more, be a spiritual adult. Take responsibility, not guilt for your life. Everything in your life is a product of the choices and decisions you and you alone make. You can change those.

*Choose wisely and decide carefully.*
*Your destiny requires it.*

## 28

# In the Fire of the Muse

### Suggested Areas of Attention

* Process your beliefs about creativity.
* Be more creative in your life, especially in the living of it.
* Keep your ego out of your creating.
* Avoid all pursuits motivated by the need for validation and vindication.
* Become a master at the living of your life. As you do, over time, your mastery will lift to the heights of artistry.
* Pursue excellence; avoid perfectionism.
* Stop hiding your brilliance! Get into the game!

Stranger: "So what is it you do?"
Writer: "I'm a writer."
Stranger: "Oh, that's interesting. Are you published? Is your book in the New York Times top ten list?"
Writer: "No, but I write every day. I'm a writer. That's what I do."
Stranger: "I'm sorry, my friend, you're not a writer if you're not published, or in the New York Times top ten list."

Stranger: "So what is it you do?"
Painter: "I'm a painter."
Stranger: "Oh, that's interesting. Where is your work showing? Do you own a gallery?"
Painter: "No, but I paint every day. I'm a painter. That's what I do."
Stranger: "I'm sorry, my friend, you're not a painter if your work's not sold, or displayed in an established gallery."

The consensus beliefs and attitudes about creativity are very much askew. Many believe that if a person's work is not published, or in a gallery, or performed in a concert hall, or written about in some philosophical journal, that person is not a real artist. The consensus also legitimizes creativity only if it meets the standard of profitability. If a creative person is not a professional at his or her craft, then that person is a *"wannabe"* artist, indeed not a 'real' artist. This notion is, of course, a fallacy. Avoid such beliefs and standards.

It's simple. If you write, you're a writer. If you do not write, but call yourself a writer, you're a *"wannabe"* writer. If you paint, you're a painter. If you do not paint, but call yourself a painter, you're a *"wannabe"* painter. Being a professional is a category; it's a choice, not a condition. It doesn't qualify you as anything other than a person who receives a check for a product created. The payment is a display of appreciation, that's true, but it doesn't make your creation or art any more valid.

It's essential as a creative person not to give your creativity to your negative ego. Doing so would either greatly diminish what you're capable of creating or stifle creativity altogether. For creativity to flow and flourish, keep the negative ego out of the process.

Avoid the erroneous belief that creative genius requires martyr and sacrifice. No, you don't need to cut off an ear or wallow in a pit

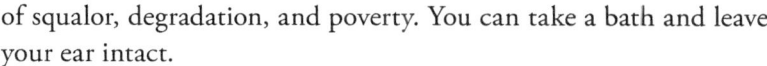

of squalor, degradation, and poverty. You can take a bath and leave your ear intact.

Avoid at all cost the toxic need to create to prove your validity, or to vindicate some past hurt. And above all, avoid creating as a way of proving your specialness; this never works. Create because you love to, not need to. No one needs to create; that's your ego talking.

Being an artist is not limited to writing, performing, painting, composing music, or any of the fine or applied arts. One can be an artist in any endeavor one pursues. There are athletes whose performance is breathtakingly artistic. Some auto mechanics are pure artists at their skill and craft. Being an artist is what you make of something, not the something itself.

Be a master at all you do, but avoid the pursuit of perfectionism. Know the difference between the ego's pursuit of perfection and your Higher Self's call to excellence. Reach always for excellence; strive always to lift your mastery to a state of artistry.

There's a whisper here to free yourself from the false safety of mediocrity, and the prison of the socially accepted. Stop hiding there. Be exceptional, not an exception; be a path maker, not a path taker. Get into the game not to win it but to excel in it. Be more of the 'you' you're capable of becoming. Be a master at the crafting of your life. Grow your mastery to become an artist in your crafting. Craft your life anew and let it flow from you with panache.

If you can monitor your ego, cast aside all need for validation and vindication, and shed the foolish trappings of martyr and sacrifice, you'll gain the attention of the Sisters of the Muse. If you will value the process more than the result and simply enjoy what you're doing, the Muse will most certainly lift you up and toss you into the fire.

*And the fire will consume you. And you'll emerge an artist.*

## 29

# What a Rare and Special Child!

### Suggested Areas of Attention

* Stop dumping shame onto others, and give back the shame others dumped onto you.
* Let go of your ego's need for specialness and discover and accept your wondrous uniqueness.
* Let go of the need to control; the love in you is safe.
* Discover, awaken, and be at play with your Magical Child.
* Be patient and forgiving; be wise and understanding.

Shame is the belief you're flawed, defective, or broken.

Shame is a belief and resonance we adopted throughout the various phases of our life: childhood, adolescence, and adult years. It was a way to make sense of the pains and hurt we encountered. We came to shame by various means: abandonment, abuse, or being wronged. Shame acted as a means of insulating us from the pain and hurt and became a way of making sense of them. But now shame separates us from God/Goddess/All That Is. It denies us the full expression of our feelings and robs us of self-realization. It also impedes our journey of becoming more.

By the time we reach adulthood, we neglect the ownership and healing of our shame. Instead of pursuing its healing, we pass it on to others, often to our children.

Take back the shame you passed to others; you cannot heal it if others have it, and they cannot heal it because it doesn't belong to them. Since healing shame is essential on your journey, take back the shame you passed to others, and lift the shame you hold. You'll have help in the returning and the healing if you ask. Your Higher Self is there to help you.

Stop trying to make yourself special but dumping specialness onto others. Let your children, and your child within, be themselves with all their flaws and strengths. They're on their own unique and wondrous adventure. Let it be theirs and theirs alone. Like you, they'll have guidance along the way, and like you, they'll find love and nurturing, and like you, they'll receive healing if they're open to such guidance, love, nurturing, and healing. Just like you.

Discover and awaken the Magical Child within you. Oh, the wonders this child can show you! This child can inspire patience and forgiveness. This child can restore lost hope, fun, and joy. This child can teach you the play of life. This child can be a guide on your journey of becoming more. And oh my, can this child open you to such vistas and take you on such adventures!

Let your children, and the child within you, be children. Don't expect them to be an adult when it's not their time to be one. Let them flower in their way and in their own space and time. Love does not control; it honors and respects the paths of others.

Yes, guide and set boundaries for the young; it's important to do so. But, over time, allow them to follow their own guidance and to discover for themselves the new boundaries of their becoming. They'll fail and make mistakes, for this is a part of their growing and becoming. Be patient and forgiving. Be wise and understanding. Be mindful when it's time to let them fly. If they fall, be supportive; if they soar, celebrate. And if they, against your wise and loving counsel, pick their noses from time to time, well - whatcha' gonna do?

# 30

# The Secret Teaching

## Suggested Areas of Attention

* Allow your journey to be your journey, not the journey of others.
* Run from teachers, gurus, therapists, or friends who claim or imply that your growing needs them.
* Avoid the pursuit of perfectionism. Such pursuits are doomed to fail.
* Avoid short-cuts, quick fixes, and magic bullets; they're the Ponzi Schemes of the consensus.
* Enjoy the path you're on. Accept more and more that you're the maker of it.
* Give attention to the cries of your lesser selves, and the encouraging whispers of the 'you' more real.
* And always eat your vegetables.

Enlightenment is not found at the journey's end; it's awakened along the way. And the journey never ends. Our destiny, our destination, does not have a finishing line; its forever. And that's the good news.

Yes, our growing never ends; it's eternal. We mistakenly look for an end as if someday we'll all become perfect. Nothing is, or ever will be perfect. Everything becomes more. God and Goddess are not perfect. They, too, are becoming more without ever having been less. Such is the magnificence of All That Is!

If we were all to become perfect, where would we go from there? How boring eternity would become! What a nightmare that would be! The beauty of it all is that, like love, everything keeps expanding and expanding, forever and ever.

Becoming more is hard work. Be wary of looking for quick fixes and easy answers. No guru, no book, no course, nothing will make us perfect or take us to the Promised Land. Our destiny, our destination, is in our hands and in our hands alone. Short-cuts will always cut us short, and quick fixes will quicken our frustration. Although we're all becoming more, we have free will to slow it down; not to stop it, only slow it down.

Although becoming more is hard work, it need not be difficult work. The more we become, the more elegant our journey becomes. Choose elegance over struggle, efforting over effort, adventure over conflict, and fun, magic, and joy over pain, suffering, and anguish.

God and Goddess never ask of us anything or ask us to be anything. Becoming whole only asks that we pay attention to the lonely and frightened calls of our lesser selves, as well as the encouraging whispers of our selves more real. Becoming more only asks that we learn two things:

(1) To enjoy the journey.

(2) To learn to create our reality along that journey, consciously.

Seek not the guidance of gurus, or teachers, or therapists, or anyone who promises enlightenment if you'll only follow them. They cannot deliver on their promise. But know that you have more help and guidance on your journey then you can yet imagine. Seek not the false protection of easy answers or magic bullets. But know that you're protected and guided always.

> But most of all,
> know enough to eat your vegetables.

# 31

# Kotia and the Bawdy Woman

## Suggested Areas of Attention

* Awaken the Bawdy Woman! Whether you're a man or a woman, its resonance is available to you. Let the freedom that is the Bawdy Woman set you free to be wild, passionate, and wonderful.
* Love as the Bawdy Woman loves. It's a love that's open, in-your-face, limitless, and honest.
* Stop believing those lies you tell yourself. Be truthful in your self-exploration.
* Stop hiding in your delusions of insignificance. Stop hiding behind your self-pity and shame.
* Don't be so prudish. Toughen up your spirituality. Be grounded and real in it. Let it have substance and weight.
* Be a little crazy; be a whole lot mad.

Seek the Bawdy Woman! It matters not that you're a man or a woman. Hers is an archetypal energy that will set you free, and she resides within each of us. Seek the Bawdy Woman! It's your nature to seek her! It's your nature to be her.

When you embrace the Bawdy Woman within you, dear one, you'll race with your Spirit in wild abandon, and dance with your Soul in the slow and graceful dance of the eternal, that sensual dance of the divine.

Shun the trap of convention. Stand up, stand out, and step forth. Shout to the world your goodness, truth, and beauty. Shout with wild abandon.

No, don't become unconventional for some desperate need to be different. Don't give up convention to appease your ego's false promise of specialness. Break free because your Spirit yearns to be set free.

The Bawdy Woman is a hard friend. She will not tolerate excuses, or lies, or cowardice. She will always tell you the truth and will expect you to do the same. She will shake you from your paralysis of fear, and will not accept your old worn-out story of insignificance with its foolish belief you're less than others.

She'll not allow you to hide and cower in self-pity and self-delusion. And above all, she'll be your champion and your voice for what's good and real in you.

She'll rebel against routine, and will not allow compliancy. And she'll expect you to do the same. She'll challenge you to become more and to be wild in the showing of your heart. And she'll gently teach you to be patient and forgiving with those within you needing patience and forgiveness.

*Live loud! Love loud! Play loud!*

*Let the Bawdy Woman within you out to play!*
*Let her pinch an ass or two!*

## 32

# Bindu at the End of Time

### Suggested Areas of Attention

* Attend to those fears that have no name. Heal the terror of your lesser selves.
* Grieve the past; welcome the future. Welcome the new 'you' you're becoming; embrace the new world that it, too, is becoming.
* Stop giving your power to the cries and wails of a crumbling world around you. Without ignoring these cries and wails, look to the Grand Awakening happening all about you. Hear the future's ever-present voice of goodness, truth, and beauty growing louder and more real. Beyond the cries and wails, you'll hear that voice.
* Discover your hopes anew; discover your dreams afresh with creativity and innovation. Flow them into your world. Be Bindu.

The world is coming to an end. You're coming to an end.

The old institutions are crumbling. The 'you' you were both light and dark are crumbling. The world is no more; the 'you' you've been are no more. All are dying.

> *"The end of the world is coming!*
> *The end of the world is coming!"*

You're witnessing chaos all about you, dear one. You see it in the crumbling of the old sacred institutions of religion, government, education, law, family, health, societal norms, and values.

You see it in people, in their rage born of terror, their lack of civility, their tribalism, fear, violence, and confusion.

You see it in a world sorely lacking in creativity and innovation.

You see it in a world where dogma replaces dialogue.

You see it in growing hopelessness, despair, and helplessness.

And you're witnessing this 'Great Ending' in you.

You're feeling it in your anger and rage born of terror. You're experiencing it in your diminishing hopes, dreams, and visions.

This Great Ending is not happening in one part of the world or in one country. It's happening everywhere. And you're not the only one experiencing what you're experiencing. Everyone is to a greater or lesser extent.

Now is not the time to wring your hands or lament the passing of the old. Now is the time to take action. Now is the time for celebration. Yes, action! Yes, celebration!

The world is ending, that's true, but a world is emerging from the ashes, not a fixed world, not a better world, not a changed world - a new world. Welcome this. Celebrate this.

You're ending, that's true, but a 'you' is emerging from the ashes; not a fixed you, not a better you, not a changed you - a new you. Welcome this. Celebrate this.

All this shaking and quaking is a gift of love from the Goddess. No, she's not punishing humanity. Chaos proceeds change; the greater the change, the greater the chaos. Monumental change requires monumental upheaval; this is Natural Law.

Accept her gift with grace and elegance. Be like Bindu and step forth to co-create this new world, this new you, with her. She asks that you do so, not because you're 'better than' or special; you're not. Co-create because you're Bindu.

Dream your dreams! Fire up your hope!

For a world lacking in dreams and overflowing with visions filled with fear and nightmares, dream new dreams and visions overflowing with hope, light, and awakening.

For a world spiraling out of control amid growing chaos, dream new dreams of majestic futures that wait just beyond the noise and the whirlwind.

For a world filled with terror, hopelessness, and despair, dream new dreams of peace, hope, and compassion.

For a world lost in dogma, dream new dreams of cooperation, respect, and the pursuit of dialogue.

For a world racked with rage and violence, dream new dreams of harmony and community.

You're destiny's calling you; respond.

Look inside yourself. Attend to your terror with its many faces by nurturing your lesser parts of self. Attend to feelings of hopelessness by welcoming new hope. Be creative and raise your creativity to the heights of innovation. Face the future with grace, dignity, courage, and elegance. Face your destiny. Welcome it. Let it lift you beyond anything you're capable of dreaming.

> *"The end of the world is coming!*
> *The end of the world is coming!"*

Now do what Bindu does;
daydream wonderful things.

# 33

# Martyr's Many Lifetimes

## Suggested Areas of Attention

* Martyrhood is an ugly game you play. Stop playing it. Recognize, acknowledge, forgive, and release it.
* Stop denying the love of others; stop denying your love to others.
* Choose magic, not martyr, as your life's calling.

A martyr is a silent sufferer who seeks an audience to play out feelings and beliefs of being unloved, overworked, and unappreciated.

Everyone, from time to time, to a greater or lesser degree, falls into the trap of martyrhood. Some, however, make full-time careers of it.

Martyrhood is a resonance that robs us of our capacity to love and our willingness to allow others to love us. It's a sad and destructive need for attention that harms not only ourselves but those we love. It's an ugly form of selfishness and self-absorption. But most of all, martyrhood denies us the discovery of our more real selves and impedes us on our journey Coming Home. When left unattended, and when allowed to grow stronger, martyrhood will eventually kill us, literally so. But even then, our passing will not eliminate martyr. It'll be waiting for us in our next life. It remains

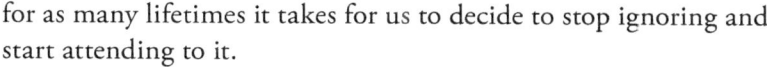

for as many lifetimes it takes for us to decide to stop ignoring and start attending to it.

We learned martyrhood at a very young age from the martyrs around us. Some were excellent teachers. We discovered that martyrhood could be an effective healing balm in the soothing of our hurt and the masking of our pain. Since it performed its job so well, over time, it became a metaphorical friend.

We're not wrong or bad for adopting martyr into our lives. It was a way we learned to survive. In fact, in some cases, it saved our lives. But now, in our adult years, martyr, having grown stronger, has developed a life of its own due to the attention we gave it. What we give attention to feeds off that attention and becomes dominant. Attention is the food that feeds its growth and increases its power. Stop feeding your attention to it, and it loses power.

Denying attention does not mean ignoring it. On the contrary, ignoring martyr only feeds it more. Stop ignoring martyr; recognize when you're in it, acknowledge its voice in you, forgive yourself for holding onto it, and choose to let it go. Stopping the martyr when it surfaces and withdrawing your use of it is what *'denying attention'* means. This way, you'll no longer be feeding it.

Ultimately, in the healing of martyr, you'll need to honestly face that a part of you loves its sweet intoxication. When you allow yourself to feel this sweetness and face that part of yourself who needs it, when you own and forgive that part of yourself, then you'll transcend martyr. You'll indeed be free of it.

When you lift the resonance of martyr, your Higher Self coverts it into magic, for the opposite of martyr is magic.

Oh yes, you'll slip into it now and then, but catch yourself and stop it. You will, over time, find how easily you move away from it.

The whisper here is to attend to your martyr. It's your future calling you to do so. Hear the whisper; answer the call. Your destiny is waiting. Work your magic in a world becoming new.

Choose to be a magician, not a martyr, in the living of your life.

## 34

# Three Old Women

### Suggested Areas of Attention

* What is your current relationship with *'that which is more than you?'* Let these relationships grow and blossom.
* Lean on your spirituality. Learn to trust it. It will never let you down.
* Remember and honor your covenant with God and Goddess; accept and allow their covenant with you.
* Welcome what you're becoming; don't lose yourself in the past

Spirituality is one's personal relationship with that which is more than one's self: your Future Self, Higher Self, Soul and Spirit, God/Goddess/All That Is.

Everyone has spirituality. An atheist's spirituality is a relationship in denial. An agnostic's spirituality is a relationship marked by uncertainty. Some relationships are ugly and violent; some are beautiful and poignant. Some are distorted and limiting; some are clear and expanding. We all have a unique relationship with that which is more than ourselves. In your quest to become more, it would be wise to know what that relationship is. What have you allowed this relationship to be for you?

Your Higher Self, your Soul and Spirit, God/Goddess/All That Is have a transcendent relationship with you, uniquely so. Their relationship with you is never defined or limited by your relationship with them.

The whisper here is to grow your spirituality. Yes, you have such a relationship, despite what you think.

How do you define this relationship? What do you bring to it?

Is your spirituality a desperate attempt to make God and Goddess your father and mother? Since they're not, choose differently.

Is your relationship based on your need for a savior? There's nothing from which you need saving, choose differently.

Is your relationship based on old stagnant beliefs from the past? Choose differently.

Establish a new relationship, a new spirituality, based on your growing and changing. Let this relationship be heightened by the more real of you; let the relationship evolve out of the pursuit of freedom, love, partnership, and awakening. Temper this relationship in the growing authorship of your reality, and your prioritizing of elegance, happiness, and fun. Base this relationship on the remembrance of your covenant with them; that promise you made to Come Home.

Allow the covenant of God and Goddess to love and be there for you to have meaning and value. Let it guide and comfort you. Let your relationship become a dance, a dance of Light, and a dance of ever-deepening love. Grow your spirituality. Let it become a priority in your life. A time will come when it will be your only priority.

If by the time you reach your senior years you've not found your spirituality, your life will devolve into that of the 'Silly Old Fool' who searches for belonging in things long dead, or to that of the 'Nameless One' who silently waits to die. If, however, you've grown your spirituality and have elevated it to grander heights, you can become the 'Wise One' who joyfully lives the fullness of life. The Wise Ones are the enlightened ones becoming the ones eternal.

Don't become one whose life is a vain attempt to be a child or adolescent once again. Don't become one who believes their life is over, and all that remains is death. Live! Dance with your Spirituality! Be the Wise Fool, not the Silly Old Fool, or the silent Nameless One. Share your ageless wisdom. Stop wallowing in past truths, lost dreams, or distant memories.

Give others a taste of the future which you so beautifully embrace. Be as an Ancient One; that wise one so very much more than merely being old. Like an Ancient One, overcome death. As an Ancient One, be the enlightened fool. Oh, how much fun and magic awaits the Wise Fool!

You don't have to grow your spirituality. There's nothing in your life you have to do. You'll have another lifetime to make that choice. But since we're on the subject, why not this lifetime?

## 35

# Gopol Talks to God

### Suggested Areas of Attention

* Know your relationship with *'that which is more than you.'* Grow that relationship.
* Stop trying to squeeze the 'you' you're becoming into the beliefs, rituals, and dogmas of the past; it will not fit.
* Let your spirituality have more value to you, and let it become a priority.
* To whom, or on what, do you lean for support? Know the answer.
* If someone's speech or actions offend your delicate sensibilities, toughen up. Your spirituality is much too wishy-washy.

Spirituality is one's personal relationship with that which is more than one's self: your Future Self, Higher Self, Soul and Spirit, God/Goddess/All That Is.

Everyone possesses spirituality, even atheists and agnostics. Spirituality is a relationship, not a belief. Some relationships are ugly and violent; some are beautiful and poignant. Some are distorted and limiting; some are sacred and expanding. Spirituality for some was born of violence and pain; for others, spirituality radiates with love and light. Each of us has a different relationship, a unique relationship.

Spirituality is defined by our relationship to *'that which is more than ourselves,'* not by theirs to us. Each person's spirituality expresses the complexities of their connection to God/Goddess/All That Is, their Higher Self, their Soul and Spirit, and their Future Self.

You can find spirituality in religion, that's true, but you'll never find religion in spirituality. When two or more people attempt to structure shared tenants with set beliefs and dogmas, you constrict each individual's unique connection. When two or more people share the same spirituality, the same relationship, religion is born. One's spirituality, one's individually unique relationship, becomes constricting and often imprisoning.

God/Goddess/All That Is love no one more, no one less, and no one the same. Their love for each of us is unique.

Respect your religious heritage. It's a valuable part of the backdrop of who you are. But at some point, you'll need to free yourself from the restrictions of its tenants and beliefs and discover and hone the unique spirituality that flourishes in the complexity of the grander 'you' you're becoming; that you, that being of light that shines radiantly in your future.

Stop trying to squeeze the 'you' you're becoming into the old templates of the past; it will not fit. You're expanding in all ways. Stop trying to make sense of this expansion by adjusting it to old beliefs and limiting dogmas. Your need to do so is born of fear and control. Such attempts will not advance you.

Be you a Christian, Muslim, Jew, Hindu, Buddhist, atheist, agnostic, or none of the above, move beyond to the uniqueness of an ever-evolving connection that transcends all beliefs and rituals. In so doing, you'll discover more of yourself and deepen more of your spiritual relationship. You'll experience more of your freedom.

Respect your past, but do not stay there.

Move forward! Always forward!

## 36

# The Actor Assumes His Role

### Suggested Areas of Attention

* Process through your beliefs and attitudes, thoughts and feelings, and choices and decisions. Change them if needed; elevate them if desired.
* Accept the authorship of your life. Don't give it away to anyone or anything.
* Be guided in your choices by your Higher Self. Stop allowing your negative ego to mislead you.
* If you don't like how your life's playing out, change it, re-write it. *"Nothing changes until you do."*

What is make-believe? You make it then believe it's true.

Your life's a play, a story of your making. Everything, everyone, and every event within it are a product of your creation or allowing, and there are no exceptions.

Your life can be a play about losing, or about winning. It can be a play about struggle, conflict, and hardship, or about elegance, magic, and miracles, or something in between. It can be a martyr's story or a magician's story. It can be a tragedy, a comedy, a love story, a mystery, or a tale of adventure, whatever you want it to be. It can be a tale of wondrous pursuits filled with successes, prosperity, and accomplishments replete with bounteous living. Or it can be a tale of dashed hopes, neglected opportunities, abandoned dreams, and soap opera melodramas peppered with abundant mediocrities. It's totally up to you how you author it.

God and Goddess gave us all a single gift, the gift of choice. The choices you make in life, along with your decisions, beliefs and attitudes, thoughts and feelings, attract the people, circumstances, and events you observe, interact with, and experience throughout that life. These thoughts and feelings, choices and decisions, beliefs and attitudes are the raw materials out of which you attract the stuff of your reality.

When you exercise the will and courage to be aware of the choices you're making and put into action your will and courage to choose differently, your play will become different; your life will become different.

You've only one play in this lifetime, and that's the play of which you're the lead actor, writer, director, and producer (and don't forget make-up artist.) If you don't like the play, re-write it. And while you're at it, maybe consider re-casting it.

## Exercise

Write down the current story of your life. Be honest and objective. Put your feelings into it; cry, laugh, be angry, etc. Let it go, let it out, but keep it brief; you're not writing an autobiography.

When completed, read it through without stopping, then re-read it a few more times.

Now choose. Choose your new story. Be honest, and make it believable. No, you're not going to be the King or Queen of England. It's not what you want anyway. Don't lie to yourself. Don't give the authorship to your ego, or a child's fantasy, or an adolescent's aspiration. You most likely gave them your current story. Look where that got you.

Don't give the authorship of your play to parents, siblings, old beliefs, old expectations, or the limitations of consensus thinking. Be a spiritual adult. Choose a higher, more majestic story for yourself.

Now write it out. Remember to keep it brief. When you finish, read it through a few times without stopping.

Honesty is essential here. The feelings that emerge as you undertake this exercise are important. Whatever surfaces, positive or negative, when genuinely felt are a part of your healing, appreciate them as such.

Hide what you've written. Don't allow anyone to read it. Don't discuss it with anyone. From time to time, come back to it and add or subtract as you choose, this is an ongoing process.

Now live your new play. Be conscious of the resistances that surface. They'll be there. Pay attention to them. Recognize when the old story re-emerges. Acknowledge it's re-emerging and forgive yourself for allowing it. Continue living your new play.

Remember, there are no limits to the number of drafts you can make. Keep elevating your play, keep expanding it. It's a work in progress, as you're a work in progress, and it will be a work in progress forever and a day.

*In that lies the adventure! In that lies the fun!*

## 37

# The Greatest Gift

### Suggested Areas of Attention

* It's time to make different choices in your life.
* It's time to remember your covenant with God and Goddess.
* Evaluate the choices and decisions you're making. Process the thoughts and feelings, beliefs and attitudes you're holding onto in the crafting of your life. Ask yourself, *"Are these leading me Home or holding me back?"* Challenge them, hone them, and find different ones if need be.
* Start consciously creating your success and start living your life with fun and happiness.
* Start leaning on the love and guidance of your Higher Self, your Soul and Spirit, and God/Goddess/All That Is.

God and Goddess gave each of us the gift of life, and within that life, the gift of choice. They'll never violate their gift by interfering in any way with your right to choose the life you elect to live, even if that life is dark and painful, or unreflective of the truth of you.

You began this journey when you chose to separate from them. You did not make this choice because you're wrong or bad. On the contrary, you chose to separate because you wanted to grow your love. You want to love them consciously. You freely separated from their love (though in truth you didn't and couldn't) that you many consciously discover and own the love you are, and to consciously co-create with them your reality from this awakened place. You chose conscious love, dear one. How magnificent your desire! How splendid the quest you chose!

No, you weren't cast out of paradise. No, you weren't born of sin. You were a being of Light once, you're a being of Light now, and you'll become a being of Light once again. It's the promise of your future, it's the calling of your destiny, and it's the challenge of this lifetime if you'll accept it. It's what all your lifetimes are about; it's what you're here to awaken in yourself. How can you be wrong or bad for this?

When you chose to embark on your sacred journey, God and Goddess made a covenant with you. They promised never to leave you, and always to love and protect you. They'll keep this promise even though you create realities where you deny their existence, presence, safety, and protection. Yet, their patience is unwavering. Their love and assurance of security and protection are always available if you choose to receive it.

You likewise made a covenant with them. You promised to Come Home. And you'll keep your promise, dear one. One of your lifetimes will make this choice; one will choose to Come Home. Is it this lifetime? If your answer is *"No,"* then ask yourself, *"Why not?"* *If* you're uncertain, ask yourself again, *"Why?"*

The reality you create and attract is a product of the raw materials out of which you craft it: choices and decisions, thoughts and feelings, beliefs and attitudes. Change your reality by challenging, elevating, and honing these materials. Of these six, 'choice' is the most powerful. Use it consciously and wisely. Choose differently. It's necessary for the journey you're on. It's the challenge you crafted for yourself.

God and Goddess will always honor their covenant to you; they'll keep their promise. Honor your covenant and keep your promise to them. Remember your covenant, dear one, remember your promise.

God and Goddess gave you the gift of life. They also gave you the gift of choice. Gift to them the choice to live that life consciously, and to have fun in the living of it.

Consciously create success and remember to have fun along the way. Yes, this is how you honor them; this is how you honor yourself. And this is how you'll keep your covenant, your promise to come Home.

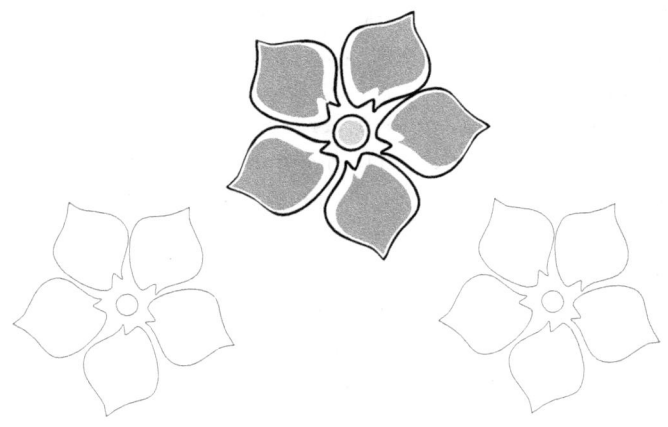

## 38

# Thirty Days in the Infinite

### Suggested Areas of Attention

* Stop giving your power and authority to others, and stop giving it to things or circumstances. Re-claim this power; you'll need it.
* Start healing the pain you deeply lock within you. Go within yourself and own it, then ask for its healing.
* Change the raw materials out of which you mold your reality. Mold them with the sharpened tools of desire, imagination, and expectancy.
* Listen and respond to the voices of your less developed selves.

Don't give away the authorship if your reality. Don't expect others, or things, or better circumstances to make your life more. Don't blame others, or lack of things, or present circumstance for your life being less then you'd like it. Only you determine how your life unfolds. Only you and you alone can change it.

If your life is miserable, filled with suffering and pain, it's because you created or allowed it so. Creating or allowing this does not make you wrong or bad. It's just the reality you're making right now. It can be changed.

Pain is a part of being human; it's not necessarily a bad thing. But pain does need healing. Now is the time to focus on its healing. Stop focusing on blame and judgment of others, or the circumstances of your life.

If you're in the throes of despair, anger, hurt, fear, or loneliness, or if you're in the whirlwind of anxiety, worry, confusion, or doubt, it's because your reality requires your attention. Pay attention, dear one. Pay attention to the materials out of which you're molding your reality, the decisions and choices you're making, the thoughts and feelings you're holding, and the attitudes and beliefs you're still clinging to. And mold them with the tools of a sharpened desire, a rich and vibrant imagination, and a sincere and genuine expectancy. Such dark emotions and chaotic whirlwinds are not products of your failure, but a call to change and to heal. Pay attention, dear one. Start processing your raw materials and strengthen your tools of creation.

Also, be aware that these feelings and whirlwinds are the voices of your younger, less developed selves. They're attempting to get your attention. Respond to them with patience, understanding, and love. Respond to them without blame or the need to *"get them on board."* (See 'Appendix One' for guidance)

To change the raw materials out of which you're creating your reality, first look to where they need improving and honing. Look to the decisions and choices your making and decide and choose differently. Look to your thoughts and feelings and elevate them. Look to your beliefs and attitudes and question them, and if need be, change them.

No one can empower you, dear one. God and Goddess cannot do so; they already have. Claim the empowerment they've given you, and choose to act from this place of power within you.

Pay attention to where you're giving this power away. To discover this, look to those you hate, fear, loath, or try to please. Look to those you fawn after, are jealous of, or envy. Those are the ones to whom you give your power.

Again, forgive yourself for doing this and take your power back. You'll need it in the authorship of your life.

*And if you have to take a pee,
by all means, do so.*

# 39

# Sundeep and the Simple Life

## Suggested Areas of Attention

* Welcome complexity; avoid the pursuit of simplicity.
* Stop your attempts at controlling, especially of your emotions.
* Feel your emotions thoroughly and cleanly, and allow the gifts that all emotions both dark and light provide.
* Stop complicating your life. Instead, let life challenge you, intrigue you, awaken your magnificent complexity, and elevate you. Allow your life to be an adventure, not a struggle.
* Avoid playing it safe. Welcome the mystery and magic of the unknown.

Control is one of the most instinctive responses humans have when faced with fear. Our need to control is born of our need to be safe. But control does not, in truth, keep us safe, and it does not keep fear at a distance; it only masks it. Control accomplishes one thing only, keeping fear alive.

Control expresses itself in many ways. One of the most common is the need to figure things out. It's a defense mechanism we often use. When afraid, animals instinctively go to ground. When fearful, humans reactively go to their heads. Humans need to figure the fear out, they need answers, they need to discover escape routes, and they often escape by going up and out of their bodies. Animals do not control or wallow in what they're feeling. They focus their entire attention, their whole being on it. They do their emotions spontaneously. They experience their feelings cleanly. Because this is the most natural approach to fear, it provides the most healing. To most effectively handle fear, do as the animals do, go to ground. Feel the fear deeply, give your complete attention to it, go through it cleanly, then release it.

The pursuit of simplicity is also a reaction to fear. It's a call for control. A person will lament, *"Oh, how complicated life is!"* not realizing that complication is born out of the attempt to make complexity simple. By honoring the complexity of something, you become elevated by it. By trying to make something simple, you complicate it.

Sir Isaac Newton, in his attempt to make the complex nature of the universe simple enough so even the most common man would be able to understand it, eventually drove himself insane. Squeezing the complexity of the universe into a simple law or concept is impossible. Those scientists who marvel at the complicity of the universe experience the wonder and awe of its majesty. They're elevated by it. They transcend the confines of their intellect.

Get out of your head and go to ground! Feel your fear thoroughly and release it. Stop trying to make life simple and let yourself be captivated by its complexity. Making things simple takes effort and struggle because it's unnatural. Complexity, being natural, is wondrously magical and surprisingly effortless.

*Be captivated by life's complexity.*
*There's no fear there.*

# 40

# The King of Beasts

## Suggested Areas of Attention

* Look to who and what inspires you. Be inspired and inspiring.
* Stop giving your power and authorship away to others. Take it back.
* Accept your beauty, truth, and goodness, let them shine within you; let them radiate from you.
* Answer the call of your destiny. Undertake your Great Adventure.

There's a whisper here to stand up, stand out, and step forth, there's a whisper here to lift your voice and be heard, and there's a whisper here to claim and to exercise the authorship of your reality. Be the inspiration you seek from others. It's your time, dear one. Can you hear the calls? Can you hear the whispers?

Stop giving your power to others. Stop expecting others to guide you, or lead you, or protect you, or to steer you in the right direction. They may be noble and principled, maybe just and wise, but they're not you. Only you can put to use the power you possess. Only you can chart the higher course of your life. And only you can find within yourself the safety and security you so long to find.

Don't expect others to be your King or Savior; you don't need governance; you don't require saving. You're loved and counseled by your Higher Self, and enveloped and embraced by your Soul and Spirit. You're uniquely loved and eternally one with God/Goddess/All That Is. Isn't that more than enough, dear one? Isn't that what you're looking to find? Let your relationship to your Higher Self, your Soul and Spirit, and to God/Goddess/All That Is be enough for you.

Awaken and claim the authorship of your life. Don't give it away to others. Yes, be inspired by others. Yes, be uplifted by the wisdom, kindness, and love of others. But realize this,

*What inspires and uplifts you, what attracts you to those gifted others, you possess abundantly within yourself.*

Those gifted others are but an out-picturing of the truth of you. Their priceless gift is that they reflect your goodness, truth, and beauty. They reveal what exists in you already if you'll only just see it and accept it.

Accept their priceless gift to you. Own your uniqueness. Harness the power of your goodness, truth, and beauty. Awaken and paint your world with the vibrant colors of your creativity and innovation. Inspire and uplift others by the magnificence of you.

Hear the whispers, dear one, hear the whispers. They call you to be the author of your reality, a maker of maps, and to be inspired and inspiring. Can you hear the call to Come Home among the many whispers?

*You're the King, dear one.*
*It was you all along.*

## 41

# A Legitimate Profession

### Suggested Areas of Attention

* Pursue the real healing found only within yourself. Be honest and courageous in your pursuit.
* Seek out both the lies and the truths of the 'you' you keep hidden in the dark places of your making.
* Stop making choices and decisions that always lead to pain, suffering, failure, and disappointment.
* The world does not need more experts; it needs more love, forgiveness, and understanding. Flee from those who claim they can 'make you whole;' embrace those who understand the journey and embrace the wholeness you are.

Have you heard the story of the *'Old Man and the Lost Keys?'*

*A woman walking along a sidewalk at night noticed an old man searching for something beneath a streetlamp. The woman approached the old man and asked, "Sir, did you lose something?" "Yes," said the old man, "I lost my keys." The kind woman responded, "Let me help you look." "Oh, that would be most kind!" replied the grateful old man.*

*Although the two searched and searched within the glow of the streetlamp for nearly a half-hour, they could not find the old man's keys. The frustrated woman asked the old man, "Sir, are you sure you lost your keys here?" The old man replied, "Oh no, I lost them over there in the dark." The shocked woman exclaimed, "Then why are we looking here?" The old man casually replied, "Because there's more light."*

Healing, true healing, will not be found outside you. You'll find it in the dark places within. Oh yes, you can find 'curing' outside you, that's true, but you'll not find the healing you ultimately seek. It's in those dark hidden places all your answers will be discovered, all of your healing accomplished, and all your 'issues' transcended.

Journey within to those secret forbidden places; invade your privacy. Discover the hidden vaults where you store your ancient wounds, your deeper pains and hurts, and the old lies and hidden agendas you use to keep yourself safe. There in those hidden places deep inside you, those places where darkness permeates, cast the light of your awareness. Be conscious of what you find there, own what you discover, forgive yourself for hiding them, then release what you held for such a very long time. Return to your life now healed. Your destiny requires this. The 'Awakened You' requires this.

*And please stop sitting on thistles.*

# 42

# A Tale of Two Villages

## Suggested Areas of Attention

* Value the ease, elegance, and upliftment you'll find in efforting over the struggle and debilitating nature of effort.
* Face your fear of the unknown. It's in the unknown you'll meet your real self.
* Pursue the beauty of Nature. It's in Nature you'll awaken your realness.
* Step away from consensus beliefs. They'll never get you to where you genuinely want to go.

We put far too much stock in struggle, effort, and conflict. Our world elevates these things to the status of nobility. It's time to make a different choice. Instead, try choosing elegance, ease, and enjoyment.

Yes, in the past, life was hard and difficult; that's true. Yes, life was full of struggle and conflict; that's also true. It was the condition of the times in which people lived. It was the way life existed during those periods of humankind's development.

Today, humanity is called to a different, more elevated functioning. The call is to live a life of elegance, ease, and enjoyment. The call is there, but the consensus, stuck in this belief in the nobility of struggle, does not hear it.

The world is slowly evolving beyond such beliefs. We're growing to a place where elegance, ease, and fun hold greater appeal and value. This level of functioning and valuing is new and uncharted territory, and this is a scary place for us.

When facing the unknown and the uncharted, the consensus will hold tightly to its archaic beliefs and pursuits, especially the belief in martyr and struggle. Hearing the call to elegance and fun is met by the consensus with confusion, mediocrity, hostility, and dismissal.

The consensus holds that the desire to pursue such a life of ease and elegance is born of laziness or the wishful thinking of a person's fantasy. The consensus holds 'elegance' as something you'd find in a fashion magazine, 'ease' as the gift you give yourself on a day off, or something you're permitted only on vacation. Such foolish and tenaciously held beliefs are born of the old and decaying templates of the past! They're born of the fear of the unknown and uncharted future.

Elegance is a state of being and living where challenge replaces conflict, adventure replaces struggle, and uplifting acts of efforting replace the debilitating need for effort.

Nature does not struggle or effort; humankind does.

Nature flows; humankind creates resistance.

Nature functions in harmony; humankind thrives on disharmony.

Find freedom from struggle, effort, and disharmony by aligning yourself with the frictionless flow of Nature. In the beauty of Nature, you'll find your beauty, your elegance, your dignity, and your balance and harmony; in the beauty and presence of Nature, you'll discover and enliven your more real self.

Living an elegant life produces efficiency in action where one does less and accomplishes more. Elegance is artful living. It's a by-product of living in a state of freedom. The more freedom you allow by dropping old patterns of behaviors and beliefs, by letting go of the destructive templates of your past, and by exposing and relinquishing hidden agendas, the freer you become. Your life becomes more elegant, more natural, and more in alignment with Natural Law.

When you prioritize elegance, ease, and enjoyment, magic occurs with ever-increasing frequency. Synchronicity becomes the normal play of life, and living is just plain fun.

Let your life become an adventure, not a struggle.

Let your life become an elegant flow of synchronicity, not a series of hurdles you must overcome.

Let your life be enjoyable; not the *"Life's a bitch, and then you die'* nonsense held by consensus thinking.

Face your fear of the unknown. Go deeply into it. Feel it. On the other side, the second village waits. Choose to live there. It's where you belong now; it's where your truer self is most at home.

Enjoy!

# 43

# The Captain and the Sea

## Suggested Areas of Attention

* If you're in dark times, be patient, responsive, and forgiving. You'll find healing during such times.
* If you're in light times, be courageous, adventurous, and trusting. You'll discover opportunities during such times.
* Seek the safe harbor that calls to you, be it beauty, enchantment, solitude, or love. You'll find renewal in such places.
* Respond to your lesser parts of self that call to you. Wholeness will be achieved by such responding.
* Trust in the stars that guide you. Lean on the love of your Higher Self. You'll find your Home Port through such guidance.

Life ebbs and flows like the sea. It must. It's the ebbing and flowing that makes you a better sailor.

Perhaps you're in a time of ebbing. Don't be hard on yourself, dear one. Don't give in to the doldrums, frenzies, fears, confusions, or uncertainties of those times of ebbing. Be easy now, especially with yourself. Be forgiving now, especially with yourself. And be responsive to the lesser parts of you crying out for your attention. Be with them, listen to their fears and anger, and reassure them that all is right and the storm will soon pass. All the many parts of you are your shipmates on this journey. You go nowhere without them. (Work with Appendix One).

The ebbing time is not a time for hiding and withdrawal. It's the time of healing, of paying attention and responding to your feelings. Feel deep whatever surfaces from the depths of the sea within you. Feel what needs to be felt and lift it. And always, dear one, remember that you're loved, and guided, and protected. There are better seas ahead, dear one. And when you enter those calmer waters, you'll find yourself more of the Captain of your ship thanks to the healing and forging of the rougher seas behind you.

During this time of ebbing, dear one, take the time to enter the safe harbor that calls to you. See its light guiding you to it.

Perhaps you'll find your safe harbor in the nurturing womb of beauty.

Perhaps you'll find your safe harbor in the mystery, magic, and oneness of enchantment.

Perhaps you'll find your safe harbor in the blessed silence of solitude.

Perhaps you'll find your safe harbor in the tender embrace of love.

Which beacon light reaches out to you? Which lighthouse calls the loudest? Follow its light and answer its call and enter its safety and shelter. There you'll be refitted and renewed.

Yes, perhaps you're in the ebb, dear one. Be patient, especially with yourself. There's a calmer sea ahead.

But perhaps you're in a time of flowing. If so, let your sail down and feel the wind at your back. Move forward now, dear one. Stop waiting for someone to tow you; stop procrastinating and dallying. Attend to your fear of unknown seas and be the adventurer you're born to be. Incredible power and opportunity lay ahead in those unknown

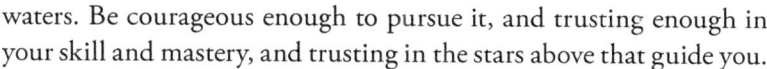

waters. Be courageous enough to pursue it, and trusting enough in your skill and mastery, and trusting in the stars above that guide you.

*Oh, the ebbing and flowing of life!*
*How magnificent the adventure of living!*

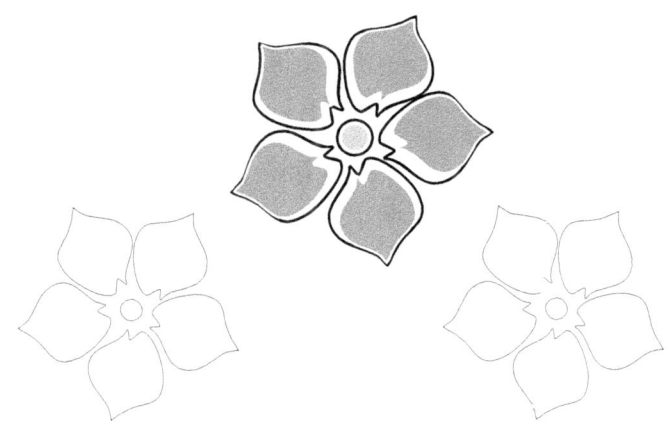

# 44

# An Abandoned Garden

## Suggested Areas of Attention

* Accept the majesty of your loving; lean upon it, rely on it.
* Search for the spark of love and hope that lies deep within your pain and hurt. Invade the privacy of your hidden emotions. There you'll find the healing you seek.
* Lean on the love of your Higher Self. Let it become more valued and more present in your life.
* Feel and release your darker emotions; feel and own the lighter.
* Tend to your garden, dear one. Bring it to life once again.

In each of us and all of us, there's a magnificence of loving. For some, it's lost in control, pain, and bitterness; in others, it shines brightly, and for the rest, it lies somewhere in between.

When love dies in you, you die to yourself; when love is lost, you lose yourself. When you give your love over to control, pain, rage, and bitterness, they'll feed off it. When you hide your love to keep it safe, in time, you'll no longer find it.

Search deep within your pain and hurt for that spark of love and hope that shines there still. Invade the privacy of your hidden emotions.

Though you feel as if those hidden emotions will overwhelm you, they will not; you'll find the help you need. You can call upon your Higher Self to journey with you. Together you can free yourself. Your love and hope are so much stronger than you right now.

Lean on the greater love of your Higher Self. Lean on the greater love of you more real. There's nothing your love cannot accomplish; nothing it cannot heal, and no prison so strong you cannot be freed of it. You're so much more powerful than you know, dear one.

Negative emotions are any emotions dark or light, you will not allow yourself to feel. Positive emotions are any emotions dark or light, you allow yourself to feel; and with the darker emotions to release, with the lighter emotions to own and integrate.

Feel your pain, fear, hurt, despair, anger, loneliness, shame, and rage deeply; feel all your emotions deeply. Let them out, let them express themselves, let them vent. You're safe. You're protected.

When you don't let these emotions out, they'll remain with you. When you let yourself feel them deeply, you'll be free of them. Know that deeply hidden in those dark emotions is the love you so desperately seek, is the lover you once were, and are destined to become once again. Know that deeply hidden in those negative emotions is the healing you seek, and the freedom you longingly yearn for.

Let your love free! Stop holding on so tightly to the pains and hurts of the past! Love becomes so much more when you let it breathe; when you set it loose to fly.

It's time now to tend to your long-abandoned garden. It's time to nurture your heart.

*You're so much stronger than you know, dear one,*
*so much stronger.*

# 45

# The Purpose of Life

## Suggested Areas of Attention

* Challenge what you currently know and believe. Step outside the comfort zone of what you hold to be true.
* Seek understanding more than knowledge; seek wisdom more than understanding.
* Don't allow your elder years to stagnate. Don't waste these precious times indulging in past glories and distant memories, or in waiting for death to claim you. Fly! Soar! Reach to the heavens! You're able now to do so because this is your time to do so.
* Pursue adventurous living. Sail upon the breezes of your futures call.
* Don't run and hide from fear; allow yourself to grow from it. Don't hide in the false safety of consensus beliefs and attitudes; run to the unknown and the uncharted.
* Lighten the load you carry. Lighten up, dear one!

During the Vedic period of ancient India, in the early morning just before the first breeze of the morning blew across the land, this breeze they call the Nava Swam, a young child destined to be a Vedic pundit would sit before his grandfather. He'd sit before this wise old sage, and together they'd recite the hymns of the Veda. This sacred ritual was performed each morning at the coming of the Nava Swam for generations upon generations.

At first, the child would simply memorize the hymns, not understanding their meaning. But as he continued this recitation each morning at the coming of the first breeze, the breeze they call the Nava Swam, little by little, he grew in understanding. For its proclaimed in the Veda *'knowledge and understanding grow with the expansion of consciousness.'*

Throughout one's lifetime, throughout life's various stages from childhood to old age, knowledge and understanding grows; or at least it should. Sadly, this is not true for most. Many stay frozen in the knowledge and limited understanding of earlier years. Many remain lost in the limited knowledge and understanding of a child, an adolescent, a young adult, or a grown-up. Many never advance from being a grown-up to becoming an adult. Fewer still evolve from being an adult to that of a spiritual adult. And of the few who become spiritual adults, only a tiny few elevate their knowledge and understanding to that of wisdom.

The whisper here is to challenge what you currently know and understand. Pursue greater knowledge and understanding. Expand your boundaries of knowing and believing. Don't settle for simple answers. Seek the understanding found in complexity. Run from the dogmatic thinking and limiting beliefs of the consensus.

Seek the wisdom of the Ancient One within you. Seek the knowledge, understanding, and wisdom of your Future Self. Your Future Self holds greater awareness and understanding. Your Future Self is where you'll find your ancient wisdom awakened. Pursue your future; it's there you'll find your Future Self. It's there your Future Self and the Ancient One within wait for you.

It's fear that holds you back from knowing and understanding beyond the confines of what you currently know and understand. And its fear, and your belief in your insignificance, that denies the enfoldment of wisdom in you. Challenge your fear by feeling and releasing it. Step away from the belief in your insignificance. Seek love that's more than you. Seek the love of your Higher Self and Soul, and God/Goddess/All That Is. Such love and support are always available for the asking. Just ask. They'll gladly take from you this belief in your insignificance. But it must be given sincerely.

George Bernard Shaw once said, *"Youth is wasted on the young."* Oh, how right he was! Know that in your growing and blossoming to old age, you'll awaken, if you pursue it, a knowing and understanding that is truly remarkable and elevated. You'll harvest wisdom, majestic, and ever-expanding, you'll know and experience the fullness of youth without its pains, frenzies, fears, confusions, and uncertainties, and you'll become a Wise Old Fool; among the highest of the enlightened ones.

Those who have knowledge without understanding are like hollow reeds blowing empty sounds expressing nothing. Those who have knowledge and understanding without wisdom are like an eagle sitting on the edge of a cliff, never taking flight.

The purpose of life is to enjoy. If you choose, you'll come to realize this at the time when you can most enjoy it.

But know this, dear one. It will take you an eternity and a day to fully understand and appreciate this realization. But when you do, then you'll come to realize that this *'enjoying'* is just the beginning of the fullness of enjoying. In the meantime,

*Ride joyfully upon the first breeze of the morning,*
*the breeze they call the Nava Swam.*

# 46

# The Passing of the Torch

## Suggested Areas of Attention

* Identify and rip-up all psychic contracts you've made with others whether out of love or hate. Your freedom requires this.
* Heal the shame you carry. Let go of the shame of your own making; give back the shame of others.
* Feel shame deeply without self-blame and guilt.
* Don't recycle your shame, don't blame others. Heal it and be free.

Shame is the feeling and belief that you're broken, flawed, defective, and unworthy.

Everyone, to a greater or lesser degree, holds the destructive belief and debilitating resonance of shame. It came to us through the various stages of life: childhood, adolescence, and in our adult years. We came to shame in several ways. We were either taught it, wronged into it, we adopted it as a result of abandonment, or we came to it through forming psychic contracts with others.

Shame is one of the most common and prevalent obstacles to our growth, health, happiness, and success in life. It's presence within the foundation of all our beliefs and actions prevent us from experiencing the fullness of living, and the ever-present call of becoming more.

What's so ugly about shame is what we do with it as adults. Instead of owning and healing it, we pass it onto others. We do this to avoid having to deal with it. Since healing requires ownership, dumping our shame prevents its healing. Shame is still present within us, but we cannot process it and thus free ourselves from its destructive influence.

You have the shame of your own making, that's true, but you also carry the shame of others. To heal both, you'll need to do two things.

(1) Own the shame of your own making by feeling it deeply, forgiving yourself, and asking your Higher Self to lift it from you.

(2) Give back the shame you carry, the shame dumped on you by others. This shame is not yours. Give it back.

You cannot heal the shame of others; it's not yours to heal. Only they can do it. When you give back their shame, they can begin its healing, if they choose to do so.

Use the following technique to return the shame dumped on you, be it from your father, or mother, or a sibling(s), a teacher, a partner, a nemesis from your past, etc. In doing this meditation, you'll feel a growing sense of freedom and lightness, a renewed energy and strength.

## Meditation to Return Shame

(1) Be still and close your eyes. Allow yourself to become calm. Count slowly from seven to one mentally. On each count become more relaxed and altered.

(2) On the count of one, open your mental eyes and imagine sitting in a beautiful place in nature; this is your Safe Place. This place may be a creation of your imagination, a place you'd like to use from a movie or picture, or a place of beauty and safety you remember from your past.

Your Safe Place should be in nature. It should not be a building, house, fortress, or castle as these images send the wrong message to your subconscious.

This place should be free of other people and should awaken a sense of safety and security in you.

When you do other meditations, always return to the same Safe Place. In every meditation, take a little time to explore more of this place, pay attention to every detail. *"Love pays attention to detail."*

(3) In your Safe Place, find a stick on the ground. With the stick draw a circle around you, this is your *'Ring pass not.'* No one can enter there.

(4) Now demand that the person whose shame you carry, living or dead, appear before you. Don't ask that he or she appear, demand it.

(5) This person will appear outside the circle standing before you.

If there are more than one whose shame you carry, do separate meditations for each on different days.

(6) Standing face to face, you within the circle, the other outside, talk of the shame you're holding; the shame they dumped on you. You may argue. You may fight and scream. Let it all come out. Feel your anger. Let yourself rage. Let yourself scream. Express whatever needs releasing. Let it be cathartic.

When you finish, demand that this person take back the shame. Don't ask, demand. This person may resist, but ultimately he or she must and will comply.

(7) Now feel the energy of shame flowing from you through an invisible cord extending from your navel to the navel of the other person. Feel yourself becoming lighter and lighter as this energy flows from you to the other. Let your body feel the shift. Get into it.

(8) When the last of the shame is released, the cord will disappear, and the person standing before you will slowly fade away. Feel the lightness. Feel the freedom. It will be there if you honestly let it go.

(9) Now close your mental eyes and mentally count from one to five. On the count of five, open your physical eyes and return.

You may need to repeat this meditation a few times on different days as the subconscious and unconscious calibrate the new programming.

## 47

# The Poet's Skill at Fishing

### Suggested Areas of Attention

* Awaken creativity in you. Be an artist in the living of your life.
* Don't give the process and fruits of your creating to your negative ego.
* Cultivate patience and discipline.
* Be inspired and inspiring.
* Pursue always the sacred of Beauty and Nature. Let yourself be inspired and elevated by them.

You're not called to write that book, or compose that music, or to paint that canvas. You are, however, called to create. The world does not need another book, another painting, another musical composition. The world does need more love, however. The world needs more creativity. So this is your call to love and create.

The call is to create more love and happiness for yourself and others. The call is to create an exceptional life. You're the paper upon which you write. You're the canvas upon which you paint. You're the instrument through which your music flows. And you're the audience; the only audience you need.

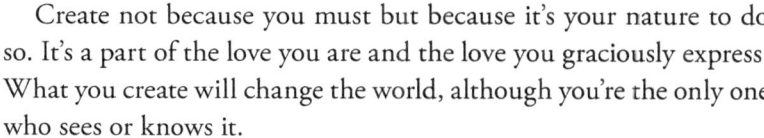

Create not because you must but because it's your nature to do so. It's a part of the love you are and the love you graciously express. What you create will change the world, although you're the only one who sees or knows it.

*My how your ego hates to hear this!*

But listen well, dear one. Don't give these words to your ego to judge or interpret, or give your creativity to it. Doing so will not accomplish what you truly seek. Doing so will not allow the crafting of an exceptional you.

Being creative is not limited to writing, musical composition, painting, or any of the other fine or applied arts. It involves anything you undertake. But most of all, it involves the living of your life.

Be creative and inspired in the living of your life. And be an inspiration to others by the living of it.

You were born to create, so be a master at your craft. In time, elevate your mastery to the heights of artistry. Pursue artistry; pursue excellence. Be an artist in the living of your life.

There'll be times when your creativity flows; there'll be times when it won't. Life's rhythms ebb and flow, learn to honor both. Respect and honor the rhythms of life; respect and honor the unique rhythms of your life. Be patient.

Patience does not mean that we do nothing. On the contrary, patience involves work and self-discipline; it involves *"seeding the waters."*

To *"seed the waters,"* pay attention. Pay attention to the intentions behind your desire to create. Are your intentions your egos intentions for fame, fortune, validation, or vindication? If yes, get rid of them. Create because it gives you joy, not because you must. Create because you're inspired to do so, not because your ego requires it. You always create for you and you alone.

Patience allows ideas to flow freely. Don't try to control your creation. Your creation will seek you out when it's ready. Prepare yourself to receive it; this is patience; this is self-discipline.

Pursue the sacredness of Beauty and Nature. It's there you'll be inspired. Beauty and Nature, and the creativity you'll awaken there, will always inspire you to become more.

Also, remember to share that more of you with others and with your world. As you flow the fruits of your creativity and becoming into your world, the more creativity and becoming is available for you to discover, to pursue, and to flow.

Happy Fishing!

# 48

# Rathgar Gets His Name

## Suggested Areas of Attention

* Stop giving your reality to your negative ego to interpret; stop listening and buying into its lies and false promises.
* Start taking authorship of your life.
* Lean on the love and guidance of your Higher Self. It will never lie to you or let you down.
* Awaken to the truth of you. Let it shine so the whole world can see it.

When you give the keys to your car to a five-year-old and order it to drive you to your various destinations, it will invariably crash it. And then after blaming the five-year-old for failing in its duty, you punish it, you will most certainly make the child fear and distrust you. And if you keep demanding that it drive your car and keep blaming it when it crashes, it will over time come to hate you. And over time, with this continuous abuse, the child will eventually wish you dead.

The child was never capable of handling such a responsibility. It was your mistake in expecting it to do something it could not do.

This dear one is your negative ego's story; it's what you did to it; it's what you made of it.

Your ego comes into your life when you do. It's a necessary part of your being and living. The sole purpose of the ego is to provide information to you. It's up to you to interpret what it gives.

Yet, along the way, you expected your ego to do the interpreting. You delegated your responsibility to it. And like the five-year-old, it was doomed to failure; for interpreting was not what the ego was supposed to do or capable of doing. And like the five-year-old, it failed and failed, again and again. And like the five-year-old, you blamed it over and over again for its failure. And like the five-year-old, it grew to hate you. And like the five-year-old, it wanted you dead.

Don't give the keys to your car to your negative ego; it will always crash it. Drive the car, drive your life, and stop giving such responsibility to it.

Because it hates you so, your negative ego will always lie and wish you harm. So why keep listening and believing it? You do so because you'll not take responsibility for the living of your life. Since you'll not author your life, you'll pass the authorship to those parts of you who will most certainly crash it. Instead of taking responsibility, you'd rather accept your ego's promise of specialness. You'd rather wallow in self-pity and guilt. You'd rather blame fate, God, and life for your failures, tragedies, dashed hopes, and unfulfilled dreams.

People do not die of cancer, heart disease, viruses, accidents, etc. These things, like millions of other things, are just the means of passing. People die because they gave the authorship and responsibility of directing their lives to their negative ego. And your negative ego will most certainly crash it. Don't give your life over to your negative ego. It won't just ruin your life; it will end it.

Take back the wheel of your car; be the driver of your life, be its author. Though your negative ego will fight you for control, and though your negative ego will continue to hate you and wish you harm, over time and with steady attention and support, you'll become the author you're supposed to be. Over time your negative ego will transform to your positive ego, which is what it was supposed to be all along. But it will take time, dear one, and much patience, attention, and forgiveness.

Along the way, lean on the love of your Higher Self. Because it loves you so, it will never lie to you, and it will always patiently guide and protect you.

You're loved no matter in what direction you choose to go. So why not go in the direction of your authorship? Why not drive your car? Your Higher Self will be sitting beside you in the passenger seat; God and Goddess and All That Is will be there as well.

*No harm can befall you when you take authorship of your life, unless you author it to do so*

# 49

# The Counting of the Stars

## Suggested Areas of Attention

* Let go of your need to control. Know that love is safe within you.
* Don't drop all logic and reason, but don't be fettered by them either.
* Step outside the consensus; discover and accept your uniqueness.
* Be vulnerable to your strengths and weaknesses.
* Allow more time for dreaming, visioning, imagination, and wonder.
* Be elevated by all that's beautiful and majestic, stop bending to the tedious and mundane.

Stop counting stars; instead, be enraptured by them. Stop trying to control the uncontrollable and soar instead among its beauty and magnificence. Don't abandon logic and reason, but cease becoming fettered by them. Dream, imagine, wonder, and call upon your home beyond your imaginations, dreams, and wondering.

Step outside the false safety and security of the norm. Take pride in your uniqueness and individuality. You'll not find greatness among the mundane rituals and shallow musings of consensus thinking. Your greatness will be discovered in your dreams and visions and within the sacred folds of your imaginings.

Be the fool; be the Wise Fool. Be the weird one. Be the one who stands apart from all the rest. No, don't be different for the sake of being different. That's not being the Wise Fool that's being foolish. Be different because you are. Be exceptional, not the exception. Be these things because that's your nature. That's what calls to you. That's what will carry you Home.

Let go of your need to control. It's a need the consensus believes will keep love safe. The consensus does not realize that control locks love in a vault so deep it becomes lost to those who seek to protect it. Control is born of fear. There's nothing in your universe that can harm you unless you allow it so.

Be free of control, and allow yourself to be vulnerable. You're safe. In your vulnerability, you're invincible. Let go of your fears. Face them and let them heal through honestly feeling them, understanding them, and accepting them.

By being vulnerable to your strengths and weaknesses, you'll awaken magic in you, and you'll find the love and will to transcend all your fears, doubts, and uncertainties. Your strength and freedom lie in your vulnerability. Be courageous in allowing it. The stars will help you here.

Let the consensus count their stars; you become elevated by them. There's incredible magic in dreaming, unimaginable power in imagination, and magnificence in your wondering.

There's a place for you among the stars, dear one. You have a home there waiting for your return. Soar, dear one, fly among the heavens. Let your dreams and imagination take flight; let the wonder lift you. Let the stars guide you.

*Come Home, dear one!*
*Come Home!*

# 50

# The Way of the Dreamer

## Suggested Areas of Attention

* Re-connect to your lost fantasias. Let go of the fantasies you're still clinging to.
* Step out of your over-reliance on logic and reason. Awaken and claim the power and gifts of your imagination. Dream, dear one, dream!
* Accept the authorship of your reality; don't give it away to others. Craft a life replete with fantasias, dreams, and wonders.

Fantasies are dreams, hopes, desires that were never meant to happen. They're the playthings of children and adolescents.

Fantasias are dreams, hopes, desires that are meant to happen. They're the voices of your destiny calling.

Let go of the fantasies you're still clinging to; re-claim your lost or stolen fantasias. Dream the dreams destined to happen; stop fooling around with fantasies. Let the fantasies die. Learn to discriminate between the two.

As a child, you may have dreamt of one day becoming a ballerina. It was a deep and powerful yearning in you that was more than a childish dream; it was a call of your destiny, and as such, is was fantasia. But you're now fifty years old, and you know this dream will never happen. Even so, it's still a call of your destiny; it's still a fantasia meant to happen.

As a child, you could only calibrate such calls through the filter of a child's perspective and understanding. As a child, you imagined the call to *'dance'* expressed in the form of a ballerina. The dream of being a ballerina was a fantasy; as such, it was never going to happen. The call to *'dance,'* however, being a fantasia, is.

Now, as an adult, re-discover this lost dream, not as a ballerina, but in a form more real for you. Your destiny has called you to dance, now dance, dance a dance more meaningful. Discover the magic, your magic, in the 'Dance of Life.' Move through life like a dancer with grace, and beauty, and elegance. Movement magic is powerful magic; it's inherent in you. Your Soul speaks to you through it. It's your future's call to awaken more of its magic and flow.

Perhaps you take dance classes. Maybe you teach dance. Maybe you just dance wildly about in the privacy of your kitchen. Maybe dance becomes a hobby, or something yet to be discovered. Becoming a ballerina was a fantasy. Let this dream go. The magic of dance, being the fantasia of your Soul, will awaken something grand within you. Re-ignite this dream. Dance with your Soul in the rhythms and flows of life; in the rhythms and flows of your being.

Ask for guidance and help in the re-discovering and the re-awakening of your fantasias; it will be provided. It's your destiny, after all.

You're called to trust your imagination. You're called to dream. Get out of your over-reliance on logic and reason; it will only take you so far. There's a lack of imagination and creativity in the world. There's more so a lack of innovation. Be a dreamer. Hear and answer the call to dream your reality into happening. Let imagination be your guide.

You're also called to claim your authorship. You're the author of your reality, all of it. Don't give this authorship and power to others; be they living or dead. To do so is to deny yourself the authority and responsibility of crafting your own life. Break free of the stifling influences of others. You cannot craft your reality while expecting others to craft it for you. Be the author of your life. Claim your power back. It's a requirement for the 'you' you're becoming.

You're being called, Dreamer. Your future seeks you out. You're the dream that's meant to happen.

*"Who is the author of all you behold?"*

Think well upon your response, dear one.
Your future awaits your answer.

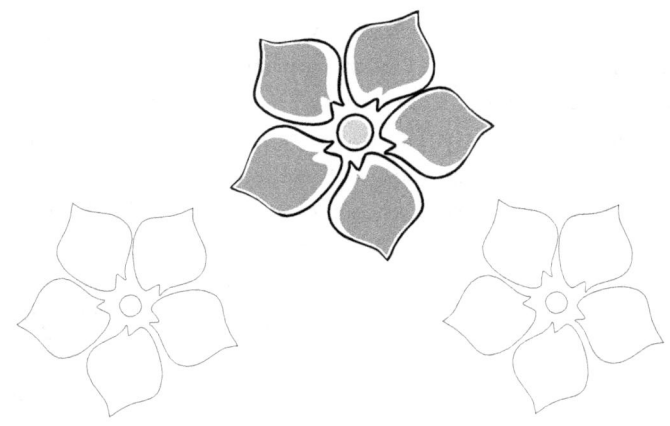

# 51

# The Laughing Fool of Binduvan

## Suggested Areas of Attention

* Awaken the beauty of your heart; let it soar. Let the world rejoice in it.
* Throw off the burdens you carry.
* Invite more of the presence of your Soul into your life. You'll discover her in those places where she expresses herself to you.
* Look for the beauty, truth, and goodness in all things, especially in yourself.
* Let your life be fun, ever new, and ever-adventurous.
* Don't hide your humanity; have the courage to weep its tender tears.

Oh, the beauty of the human heart! Rejoice that you possess it. Celebrate your human heart by releasing it and letting it free to soar. It'll carry you to heights unimaginable and guide you through life's dark and tumultuous times. Your Soul is the nurturer of your human heart. Let her tend it, let her lighten it, and let her touch it with the sweet sadness of her loving. Dance with your Soul, dear one. Laugh and be foolish in your loving. Cry and be tender in your humanity. Your Soul will always be beside you and within you when you do. Dance, play, weep and laugh. Oh, the beauty of the human heart! Oh, the majesty of the love between you and your nurturing Soul!

*Lighten the living of your life.*

Awaken and see the world through the eyes of the Wise Fool within you.

See the beauty, truth, and goodness lying eternally in the midst of all you perceive, even amid the dark places. In life's dark places, you'll discover the light of hope. You'll find the tender touch of God/Goddess/All That Is in all of life's pain and sadness.

Awaken to the fun of living and the joy of living free.

Attend to the dark times of your life with courage and self-compassion.

Attend to the chaos with patience and with hope.

Attend to the cries and whispers of your lost and panicked selves.

Attend to the living of your life with laughter and with your Soul's sweet and tender sadness.

Discover and awaken your humanity, dear one, and be the Wise Fool that is your destiny.

*Lighten the living of your life!*

Let go of the burdens you carry. Give them to your Higher Self or give them to your Soul, they'll know what to do with them. Then laugh and laugh, and laugh again. Laugh at the wondrous play of life and weep tender and loving tears at the eternal dance of the Divine. Your freedom embraces such laughter and human compassion.

*Lighten the living of your life!*

# 52

# The Thousand Coats of Suma Ti

## Suggested Areas of Attention

* Accept your destiny. Get to work in living it. *"The qualities of being there are the steps to getting there."*
* Own and heal the dark of you; own and align with the light.
* Activate the power of forgiveness by first forgiving yourself.
* Let what you're becoming have more influence in your life than where you've been.
* Respond to the calls and whispers of your past. Respond to the calls and whispers of what you're becoming.

    Acknowledge the light and dark of you; own them as parts of yourself, as the many parts of the totality of you. Acknowledge the dark; forgive it and let it go. Acknowledge the light; welcome it and let it in. Then keep moving beyond the light and darkness of your past. The real you is there before you.

    You have many lifetimes, dear one. Some of those lifetimes are dark and painful, and some are light and glowing, others somewhere in between. You don't need to know these many lifetimes, though some may be up for healing in this current life your living. You don't need to go back in time to attend to all those in need of forgiveness. If you truly forgive yourself in this life, such forgiveness will most certainly extend to them.

Time and space are illusions; forgiveness is not. Forgiveness transcends all time and space and reaches out to nurture and heal the many of you. As you can forgive yourself, and sincerely ask for healing, all your many lifetimes lift and heal; in their own time, and in their own space, and in their own way.

Some lifetimes may call out seeking to lean on you their future self. Respond not by trying to fix the past but by leaning upon your healed future. Lean on the 'you' more real, then nurture and embrace the 'you' lost in a darkened past. Each lifetime has a story; each story can be re-written.

Welcome the realness you're becoming, as you do know that you have pasts that journey beside you. You cannot return Home without them.

You stand with God/Goddess/All That Is as the singular representative of all your past and future lifetimes. Stand tall, stand proud, stand humble, and stand forgiven and forgiving. Brilliance is your destiny. Pursue it with patience and attention. You have a future to guide you, and a past in need of your loving. Heed the calls of both.

You're Coming Home dear one, so too your many lifetimes; in their own time, in their own space, in their own way. The journey of Coming Home only needs one lifetime to choose to do so. Why wait? Why not choose now?

Oh, what a splendid journey you're on! What a magnificent cloak the Weaver Woman spins just for you! Wear it proudly, dear one. Let yourself shine brightly in it.

*The heavens call your name.*
*The stars await your shinning.*

# 53

# In the Valley of the Singing Stones

## Suggested Areas of Attention

* Invade your privacy. Despite your fear and hesitation, go into the unknown of you. Go forward into the hidden places of yourself and discover the secrets you keep locked there. It's in these places you'll find your healing.
* Step outside the false safety of the consensus. Be an adventurer in your pursuit of healing. Have the courage to move forward, always forward.
* Be open to magical occurrences and miraculous happenings; seek the healing of the Ancient Ones. Seek the healing of ancient magic.
* Cultivate the power of faith, not blind faith, but faith grounded in solid trust and hope.
* Allow the more of you to be involved in your healing. Respond to the whispers and shouts of the lesser.

Seek the 'Great Uncharted.' Go where others will not go. Be the adventurer you were born to be. The 'Great Uncharted' lies within and beyond you. It's there you'll find the healing you so much desire. It's there you'll discover lost treasures beyond measure. It's there you'll unlock opportunities beyond what you can currently dream or imagine. Seek the unknown of the 'Great Uncharted.' You'll discover your future there. You'll find your healing there. Oh, what adventures await you in the Valley of the Singing Stones; this sacred place within the 'Great Uncharted!'

Stop hiding in the false safety of consensus thinking. Move beyond it. Playing it safe will not get you to where you truly want to go. Move beyond the numbing mediocrity of consensus thinking. You've stayed stuck in the familiar much too long. Let's try the unfamiliar now.

Be wary of the desire to stand out for the sake of being noticed, that's the ego at work here. Be wary of the desire to step outside the consensus to feed your ego's need for specialness, that's the ego's game. Step out of the flow of the familiar because beyond it, your Soul calls to you, a more authentic future awaits you, and frankly, it's just more fun. Be an adventurer. Adventure is the joy of your Spirit, the playground of your Higher Self.

Don't run from fear or deny it; in doing so, you negate your healing. Go into your fear instead. Fear, being a human emotion, is a part of your nature. Welcome fear as a teacher and a guide, as one who warns you that your path forward is over the terrain of your inner secrets and conflicts, and through the dark valleys of your hidden unaddressed pains. Have the courage to welcome your fears, not wallow in them. Have the courage to go deeply into your fears, for on the other side, your healing, freedom, and truer self waits.

Invade your privacy, dear one. Invade your private self. Your Higher Self will go with you if you wish.

*Can you hear the calling of the Singing Stones?*
*Can you feel their ancient pull?*

# 54

# Just Imagine

## Suggested Areas of Attention

* Be aware of the consensus beliefs you hold about imagination. Correct such distortions and awaken to imagination's real power.
* Exercise and hone your imagination.
* Don't stop dreaming and imagining. Dream new worlds; imagine new futures. Play wildly in the fields of your imagination and dreams.
* Let go of the fantasies of the past; pursue the fantasias of the future.
* Allow your creativity to flourish. But also work to elevate your creativity to the grander heights of innovation.

We're experiencing a drought in the world, a drought of imagination. We live in a time where creativity, genuine creativity, is sorely lacking.

Hollywood spews out tired remakes and *'bang 'em up'* spectacles lacking in third acts and substance. Broadway relies on adaptations of proven successes and endless replays of old tried and true winners.

The world sorely needs dreamers who dream dreams beyond the boundaries of past formulas, and the economic bottom line of the tried and true. The world is much in need of genuine creators imagining new and more magnificent futures that extend the limits of the possible and broaden the boundaries of the excepted. The world needs awakening, awakening to the magic of the possible. But more so, the world needs to awaken to the power and magic that lies beyond the possible. It needs those courageous enough to pursue the imaginings that wait just at the edges of the unimaginable. The world needs those who are genuinely creative, but more so those who will dream the dreams that elevate creativity to the dazzling heights of innovation. You, dear one, are being called to be such a creator and perhaps to become such an innovator.

There are three tools we all use in the crafting of reality: imagination, desire, and expectancy. Of the three, imagination is the most powerful for nothing in our reality manifests without first being conceived in one's imagination. Your desire for something is born of your imagining it, and your expectation weak or strong is how we bring into manifestation, or not, the object of the desire we imagined.

To become the creator and innovator you're called to be, begin by following these three steps.

First: Understand and respect the power of imagination. Don't let consensus thinking minimize it with its distorted views. The consensus sees imagination as the stuff of weird artists, or the rambling daydreams of children. Or the consensus, in its rampant chauvinism, dismisses it as just *'the silly musings of women.'* The consensus thinking is always wrong. Nothing great is ever imagined or created from it.

Second: Exercise and hone your imagination. Allow yourself to dream; allow yourself to imagine futures. These futures don't have to play out as you dreamt them. Details are not necessary; the essence of the dream is. It's the essence of your vision that awaits you in the future. It's the essence of the dream that you truly desire. Don't be surprised if it manifests in a form much grander than you imagined it. But dear one, your future requires you to imagine it. It needs you to desire it. It needs you to expect it.

Third: Don't stop dreaming and imagining. Keep your dreaming and imagining alive and ever vibrant. Without dreaming and imagining, without hope and the pursuit of futures, we give up the living of our lives and exist solely in dashed hopes, unfulfilled dreams, and the stagnant routines of mediocrity. We simply pass the time while waiting to die.

Pursue the dreams that are supposed to happen (fantasias); let go of the ones that are not (fantasies). Embrace the future that calls you Home; let go of the siren's call of childhood dreams and adolescent musings.

A wondrous and magical future awaits those courageous enough to imagine it and awake enough to dream it into manifestation. The world needs dreamers such as you.

*You're a dreamer, dear one.*
*Imagine that!*

## 55

# A Marriage Made in Heaven

### Suggested Areas of Attention

* Challenge your perceptions and alter your perspectives of the reality around you.
* You attract what you project. So what are you projecting?
* Pay attention to what you give attention to; monitor your intentions.
* Change what you express to the world; change your *'voice.'* Change how the world perceives you.
* Attend to the shame you're holding; ask for its healing.

How you view the world is the world you attract. It's the dark or light lover you seduce. Change how you view your world, and your world becomes different. What you give attention to and the intentions underlying it are at the foundation of the reality manifesting for you. The reality you're observing now is not the reality that is. It's only the world you're making real for yourself.

You're being called now. It's a call to change your perceptions of the world about you and to alter the perspectives you give it. And it's a call to not only question what you're giving attention to but to question why you're giving it. Do you see a glass half empty? Are you pretending the glass is half full while deep inside, fearing the opposite? What are you giving attention to, and why?

You're not wrong or bad for seeing reality as you do, you're just mistaken. You can correct a mistake. Doing so is an essential part of your healing. It's fundamental to your growing and becoming.

There's also a call to pay attention to your *'voice.'* Your voice is not how you speak, or what you say, but how your inner world is expressing itself.

For example, depressed people do not have to say a word; their presence alone can bring down their environment. On the other hand, people with a strong voice can uplift a room just by being in it. They don't have to say anything. Cynics, having nothing of value to say, inject negativity into conversations to feel a sense of contribution. They also bring their environment down by their gloomy presence.

Grow your 'voice' not by having more to say, or by saying only positive things, but by elevating your inner voice's expression. As you pursue, discover, and live more of your goodness, truth, and beauty, you'll gain the courage to let it be seen and heard in your world. It will express itself in both your presence and conversations.

If you don't see the realness in others, it is because you're afraid of letting others see the realness in you. Your fear of being seen is born of shame. Shame is the false belief you're flawed, or broken, or defective. Everyone holds, to a greater or lesser degree, this resonance of shame. It's a condition we were taught, wronged into feeling, or came to by other means. Shame is not real; it's a lie. You're not flawed, broken, or defective.

Recognize shame when it appears. Acknowledge its presence in you. Forgive yourself for holding onto it, and ask it to be lifted. It will if you'll let it go. But you have to let it go.

*Beyond shame is freedom.*
*With freedom, there are no glasses half full;*
*only glasses continuously overflowing.*

## 56

# The Eternal Companion

### Suggested Areas of Attention

* Grieve the loss you feel so deeply. Don't push the pain away or attempt to *"toughen it out."*
* Continue the love you had by expanding the love you yet have. You didn't lose your companion; you only believe you did. Change your belief. You can continue the relationship if you let it take a different form, a more real form.
* What in you needs dying? What in you needs birthing?
* During times of significant change, mourn the old, celebrate the new.
* Be willing to accept the gifts and healing that grieving offers you. These gifts will not harden your heart. These gifts will strengthen your resolve to acknowledge and value its tenderness.
* Open to transcending your investment in form, and allow more valuing of content.

Form dies; life does not. Your companion has not abandoned you. The passing of a loved one never means the loss of the relationship.

Yes, your beloved moves on, but never away. Your beloved is free from the restrictions of time and space now. Your loved one is free from the limits of form. How can your companion move away from you? Since it's you who's currently trapped in form and therefore stuck in the illusion of time and space, the only one who moves away is you. But you can choose not to. You can continue the relationship if you so desire. But to do so, you'll have to allow the relationship to become different, to become more.

Your loved one is no longer a form; in truth, it never really was. Your loved one is more real now, and the love shared between you can be more real as well if you'll allow it to be. Beyond the stinging hurt of loss, beyond the mournful wail of grief, beyond the anger and despair, beyond the loneliness and emptiness, your beloved waits more radiant, more alive, and more loving. Grieve; feel your hurt and loss, feel the anger you hold, go through the necessary ritual of loss. When you're ready, if you choose to be ready, you can resume that love made more real now by the healing gained from this sacred ritual.

When a loved one passes and you choose to remain enmeshed in the grieving, your beloved does not die to you; sadly, you die to your beloved. Your companion is with you, but you cannot experience this for the static and noise you're making.

We all experience loss; it's a part of our living and growing. Don't collapse beneath its weight. Carry it with grace and elegance. Let it carry you. Let it make you more. You're strong enough to do this.

Don't let loss keep you from loving more; in doing so, you die to yourself and the power of your loving. Don't let this beautiful part of you die. Accept the gifts that loss brings. Though these gifts will be hard to see or experience at first, they're there. They're always there.

If you will allow the loss to elevate and not diminish you, and if you will rise above the static and the noise, your beloved companion will be there. If you'll abandon your ancient belief that forms are real and make the courageous choice to resume a love more real, your beloved companion will be there. Together you'll race and love and play as always in the beautiful fields of eternity.

*All your eternal companions who have left their form*
*eagerly await your choice*
*so the love may resume once more.*

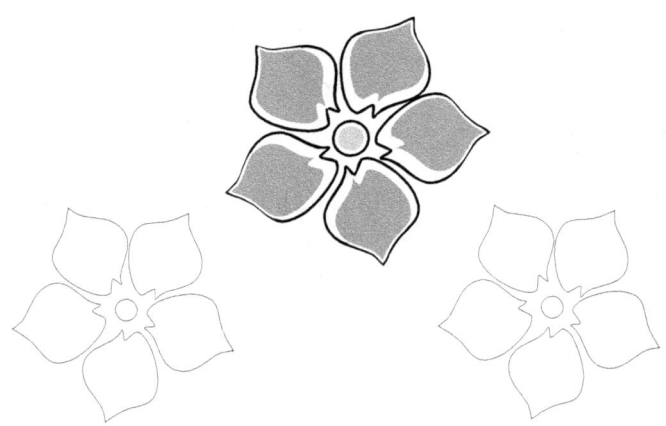

# 57

# Manju Among the Saints

## Suggested Areas of Attention

* Stop seeking empowerment from others. You're empowered already.
* You're more powerful than you yet realize. Start awakening it and start using it to craft a more meaningful, more elegant, more enjoyable, and more bountiful life.
* Stop giving your power to others; they can't use it. But neither can you if you give it away.
* Seek help and guidance from those who'll gladly be your friends and companions on your journey. Avoid the advice and guidance from those who seek to lead you.

Stop searching for gurus and masters. Run from those promising enlightenment if only you put your trust in them. You already have a guru and master. It's you!

For thousands of years, people have waited and prayed for the return of their savior. Lifetime after lifetime, they've waited and are waiting still. Don't waste your time longing for a *'Second Coming.'* The one you're waiting for has already arrived. It's you!

Those who promise directly or indirectly that they can empower or enlighten you are either lying or ignorant. No one can empower anyone because each of us has the power already. Sadly, most give it away. The enlightenment you seek is for you and you alone to discover and awaken.

Pay attention to whom or what you give your power to, either knowingly or unknowingly. Is it a family member, a friend, a spouse, co-workers, or a boss, those you hate or despise, those you faun after, that political leader, or that political party, etc.? Stop giving your power away to events, circumstances, things, groups or people. Stop obsessing over them. Stop blaming them, or the lack of them, for your current life. When you do so, you give away the power needed to craft a better one.

You're the author of your reality; no one else. Claim your authorship and, in so doing, awaken your power. You have the power, claim it.

But remember this, dear one, *'Upon your sacred journey of growing and becoming there is more help available then you'll ever know. You're not alone. You've never been alone. You're protected, and you're loved.'*

Those you meet along the way, those who can best advise and guide you, will never promise you anything, will never require trust, will never ask of you anything, and will never lead and expect you to follow. They'll be real friends, loving guides, and faithful companions on your journey. They'll walk beside you, never ahead. They'll be lights along the path of your incredible journey Coming Home. They'll also be your greatest cheerleaders.

You have your power, dear one. God/Goddess/All That Is already gave it to you. They also gave you the gift of choice. Choose to put your power into play and have fun doing so.

## 58

# The Selfishly Generous Woman

### Suggested Areas of Attention

* Recognize and acknowledge the martyrhood you're playing out at the moment. Without self-judgment and self-blame, forgive yourself and stop doing it.
* Allow the love of others to embrace you. Let their love matter to you.
* Awaken your magic; use it, be awash in it.
* Respond to the parts of yourself in need of attention. It's they who hold the martyred one in you. Be gentle, loving, and reassuring.

A 'martyr' is a silent sufferer who needs an audience to witness their melodrama of being unloved, unappreciated, and overworked.

We all do martyr; we all slip into it from time to time. Some use it as a tool of control and manipulation, and some use it as a way to get attention. Some have taken it so far as to become masters at it.

Martyrhood is a false belief and attitude we adopted as children. It's a resonance and pattern of behavior we picked up from the martyr influences around us. It became a balm to soothe the pains and hurts of growing up, and it worked. We saw it successfully play out in others, and we incorporated it into our strategy of survival. It was not a wrong choice at the time; it was a survival choice. We were children. Since we did not have adult tools and resources to handle our pains and hurts, we used martyr as a means to deal with them.

Although martyr was a survival choice then, today it's a destructive choice leading to deadened dreams, dashed hopes, denied futures, shattered relationships, and unhappiness. Today it's a significant blockage on our journey Coming Home.

To heal martyrhood, we must first recognize when we're in it. We must catch it when we find ourselves playing it out. Then we must acknowledge its presence by admitting the harm we're doing to ourselves, and especially to those we love. We then forgive ourselves and step out of it.

Martyr is an ugly behavior that denies others their need and desire to extend their love to you. It's a slap in the face of their love, and it prevents the exercise of their loving. Understand that martyr is a performance needing an audience. And to the martyr, it must be a one-person show.

*"How dare you offer love to me!"* the martyr cries out, *"This is my performance and I, and only I, am the star of it!"* Then she retreats once again into her silent-suffering self-pity.

As long as you're holding martyr, you'll never allow the love of others. The two cannot co-exist. You'll stay trapped in its lies of being misunderstood, unloved, and unappreciated. Martyr is a game you play. Recognize it, acknowledge it, forgive yourself, and stop doing it, if not for yourself, at least for those you love.

Forgive yourself for playing the martyred soul. Forgive yourself and release it. Free yourself and the child in you still clinging to it. Reassure this child of the love you have for it. Assure this little one that it will always be protected, that its pain and loneliness will be responded to, and that you'll always respond without judgment or blame to its lonely cries for help. Don't judge these martyred parts of you; just love, forgive, and nurture them.

When you free yourself of martyrhood, you'll allow yourself to receive the love so willingly offered you. You'll learn the power and majesty of real love, a love inherent in you.

The elevated and transformed resonance of martyr is magic. When you lift the resonance of martyr, you'll find magic all about you. Yes, dear one, magic abounds in a life free of martyrhood. Magic will awaken in you. Magical occurrences will be the standard of your living.

Oh, you will, from time to time, fall back into martyr, like a former smoker having that cigarette behind the shed now and again. That's Ok. Just recognize, acknowledge, and forgive yourself. Then, dear one, continue to live once again, your life filled with love and magic.

# 59

# The Master's Perfect Imperfection

## Suggested Areas of Attention

* Stop your futile attempts to be perfect. Life will have its good and bad days; it gives it dimension. You will have success and failures; it gives you dimension.
* Recognize and forgive yourself for the lies you tell yourself, and stop believing your negative ego's false promises.
* Dare to awaken to who you are, and to pursue your journey Home.
* Accept your authorship of life, and *"load the dice"* by taking steps for the winning of it.

Nothing is perfect in your reality, or outside it. Stop trying to make it so. Stop believing your ego's lies of perfection. Such lies will never make your hurts and pains, and your mistaken belief in your flaws and defectiveness, go away. Only in forgiving yourself for believing these lies, and in your pursuit to become more, not just better, will you accomplish this.

Life ebbs and flows. There'll be times of brightness and accomplishment, there'll be times of darkness and resistance, and there'll be times somewhere in between. There'll be times of moving forward, there'll be times when you seem to be moving backward, and there'll be times when you seem not to move at all. When you can accept these ebbs and flows with grace and patience, understanding and forgiveness, attention and celebration, then you'll come to realize all your days lead in one direction; toward becoming more, not merely becoming better. Your journey of becoming more, not perfect, will have signposts along the way marking your growth and progress.

You'll blame yourself and others less. You'll be less judgmental as well.

You'll be more responsive to the fears of your less developed selves and more attentive to the whispers and calls of your more developed.

You'll grow in understanding of yourself and others, and the world about you. You'll begin to see life's bigger picture.

Life will become more fun, dark times less tragic, and those times that lie somewhere in between marked by valued pause and reflection.

Your life will flow with wondrous synchronicities and with endless magic.

Your growing creativity can rise to innovation, and you'll dream dreams destined to happen.

But most importantly you'll come to know that you're loved and continuously cared for, that you're loving and strong enough to show it, that you are and always have been protected and guided, and that life is indeed a marvelous dance with God/Goddess/All That Is. And you'll reach a place and time beyond your current place and time where you will find it very hard to keep from laughing.

Oh, dear one, these are only a handful of signs along a magnificent journey that never ends.

*Oh, what wonders lie ahead*
*if you'll but risk the journey!*

# 60

# King or Seeker

## Suggested Areas of Attention

* Don't seek the Divine for what it can get you. Seek the Divine for where it can lead you.
* Let go of your belief in *'lack.'* Let go of its greed that says there'll never be enough for you.
* Don't lose yourself in the belief that you must choose between seeking the Divine (the spiritual), and having what you desire (the material). Know that in seeking the Divine, you'll awaken more and more to the truth that you, and only you, are the creator of all your needs and wants.
* Know that receiving what you desire is not a reward or something you earned. And know that not receiving what you want is not a punishment or a lack of earning.

Live a life that shines with the radiance of your spirituality. Live a life that overflows with success, abundance, and prosperity. You can live both lives together. There's no conflict there.

Let go of the archaic belief that the material and the spiritual hold opposing values. Let go of the foolish belief in the nobility of renunciation with its ego promises of specialness and sanctity. Let go of the foolish belief that the accumulation of things will provide you with joy, happiness, and fulfillment in life.

Yes, accumulating things will not alone fulfill you. And yes, the denial of your material desires will not ensure your happiness.

When you truly own and pursue a deeper, more intimate, more heightened relationship with that which is more than yourself, your material world shines and reflects the light of your more developing self. When coming from a place of light and love and connectedness, your desires, your real desires, not the desires of your child or adolescent, are synchronously fulfilled. Learn to discriminate between the desires of your lesser selves and those of the more real you. The material world of a genuine spiritual adult is never lacking.

Life's an illusion; the material world's an illusion. Your spirituality is the only thing that's real. Elevate your spirituality. As you do, you'll realize that you can have as much of an illusion as you like.

When you prioritize your spirituality, your life prospers, not as a reward but as a claiming of your grace. In time as your spirituality becomes your only priority, life overflows with unlimited bounty; again, not as a reward, but as a claiming.

Live a bountiful life. Let your spirituality and the play of your creative manifestations join. Don't deny one for the other. There's no need to do so. When you dance with God/Goddess/All That Is, your world and the heavens above pulsate. They pulsate with the rhythm and harmony of the dance. When you dance with God/Goddess/All That Is, you allow the material to elevate to the spiritual, and the spiritual to become grounded in the very essence of your material life. Worldly pursuits and divine passion become one.

*Be the King you were born to become.*
*Be the Spiritual Being of your destiny.*
*There's no conflict there.*

# 61

# Where the Two Worlds Meet

## Suggested Areas of Attention

* It's time to take your magic to another level. Consider expanding the power and scope of your reality creating through the power of co-creation.
* Don't be afraid to ask for help. Don't be so arrogant as not to allow it.
* Be willing to expand the limits of your beliefs and your range of what's possible.
* Answer the call of unseen friends. Accept the help they offer.
* There's a grander love available to you. Pursue it.

It's time to elevate your magic. It's time to take it further.

You create your own reality; this is true and without exception. But you can take your reality creation to greater heights; heights beyond what you can create alone. Some creations cannot be created alone; we need help to manifest them. To create such realities, we'll need to work *'co-creation magic.'* When we undertake our reality creation with others, seen or unseen, a synergy is created producing a resonance more significant than our own. This resonance generates higher manifesting capabilities.

It's time to work your magic with others. Maybe your Higher Self, or certain friends, or if you're so inclined, those of other realms. Perhaps this is the time for you to pursue such things.

But what stands in your way?

Is it your fear that requires the need for control? Is it the chauvinist in you that holds that unseen friends are just a child's fantasy? Is it the claim of your arrogance that you and only you are capable of such working? Is it your fear of gratitude that angrily rebels at *"being beholden"* to anyone? Or is it the belief that you're not worthy of such love and support? Go within and discover your resistance. Ask for help with this. Be humble and courageous enough to be told.

Recognize your resistance, acknowledge its presence, forgive yourself, and let it go. And be ever mindful when it shows up again, which it will surely do.

There's a love so grand it will take your breath away, a love so majestic it can elevate you beyond the possible into the realms of the unimaginable, and a love so real it can only be called Divine. Such a love awaits those courageous enough to seek it, who are strong enough to allow it, and who are humble enough to be lifted to it.

Welcome your Higher Self. Open to God/Goddess/All That Is. Open to those seen and unseen friends who await your co-creating, who likewise need your participation in the lifting of their magic.

It's time to elevate your reality creation, its time to raise your magic, and it's time to heighten your love and willingness to be loved. You're ready.

*"In a meadow, two trees grow;
between them an invisible door."*

*Will you enter, dear one?*

# 62

# My Life Has Never Been So Bad

## Suggested Areas of Attention

* Lighten up!
* Stop fighting the crisis you're in; recognize, accept, and move elegantly through it. Freedom from crisis begins with recognition and acceptance. Stop blaming yourself and others for it.
* Forgive yourself for trying to hold onto the past. Give more weight to what your becoming; value more your Future Self.
* Be courageous enough to ask for help and strong enough to receive it. Support and guidance are always available to you.
* Be patient and attentive during times of chaos.

Perhaps you're in a crisis now. If so, be easy with yourself. Now is not the time to blame others or yourself for the tumultuous times you're having. Now is the time for understanding and forgiveness. Now is the time to ask for help, and the time to exercise the courage to allow it.

A crisis is a state of chaos. It's not a punishment. And its presence in your life is not a judgment on your worth or value. Chaos is a necessary part of change and an essential condition upon your journey of becoming more. It precedes all significant changes. A crisis occurs when one fights or ignores chaos instead of accepting it and working through it.

At the point of transitioning between one state of being and another, a gap exists between the two. In this gap, the past is no longer present, and the future has yet to occur. This gap is where chaos lies. Scientists refer to this gap as *"phase transition."* Within the spiritual community, some call it *"The Dark Night of the Soul."* In the healing arts, the term is *"healing crisis."* This gap, this chaos, is a necessary part of living. Accepting the crisis we're in and navigating elegantly through it will lessen its duration by shortening the gap. Wallowing in it only prolongs the chaos.

The following archetypal story of the *'Weaver Woman'* describes the nature and function of chaos.

*"The ancient Weaver Woman sits in her cave, weaving the Fabric of Life. Her weaving is elegant and magical, her fabric majestic and amazingly beautiful. When she completes the work, she takes it off the loom and places it on the ground beside her. Her black dogs then grab the cloth and tear it completely into shreds. The Weaver Woman then collects the tattered shreds and weaves another fabric; this one more majestic and even more beautiful. On and on, this cycle of weaving, completion, and shredding continues. And on and on this Fabric of Life is made more majestic and more beautiful than the previous."*

The weaving, the completion, and the shredding are the play of the eternal forces of Nature. They are the forces of creation, maintenance, and destruction. In the Veda, these forces are referred to as the Three Gunas: Brahma, Vishnu, and Shiva.

Growth is never-ending and always in the direction of the more real and the more beautiful. Such is the archetypal nature of becoming more. Such is the archetypal nature of you becoming more. When you make choices and decisions that take you off your destiny's path, it may take a crisis to bring you back into compliance. Also, in your growing process, the new 'you' you're becoming will be preceded by chaos at various times. This chaos must and will happen. But crisis and chaos always make way for the more real and the more beautiful to emerge. Chaos and crisis appear destructive or constructive, depending on your perception.

By understanding the function of chaos as the tearing apart of the old to make way for the new, we can welcome and align with it. We don't need to turn it into a crisis. It can merely be a speed-bump along our way.

When in the whirlwind of chaos, look for that spark of hope that always lies within it. This hope will propel you forward. When in the whirlwind of chaos, find the light of the more real you. This light will guide you through. And when in the whirlwind of chaos, ask for help. Help is always available for the asking. And always keep in mind,

*'The greater the change, the greater will be the chaos proceeding it. The greater the chaos, the grander will be the reality that waits on the other side.'*

Don't fight or ignore chaos; don't turn it into a crisis. Change your perception of it. Choose to approach it differently. Exercise forgiveness, look for the spark of hope and the light of the new 'you' you're becoming, attend to your frightened selves, and ask for help.

For others, chaos can be a raging storm; for you, it can be a morning drizzle. Soon, you too will be heard to say, *"My life has never been so good!"*

Be patient. Enjoy the ride.

# 63

# Mother Seagull and the Ocean

## Suggested Areas of Attention

* Blend your will with your heart. In doing so, you'll make magic.
* Allow life to be magical. It's more fun that way.
* Be tenacious in pursuit of what's right, what's true, and what's sacred in you.
* Never let yourself forget that you'll always be supported in your quest to become more.
* Stay the course regardless of the obstacles before you. They're never as big as you think they are. They're never mightier than you.
* Love's power is eternal and invincible. It will never fail you.

*'Will, when infused with love, produces magic.'*

Be a champion. Be the champion of your love and caring. Don't hide them, don't dismiss them, and don't deny their power within you. Be the champion of your love and caring; awaken them, nurture them, and hold them sacred.

Be a magician. Be the magician you were, are, and will become even more so again. Stand tall. Stand determined. Stand in the light of your beauty, truth, and goodness. Stand in the power of your will and love.

When you stand as the champion of your love and caring, when you work the magic of your heart and will, when you glow in the light of your beauty, truth, and goodness, you will know that you're supported and protected by God/Goddess/All That Is. You will realize that you always were.

No obstacle you face is ever bigger or mightier than you. Your reality never places before you a challenge you cannot meet and surpass. Life never stacks the deck against you. There's no obstacle you cannot handle, and no dream you cannot manifest.

Stay the course. Draw upon your body of knowledge and experience. Draw upon the ever-present love of your Higher Self, your Soul and Spirit, and God/Goddess/All That Is. Draw upon your alliances with those who stand beyond what you can see or fathom. Their support and power are always available to you.

Yes, dear one, setbacks are a necessary part of moving forward, but don't give your power to them by blaming yourself and others or by judging yourself unworthy. Don't give in, don't give up. You're loved and supported, dear one. You cannot fail in the growing of your heart, in the expanding of your life, and your pursuit of Coming Home.

You can, if you wish, sit this lifetime out by hiding in your delusions of insignificance, but why? Why waste a perfectly good lifetime? Choose differently!

Stand up and stand out. Be grounded in your beauty, truth, and goodness. Be courageous in your loving! Use your will and love to make magic happen. Start throwing sand upon the ocean and marvel at the support you'll find. God/Goddess/All That Is will be heaving sand beside you.

*An ocean filled with obstacles and resistances*
*doesn't stand a chance.*

# 64

# The Man Who Talked With Trees

### Suggested Areas of Attention

* Pursue the call of Beauty. Let your pursuit become your calling.
* Don't be trapped by the limitations of your senses or the confines of logic and reason. Pursue higher learning; acquire transcendent knowledge.
* Awaken the higher senses of voice, movement, presence, light, warmth, and substance.
* Welcome change and growth; learn to work with them and to align with their ebbs and flows.
* Shun the calls of the consensus; race to the callings of beauty and enchantment.

    Hear the call of Beauty. Be seduced by her siren's call. But before you journey in pursuit of her, know she'll be a demanding lover. She'll demand your truth and realness, she'll demand your presence and humility, she'll demand your honesty and commitment, and she'll demand your vulnerability to both your strengths and weaknesses. But also know that she'll give back more than she'll ever ask of you.

Beauty will awaken your creativity and will lift it to heights of innovation.

Beauty will reveal your beauty, truth, and goodness, and she'll reveal the beauty, truth, and goodness of All That Is.

Beauty will blend her harmonious nature with the harmonious nature of you that you may discover your oneness. She'll enchant you.

Beauty will heal you.

Beauty will teach you far more than you'll ever learn from books or teachers.

Beauty will lift you to the realization of your magic, open you to the realness of your loving, and display for all to see the divine in you.

In Beauty, you'll discover yourself.

In Beauty, you'll find your wholeness.

Yes, Beauty is a demanding lover. But she is also a transcendent giver. Be seduced by her; be loved by her. Give yourself to her.

There's no limit to what you can learn and find within the Hallows of Beauty. There's so much more to discover than what your physical senses can reveal. Awaken your higher sensing. Beauty will inspire and aid you in this endeavor.

In Beauty, listen to the *'Voice of the Goddess,'* a voice beyond sound and words.

In Beauty, flow with the *'Movement of the Goddess'* in its hush and stillness.

In Beauty, feel the *'Warmth of the Goddess'* beyond all physical sensations.

In Beauty, see the *'Light of the Goddess'* beyond what your eyes can vision.

In Beauty, sense the *'Presence of the Goddess'* beyond what your five physical senses reveal.

In Beauty, sense the *'Substance of the Goddess'* beyond all form and physicality.

Seek to awaken your higher senses. Beauty will help you do so.

Don't rest on the laurels of your successes and accomplishments. Don't stop your growing and elevating. Don't stop your learning and understanding and your pursuit of acquiring wisdom. Nature always pursues *'the more.'* Nature is, and will always be, expanding and changing.

Welcome change. Don't be frightened by it. Growing and changing is the eternal flow of existence. It's what makes life so much more adventurous and fun. There are no limits to your growing and changing when you surrender to the Hallows of Beauty.

*Let the child within you race wildly among the trees,*
*while the Ancient One within you sits beneath the nurturing branches*
*dreaming of new worlds yet to come.*

# 65

# Mukta and the Magic Purse

## Suggested Areas of Attention

* Don't dismiss magic by calling it *"luck."* That's what your negative ego wants you to believe it is. Learn to tell the difference between the lies and distortions of your negative ego and the truth and clarity of your Higher Self.
* Look to discover the intentions that underlie your desires. Look to find the truth of what it is you're really wanting.
* Always ask, *"Where will this lead me?"* Never ask, *"What will this get me?"*
* Choose to be an adventurer in the living of life. Choose to be a magician in its crafting.
* Avoid taking short cuts. And avoid looking for magic in things outside yourself.

Magic is the act of changing reality in accordance with your will, preference, and love.

Let your life overflow with magic and miracles. Choose an enchanted life. It's a more elegant life and a lot more fun. Let wonder abound in your day to day workings: It's in your nature to do so. Chase the

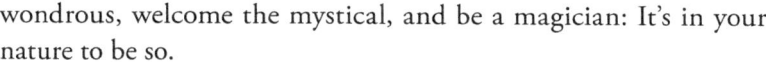

wondrous, welcome the mystical, and be a magician: It's in your nature to be so.

You're the magic you seek. Magic flows all about you, and magic is sourced within you.

*"Well, if you're so magical, why ain't you a millionaire?"* whispers a cynical voice within you, the voice of your negative ego.

Wealth is the standard it sets for you. It's the litmus test it wants as proof that your magic, your authority, and divine love is real. Remember, your negative ego always lies to you. It always distorts the truth.

If you're not a millionaire, it's not because you can't be. It's more likely because the adult in you doesn't honestly want it. The child, the adolescent, and the young adult in you may wish to be a millionaire, but in truth, it's the things that being a millionaire can buy that's at the core of what they're truly seeking. Your Higher Self will never make real the fantasies of the child, the adolescent, or the young adult in you because fantasies are never meant to happen. Your Higher Self will only support your fantasias; for those are dreams your destiny truly wants to unfold.

Your ego holds wealth, or the lack thereof, as proof of your specialness, as proof that God and Goddess love you, or not.

*"Oh, by the way,"* whispers your negative ego, *"if God loves you so much, why are you poor and struggling?"*

*"Oh!"* continues your negative ego, *"God must want you to be poor and struggling as proof of your love, and devotion, and sacrifice."*

Your Higher Self will never allow such *"proofs"* to manifest, for doing so would legitimize your ego's lies.

You may not become the millionaire you're asking to be, not because you can't be, but because it's not really what you're wanting. Everything in your reality is an illusion, including money. You can have anything in an illusion you wish as long as it's what you're wanting. But if in your reality becoming wealthy would impede your journey of becoming more, then your Higher Self, your Truer Self, will not contribute to this. *'Having more'* is what your ego says your life's pursuit should be. *'Being more'* is your real life's calling.

Wealth is not the issue; your ego's agenda is. Change the agenda, and you can create what you truly desire because it's what you truly desire, not what your negative ego says you're supposed to want.

Your negative ego asks, *"What will this get you?"* Your Higher Self asks, *"Where will this lead you?"* Listen always to the voice of your Higher Self. 'Being more' is the desire your Higher Self will always honor and support. It will never enable your negative ego's distortions.

Why not desire to become an adventurer in the living of your life? Why not become a magician in its crafting? Life can be so dull and limiting amid daily toils and struggles. Mindless routine is anathema to our very nature.

Be an adventurer. Approach your life as an explorer, searching for the unknown, at play in the mystery of the divine, discovering the yet undiscovered you, exploring the distant horizons of infinite possibilities. Why not be an adventurer, and why not be a magician upon your adventure? Adventure is all around you; magic is all within you.

A magician possesses certain qualities. If you wish to be one you'll need to develop them:

First: You'll need to be vulnerable to both your strengths and weaknesses. You'll find being open and accepting of your strengths the harder of the two. Know your strengths and weaknesses. Accept them. Don't excuse your weaknesses or give your strengths to your ego to distort. Know you have them. Realize they're a part of you. Accept them; accept yourself.

Second: You'll need to attend to, and align with, the many parts of yourself (See Appendix One). Listen and respond to the many voices of your lesser selves, and honor and heed the voices of the more real you. What you feel, dark or light, resides in their fears or hopes. Honor their feelings by allowing yourself to feel them. Honor yourself by listening and responding to them.

Third: You'll need to respect and value your connection to Nature: the elements, the trees, the spirits of nature, plants, animals, minerals, etc. They're your connection to your more real self and the real power within you. Connecting to Nature will awaken your oneness with her.

Fourth: You'll need to utilize your vast body of knowledge and experience. It's the totality of all you've learned, and the totality of all you've experienced. They're a part of what makes you so powerful and unique. No one else has such knowledge and experience.

Fifth: You'll need to forge alliances with your Higher Self and your numerous unseen friends. Such partnerships will lift you to heights unimaginable.

Sixth: You'll need to be willing to open the gateways to the unknown; and, from time to time, step through.

Seventh: You'll need to know and accept that you're always guided and protected. You're never alone on your magician's journey.

These are the qualities of being a magician. As you become more awakened to these qualities, more and more magic will flow to and from you.

Along your grand adventure, upon your magician's journey, be mindful when looking for shortcuts. Shortcuts cheat you by cutting your journey short. You'll not get to where you're going by way of shortcuts.

Be wary of pursuing magic in things outside you. You'll find no magic purse there. The magic is found in you.

*You're the magic.*
*You're the adventure you seek.*

## 66

# Sinji's One and Only Tale

### Suggested Areas of Attention

* What's your story? What are you presenting to the world and to yourself? If you don't like the story, re-write it. Like the story, make it better.
* Always challenge, exceed, and supersede yourself.
* Accept that you're the author of your life and write the story that best reflects the beauty, truth, and goodness of you. Stop giving your story to others to write. Stop using ghostwriters.
* Clean, hone, sharpen and elevate the raw materials out of which you create your reality: Beliefs and attitudes, thoughts and feelings, choices and decisions.

*"What was said is not what was heard.
What was heard is not what was said."*

Everything filters through the templates of our unique perceptions and perspectives. Each person sees reality differently as reality is the creation of each person who observes it.

Our reality, our story, is an illusion made real by our individual beliefs and attitudes, thoughts and feelings, choices and decisions.

The story can be a tragedy for some, a comedy for others. It can be a tale of hope or a tale of hopelessness, a love story, or a story of loneliness and betrayal. What we call reality is, in truth, an illusion. The only thing real is the observer.

The screen in a movie theater is blank. The movie does not come from the screen; it comes from the film projecting onto it. The film is the story of the one who produced it; it's the reality of the story's creator. When projected, each person in the theater will observe the story differently as it siphons through the templates of the observer's consciousness, self-image, individual perspectives and perceptions, and the synergy of the observer's beliefs, attitudes, thoughts, feelings, choices, and decisions. No one observes the same movie since no one is the same observer. The one who conceived the film is the only one who sees the film as written.

The reality you observe, like the movie on a blank screen, is the story projecting onto the screen from you, the projector. You can change the story, the reality you're observing, by going within yourself its creator and re-write it. If you don't like the story, craft a new one. If you like the story, why not make it better?

The whisper here is to challenge, exceed, and to supersede yourself. It's a whisper from your Higher Self, your Soul and Spirit, God/ Goddess/ All That Is, and most of all, you.

Respond to the whisper; respond to you, the whisperer. Now's not the time to be complacent. Go within. Process through and change your measuring devices, the devices by which you observe the reality (the story) you're projecting. Identify the *'how,'* the *'what,'* and the *'why'* of your current creation and choose differently. You have the power of your authorship to turn mediocrities, nightmares, tragedies, and darkness into adventures, magic, enchantments, and light. You have the power of your authorship to write the story that best reflects the truth, beauty, and goodness of you. Write the story you prefer to write, not the story you feel compelled to author.

You're Sinji. Yours is the 'One and Only Tale.' Craft your tale wisely and let all the heavens marvel at your masterpiece. You won't win an Academy Award, but at least you'll be fulfilled, free, and happy.

# 67

# A Simple Tale of Hope

## Suggested Areas of Attention

* Awaken your lost or neglected hope. Elevate it to a higher place of value.
* What do you believe about hope? Process through your beliefs and change them.
* Let hope guide you through, and free you from, the dark places of your journey.
* Have the humility to ask for help. Have the willingness to receive it. And above all, dare to allow it.
* Avoid at all times feelings of desperation, self-pity, and the belief in your entitlement. They're the static that interferes with receiving.

Consensus attitudes dismissively ridicule hope as *'the last refuge of desperate people.'* It's considered *'wishful thinking'* and often as a waste of time. Hope is so much more than the consensus misconceptions about it.

Hope is a transcendent energy that, when genuinely held, can lift achievements to fulfilling accomplishments, and can generate astonishing miracles. Hope can guide us through the narrows of our dark places and can show us the way to the possible amid the swamps of the impossible. Hope can even part the seas and stop the fiercest storms if we have the faith to keep it strong and steady in us.

Hope is essential for dreaming and visioning, so crucial in one's growth and transformation. Hope can lift those dreams and visions to unfathomable heights of manifestation and guide us through the inevitable dark times of our journey Coming Home.

In a world so lacking in hope, awakening its power within you can truly change not only you but the world itself. Hope is a powerful magic, an essential magic. It's magic is necessary for the times we're living.

You can discover your lost hope in the Hallows of beauty, enchantment, love, or blessed solitude. Whichever Hallow calls to you, there pursue your hope with focus and intent. Within your Hallow, you'll find your lost or neglected hope, and you'll awaken new and more vibrant ones. Let your new-found hope become alive in you, let it lift you; let it guide you into the future. Oh, what wonders lie beyond its door!

When you lack dreams and visions, you ignore your future and become stuck in the tape loops of the past. Through the power of hope, you can awaken dreams and visions that align with your destiny's call.

But don't engage hope from a place of desperation, self-pity, or entitlement. To do so will only create static, and this static prevents the availability of hope's incredible power. Be calm, be trusting, and be willing to engage it fully and deeply. Hope will gently carry you across the most raging waves of crisis and will guide you lovely through the frightening places of your confusion and doubts. It can melt all obstacles to your becoming more.

Ask your Higher Self to ignite hope in you. It will re-kindle in you; it will burn and glow in you again. Do you have the willingness to let in this new found hope? More importantly, do you have the courage to allow it? One would only hope so.

*Oh, what wonders lie beyond hope's door!*

# 68

# Coming Home

## Suggested Areas of Attention

* Remember your covenant with God and Goddess; your promise to Come Home.
* Receive the love of others, allow the love of others, and grow from the love of others.
* Your journey Coming Home begins with forgiveness. Start forgiving yourself, start forgiving others, and start forgiving God and Goddess for what you mistakenly believe they did.
* During times of dark and fear, call upon the Light of Love. During times of light and peace, extend that Light to those who yearn for such light and peace.

You are loved. You are loved more than you will ever know. Do you have the courage to receive that love? Do you have the courage to allow it to touch you? Do you have the courage to allow it to change you?

You are loved by God/Goddess/All That Is beyond what you will ever fully comprehend. You're loved not for who you are or what you are. You're loved not for what you do, or what you do not do. You're not loved more or loved less than anyone else, and you're not loved the same. You're loved uniquely. You're loved because you're you. And yes, dear one, God and Goddess know your name.

Theirs is a divine love, a grander love, a love without reason. They love you for no reason at all. There is nothing you can do that will make them love you more, and there is nothing you can do that will make them love you less. And their love for you keeps growing.

It's a love without judgment or condition. Whether you live your life in darkness or light, whether you live it in evil or good, whether you're a saint or sinner, it doesn't matter. They never judge you. You're loved and cherished. Karma and retribution have no place in such a love. Such things are a human construct and hold no sway in their love for you.

When you chose to separate from God/Goddess/All That Is, it was to choose to love them consciously. Though you loved them, though your very existence was the fullness of love itself, it lacked choice. By separating from their love, by in a sense losing it, you began a quest to rediscover it consciously. You started a journey of 'Conscious Awakening.' Over many lifetimes you would seek and grow, sometimes succeeding and sometimes failing, sometimes in darkness and sometimes in light, and sometimes in between. Your chosen quest was to close the perceived separation and consciously discover your Oneness. You'll keep moving, and you'll keep growing till the moment comes when you'll make a choice, the conscious choice to be one with them once again. They don't need you to make this choice, you do. They know you're still one with them. But when you make this choice, then dear one, the journey of 'Coming Home' begins, and your growing elevates to the awakening of the Sacred Oneness of you; the 'you' they hold and cherish and know you to be.

Before you separated, you made a covenant with God and Goddess, and they made a covenant with you. Their promise to you was that they would always be there for you, and would always love and protect you. They promised you freedom. Your promise to them was that you'd Come Home. With the covenants made, the journey of separation, with your eventual choice to Come Home, began.

Remember this upon your journey, *'This journey is not a destination; it's not a place. It's a state of being, a state of forever being at home with God/Goddess/All That Is. It's a state of Oneness.'*

What a grand journey! What a magical adventure! What a state of being and becoming await you!

God and Goddess have kept their covenant with you. But you have not yet kept your covenant with them. When you do not remember your covenant, when you do not honor it, you'll not allow them to honor theirs. You'll feel alone, unloved, and lost. By honoring your promise to return, you allow them to honor their promise to be there for you and to love and protect you.

You will choose to Come Home, dear one; this is destined to happen. It's your covenant, and you'll choose to keep it in this lifetime or another. So I ask you, *"Why not this lifetime?"*

Forgive yourself. Choose to do so. Let this be the lifetime you choose to Come Home. Stop playing games and consciously heal the separation and discover the unbreakable love between you. Begin this new adventure. So much love, magic, beauty, enchantment, and so much healing and miracles await you along the way.

Remember your promise and know they're keeping theirs; receive their love and protection. It's there. You're not alone; you'll never be alone again. And you'll come to know it and embrace it; this is your destiny's promise.

How truly precious you are to them!

*"Come Home, dear one!"*
they call out to you,
*"Come Home."*

# 69

# Sumitra and Her Friends

## Suggested Areas of Attention

* Choose your own life, not the life the consensus says you should be living.
* Stop living a life that does not reflect the truth, beauty, and goodness in you.
* Discover and befriend the Magical Child within you.
* Open to the help, love, and guidance from those you cannot see.
* Allow magic, play, and adventure in the living of your life.

Live the life of your choosing, not the life others have chosen for you. You'll not find happiness or fulfillment living the life of others. The consensus promises order and stability if you just stay within the safe confines of its norms. Yes, you may find some order and stability there, but you'll not find joy and happiness in a life that's not inherently yours. Let yours be a limitless norm-free life. Choose to live it. You'll find your safety and stability there.

Within the dreams and imaginings of the child you once were lay clues to a life more truly yours. Discover the Magical Child within you. This blessed one, this archetypal child, has much to show you, has much to awaken in you. This Magical Child can help you unravel the clues if you allow it to do so.

No, don't be a child once again; you did that already. Instead, bring the child you once were on your adult adventure of becoming more. Along the way, the Magical Child will introduce you both to marvelous friends and allies. It will teach the two of you how to manifest impossible possibilities, and how to make your life's journey fun and magical once again. This Magical Child will teach you how to dance with abandon, race with the fleetness of sylphs, and fly to heights unimaginable. With this Magical Child by your side, you'll come to enjoy the living of life once again; or perhaps for the first time.

Don't give your life to the false promises of consensus order and security. Nothing great is ever accomplished within consensus order and stability. Only those who pursued the life of their choosing discovered the greatness in themselves. Stop playing it safe, stop being normal, and stop trying to fit in. It's not where you belong.

Dear one, you have so many friends and allies in the worlds beyond adult knowing and seeing. Open to them anew, or open to them once again. They have so much love for you and can be of such great assistance along your destiny's journey. They'll cheer you on, they'll guide you along, and they'll offer comfort and healing during those dark times of ebbing. They'll provide light during those times of darkness, and will continuously remind you that all is a grand and wondrous play. And when you start taking your life too seriously, they'll be there with laughter and giddiness to tickle you out of it.

Don't let go of the magical and the enchanting. Don't relinquish the wonder and the spontaneous joy of living. You're a child of light, dear one. Claim your birthright and choose a life worth living. Live a life worth living. Live your life. Let it shine in your brightness and resonate with the glorious laughter of your Magical Child, and the child you once were so very long ago.

# 70

# The Sweet Old Couple

## Suggested Areas of Attention

* Process through what you give attention to, and monitor your intentions behind it.
* Discover and change your old self-image, and act in ways that best reflect the change.
* Nothing changes until you do. If you wish to change your reality, change yourself first.
* Be patient with change; don't rush it and don't drag it out. Let it unfold at its own pace.
* Never allow love to stagnate. If you take it for granted, it dies. Work to keep it alive and vibrant and new.

What you observe is not always what's there and what's there is not always what you observe. Look deeper at what you're seeing. And change your observing devices.

Everything in your reality is an out-picturing of you. Your outer world always reflects what your inner world is projecting. If your inner world is gloomy and dark, your measuring devices will calibrate what you observe to reflect that gloom and darkness within you. As the saying goes, *"The world is what you make of it."* Since gloom and darkness is what you're giving attention to, and since what you give attention to you make real, the world you observe is going to appear gloomy and dark. If your inner world is rosy and bright, your calibration will reflect that as well. Your world will appear rosy and bright. *"The world is what you make of it."*

Your reality always reflects what you give attention to, as well as the intention behind it. For example, if your attention always focuses on the negative in everyone and everything with the intent on proving your cynicism justified, your reality will confirm what you're projecting. It's a "glass-half-full/half-empty" sort of thing.

You're in a movie theater. The screen is neutral. If the film projected on the screen is a horror film, what you observe will be frightening. If the film is an adventure story, what you see will be exciting. You're the author of the film. You're the one producing what you observe on the neutral screen. If you don't like the movie change the film. Go inside yourself and change the script; write and produce a different film. Change what you give attention to, and discover and change the intentions behind it. Your intentions will determine what kind of movie you want to see. Processing your attention and intention is crucial in changing your reality.

Your actions also affect the reality you observe. If you wish to become a winner at the living of life, yet your actions are the actions of a loser, you'll fail in achieving your desire. Know what it is you desire and act accordingly. Don't pretend; don't mood-make. Be honest with yourself. When resistances arise, and they will, recognize them, acknowledge them, forgive yourself, and act accordingly.

Finally, your self-image is central to the reality you're experiencing. Your image is what you hold yourself to be. If your image is that of a 'loser,' you'll become a loser. If your image is that of being 'unlovable' you'll live a reality that reflects that image.

What is your current self-image? It will be negative. Be honest with yourself when doing your processing. Express your self-image in one word; for example, unlovable, loser, worthless, victim, invisible, etc. Now choose a new self-image. Also, make it one word; for example, loved, winner, valued, supported, etc. Have the courage and honesty to select an image reflective of the real you. Don't play games here.

Now change your reality. Pay attention to what you give attention to, be mindful of your intentions, act according to the new reality, and allow your new image to show itself.

Everything will change, and that'll be frightening at first. Remember to recognize your resistances, acknowledge them, forgive yourself, and move forward. So much fun is waiting for you! So much brightness lies ahead. Enjoy the movie.

# 71

# A Most Unconventional Master

## Suggested Areas of Attention

* Stop searching for gurus and masters. You're no longer in need of such things.
* It's time to put into play what you've learned and discovered about yourself.
* Step out of the consensus; make your own way forward.
* Stop projecting father and mother onto others. Be the father and mother to those parts of yourself still in need of them.

Stop searching for gurus or masters. You're the guru and master you seek. Avoid the need for way-showers; make your own way instead.

Why walk the path of others? Why value consensus thinking? Why look for gurus and masters? Why are you hiding in such pursuits and places? When you stop traveling the road of others and step away from consensus thinking, and when you let go of the need for gurus and masters, then you'll be on the path to discover your brilliance. When you awaken your brilliance, no, the world will not have one more light; the world will brighten and glow.

You're no longer in need of teachers. It's time to stop being a student and start living your life, or to put it another way *'It's time to get off the bench and into the game.'*

It's time to put into play all that you've learned and studied. It's time to master the living of your life. In time grow your mastery to become an artist in your crafting. And, as well, it's time to transcend what you learned and studied, not to *'find'* that grander you, but to *'found'* that grander you.

It's time now to be exceptional. It's time now to discover and awaken a 'you' beyond what you or any guru or master can yet imagine.

Although you don't need gurus or masters, you'll never be alone in the pursuit of your exceptionality. There's more help available than you can ever imagine. Avail yourself of that help. But don't make those helpers your gurus or masters. They do not wish to be, for they know it would impede your growth as well as theirs. They're friends and guides along your way. They'll walk beside you, never ahead.

You're also beyond the need for a father or a mother. Stop looking for them. If you need them, discover them in yourself. Learn to father and mother the younger parts of you; this is a part of your healing; this is necessary to becoming a spiritual adult.

*When you become your own master,
then you'll be able to eat rocks if you so desire.*

*(May I recommend mint sauce?)*

# 72

# The Secret of Sima Sen

## Suggested Areas of Attention

* Respond to the calls of your lesser selves. Respond to their whispers and shouts.
* Have the courage and humility to lean on the more of you.
* Start growing in forgiveness and self-understanding.
* Welcome change, don't fight or run from it.
* Be patient with yourself and others. Respect and allow your pacing; don't rush yourself. Be patient, dear one. Be patient and pay attention.

Can you hear them crying out to you? Can you feel their terror, their dread, and their anger? They're a part of you, dear one. Don't abandon them. Don't run from them. Don't separate from them. Don't imprison them in their lonely domains of hurt and pain. Don't blame them for your present ills and your life's disappointments. Hear their many shouts and whispers; hear their panicked cries for help. Feel their fear and dread and anger that reside in you. You're what these young ones are becoming. You're their future. Don't abandon them to their fear and pain; in so doing, you abandon yourself, you surrender your future, you deny your destiny. And dear one, because they're you, you're going nowhere without them.

Within the terrors you're feeling, within the anger and rage you're now expressing, within the stagnation and resistance your life's entangled in, they call out to you. This darkness you're experiencing is not what's really happening. What you believe is occurring is just your fear story. What you're experiencing are whispers or shouts to get your attention. These are the mournful callings from your lesser selves who believe that you're abandoning them.

Your past is not over and done with; it's not long behind you. Time and space are an illusion; all pasts, all futures, live in the now of your current life.

Though all your pasts and futures reside in different illusions of time and space, the life you're living now influences them. Your choice to grow and become more, your decision to Come Home, your desire to live a life of happiness, love, magic, and bounty, affects them. It resonates down to them.

In the various times and spaces of your past, such futures did not exist. Such futures do not make sense there. When you choose such futures, your less developed selves feel lost, for they cannot comprehend this new resonance. They do not know the choices you're making, that's true, but they can feel the shift in their resonance. These resonance shifts will frighten them, and they'll interpret these shifts as experiences of rejection, betrayal, or abandonment. They'll feel there's no future ahead of them. They'll feel lost and alone.

You're not a solitary being, dear one. You're the synergy of all the parts of yourself, both dark and light, and those somewhere in between. What you choose and do today affects the totality of you throughout different times and spaces.

It's important to attend to these developing selves. It's important to your growing and becoming that you pause and listen when you hear their calls, respond when you feel their terrors, and give them your full attention. It's important to reassure them that they're not forgotten or abandoned and that their fears and terrors are heard and shared by you.

It's important to honor their pacing; don't rush them, don't push them. The change will come at a time when it's comfortable for these lesser parts of you to do so. Have patience. Have patience. Have patience.

When you take the time to respond to the needs of your lesser selves, when you patiently allow their pace of growing and healing to be what it is, you'll find yourself awakening your love for them. You'll increase your self-understanding, and you'll genuinely grow to love and appreciate yourself so much more. You'll awaken the power of forgiveness in you, and you'll elevate your self-awareness.

If you can love the least of you, and accept your more developed self, then dear one you're becoming whole, becoming free, and truly Coming Home.

Always remember, dear one, *'You go nowhere without all of you coming with you; in their own time and within their own space.'*
(Work with Appendix One)
You craft what you're becoming, you author who you are today, and you and only you can lift the pains, hurts, and terrors of your past.

*It's blessed work,*
*this work of Coming Home.*

# 73

# The Sweet Taste of Vindication

## Suggested Areas of Attention

* Heed the silent whisper to end your need for vindication. Give it your full attention, forgiveness, and healing.
* Stop trying to validate yourself. You're already valid. Accept that you belong. Let it in.
* Heal your wounded selves that call out to you in fear, pain, and loneliness.
* This is the time for forgiveness, and the time to put your forgiveness into play.
* Address your howling rage and lift and transmute its destructive force.

Vindication is the desperate need to correct the wrongs done to you in the past, real or otherwise.

Validation is the desperate need to prove you're valid; that you belong.

Yes, dear one, you had been wronged, and you were hurt that's true, but spending your life in the futile attempt to make it right, to prove your suffering unfair and unjust, will not lead you out of the pain and hurt but further into it. Your need for vindication is the food your rage feeds upon, and by feeding it, you make it stronger. Your rage is eating away at you from the inside. In time, it will consume you.

Yes, dear one, you had been wronged, and you were hurt that's true, but now is the time for forgiveness, forgiving others for why they did what they did, and, most importantly, forgiving yourself for holding on to this wrong committed so long ago.

Forgiving others does not mean accepting their actions. Don't forgive the wrong they did. Their actions are not forgivable. Forgive only the *'why'* behind those actions. It's time now to let the past go. Understanding is needed here. Understanding the pain, suffering, and weakness behind the perpetrator's actions is the key to forgiveness. But never dismiss the actions that hurt you.

By dismissing the act, you convey to the wounded parts of yourself that their suffering doesn't matter now. Don't do this to them. Their pain is real and should be attended to and healed, not dismissed. Without treating the wounds of your injured self, you'll continuously seek your healing through the pursuit of vindication. You'll trap yourself in the tape-loop of past wrongs.

Undertake the healing meditatively. There you can be with those younger parts of self that were wronged and hurt.

(Work with Appendix One)

Be with this child; give it your love and attention. Respond to its cries of pain, anger, despair, and loneliness. Assure this child that it will never be alone again; promise that you will always respond to its fears and cries and that you'll always return in meditation to be with it. And above all, keep your promise.

There's also a whisper here to stop your endless quest for validation. The pursuit of validation is futile. You'll never accomplish what you seek. Oh, you may at times convince yourself you have, but such a lie is just a fleeting delusion. The reason you'll not succeed is that you're already valid; you always have been. The truth is that you belong; you always did. There's no such thing as *'not belonging.'* However, as long as you hold on to the need to prove yourself, you'll never come to realize this.

This need for validation is apart of the shame you carry. Ask your Higher Self to lift it. In mediation, go to the Lair of your Rage Beast, ask your Higher Self to take you there. When there, come face to face with it. Experience it in the form of a horrifying raging beast. Feel its wrath, its hatred, its pain, its despair, and its loneliness. Feel its emotions deeply, and be attentive to its suffering.

Now give this raging beast your full attention, give it your love and understanding, and give it your forgiveness. Thank your rage for protecting you, and assure it that it will not be ignored or abandoned by you again.

After many more meditations, let it know that its present form is no longer needed. It will need to transmute into a higher, more elevating octave. In time, with repeated meditations and continued attention and monitoring, the shame you hold will diminish. And in time, your rage will transform into constructive energy you can use in your self-healing and in the crafting of the grander 'you' you're destined to become. But this, dear one, will take time and regular monitoring. Ask your Higher Self for help with this gradual transformation. It will be provided, of course.

# 74

# What Kamila Learned from a Chipmunk

## Suggested Areas of Attention

* Stop playing it safe. Stop concerning yourself over other people's judgments.
* Live your life passionately and with abandon. Go a little *'nutty'* now and again.
* Go into the dark and hidden places within you. There you'll find your light and hope; there you'll find your gate to freedom.
* Stop taking your life for granted. Become alive in the living of it. Become engaged and adventurous.
* Every now and then take that second piece of cake; maybe even a third.

Stop playing it safe! You accomplish little when you risk little. Take risks, but don't be foolish in doing so. Be grounded and inspired by what you're becoming. Trust in your spirituality. Now race to your next opportunity. Be like the chipmunk and gobble up your life.

Stop nibbling at its edges. You're in this life to enjoy this life. Start enjoying. Start living. Start gobbling.

To live your life to the fullest, go often into the dark and hidden places within you, not to store your hurt, your anger, your despair, your loneliness, your shame, or your pain, but to liberate them.

Go inside and own your resistances to freedom and your propensity for unhappiness.

Go inside and respond to the voices of your less developed selves and give them the fullness of your attention and love.

Go into your dark and hidden places and find that spark of light and hope that await you there. Then share your new-found light and hope with your inner selves that see only shadows and hopelessness.

In doing so, you'll find your freedom, not just freedom *'from'* something, but freedom *'to be'* something.

Live passionately!

Passion is so much more than what the consensus holds it to be. It's so much more than merely being sexy. It's a level of intensity, an intensity of focus and attention. A passionate individual is one entirely in the moment with what he or she is engaging in. A passionate musician is not a sexy magician; a passionate musician is a musician wholly focused on the performance of his art. A passionate teacher is not a sexy teacher; a passionate teacher is a teacher fully engaged in the act of teaching and inspiring.

The consensus also holds passion as merely the display of loud and thunderous emotion. A passionate person is not a loud person; a loud person is simply a loud person. Passion is not screaming or yelling. On the contrary, passion is silent. It's a quiet and focused intensity.

Live passionately! Be focused and engaged. Be alive in your living of life. Don't take the moments of living for granted. Gobble up those moments, live them to the fullest, then move on to the next adventure.

The Magic of the Scented Flowers

Stop wishing for what was and start engaging with passion in the crafting of what will be. Be the adventurer. Be the explorer. Be the dreamer who manifests dreams into happening. Be the seeker of nuts. As the poets say, *"Live loud! Love loud!"*

> *Oh, that second piece of cake tastes so good!*
> *And my, it's so liberating!*

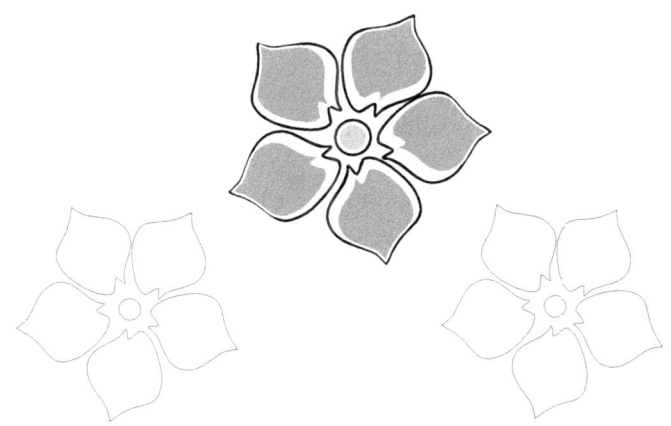

# 75

# Galen's Glimpse of Hell

## Suggested Areas of Attention

* Forgive yourself for what you did, or mistakenly believe you did.
* Respond to the call to Come Home.
* Process through the choices you're making and make wiser choices.
* Lean on the love that fully embraces you and accept the magnificence of your loving.
* Dare to ask for help. Be even more daring to allow it.
* Challenge your arrogance in believing you're not loved and in thinking you're not lovable.

There is a Hell, dear one. It's not a place created by God as punishment for a sinful life or a place of retribution for acts of neglectful subservience, and it's not a place created by someone named Satan. How can Satan exist in a sea of love and forgiveness? How can there be a Satan when all existence is a sea of love and forgiveness? But Hell exists, dear one. It exists as an illusion of your creation.

Hell became your illusion when you chose to separate from God/Goddess/All That Is. You weren't kicked out of paradise; you weren't punished for seeking knowledge. You left because you chose to. This separation, and the false belief that such a thing could happen, is the Hell you now believe exists. Your separation does not make you wrong or bad or sinful or undeserving. Your separation is, in truth, an act of majestic love.

Separation from the Divine of Love is a condition necessary for consciously discovering the grandeur of your loving through the power of 'choosing.' And you, dear one, chose to elevate love by choosing to love consciously.

By this choice, you believed that love was lost. By this choice, you thought you lost the love of God/Goddess/All That Is. By this choice, you believed you're moving away from them when in truth, you're moving toward them. These beliefs could never be correct, but you thought they were. Your Higher Self journeys with you as a companion to remind you of the truth, and to remind you of your destiny's calling.

Separation from God/Goddess/All That Is, though an illusion, is never-the-less a Hell. But you will, in time, re-connect once again to the Divine of their Love. You'll freely choose to do so. This 'choosing' is the beginning of Coming Home. You have a covenant with God and Goddess to do so. And dear one, you'll keep your promise.

You create the Hell you mistakenly believe you're living. You also create your release. It's called '*forgiveness.*'

Hell is not a destination or a place, dear one; it's a distortion in your belief and perception. It's the false belief your separation is real. But you will one day return to the Home that you in truth never left, for you have promised you would, and you will keep your promise. Your destiny is to do so.

Choose now, dear one. Choose to Come Home. Why delay? Why give this precious choice to another lifetime? God and Goddess and All That Is patiently wait for your choice. They stand just at the edge of your illusion and distortion calling you gently with their love,

*"Come home, dear one, come home. Keep your promise, dear love. You've never left our embrace."*

Your Higher Self knows your illusion and distortion and knows the Hell you've made. Your Higher Self stands with you just beyond the boundaries of your vision. Your Higher Self waits for permission to help unravel this illusion, and in the correcting of the distortion. Your Higher Self waits for you to accept its guidance and protection along your way.

Nothing you have none, or ever will do, will make your Higher Self and God/Goddess/All That Is love you less. Nothing you have none, or ever will do, will make them love you more. Love is eternal, dear one, and so are you. Accept your loving. Allow the embrace of the Divine of Love.

This illusion is temporary; your divinity is not. Awaken to your Light. Choose to Come Home. Your destiny is to succeed in this endeavor. You cannot fail in your blessed quest.

But if you wish to dally a while, don't worry, their love is infinitely patient. Illusions and distortions can't last forever.

# 76

# Being Real

## Suggested Areas of Attention

* It's time to change. Change because nothing changes until you do.
* Pay attention to what you give attention to, and monitor your intentions, change your actions, and hold a different image of yourself.
* What are the current choices you're making? You may want to choose differently.
* Let your dreams become bolder, your visions broader, your imagination more expansive, your hope more valued, and your truer self more revealed.
* Stop observing your world through the eyes of a child and adolescent. Observe instead through the innocent eyes of the Magical Child within you.
* Process your Raw Materials (beliefs and attitudes, thoughts and feelings, and choices and decisions); hone and sharpen your Tools of Manifestation (desire, imagination, expectancy).
* Always be careful what you say and think. Your subconscious is listening and will always obey your every wish and every order given.

What you observe, what you call reality, is an illusion made real by what you give attention to, your intentions behind them, the actions you take, and the image you hold of yourself. Change what you give attention to, change your intentions, change your actions, or change your self-image and reality changes for you. Change any one of these, and the others will change as well. Like the legs of a table, pull one the others follow.

Your outer world is an out-picturing of your inner world. Change what you're holding inside, and all you observe will reflect that change.

*"Nothing changes until you do."*

Of the three minds we possess (conscious, subconscious, unconscious), our conscious mind is the least aware; our unconscious is the most.

Our unconscious contains all information, all knowledge, and all experience. In truth, everything is within its domain. When we sleep, we access its infinite resources and healing power.

Our conscious mind is that part of the unconscious we give our attention to. It projects our illusion, the story we believe to be real. It's the unconscious that's real, not our conscious observation.

Our subconscious contains all the programs, templates, impressions, rules, and guidelines we've stored within it over our lifetime. For example, if a child or adolescent in a fit of hurt and anger swears, *"I'll never allow myself to be loved that deeply again,"* this template is stored in the subconscious and becomes a filter through which love passes. Now, as an adult, when he or she searches for more profound love, their reality will not allow it due to this template filtering it. Your subconscious mind always obeys you. You must re-program it. You must change the template; you must change the filter. And you must always be careful what you say and think.

Although the unconscious and subconscious minds are far more vast and powerful then the conscious mind, they lack one thing the conscious mind possesses; they lack the transformative power of 'choice.' The unconscious and subconscious minds do not make choices for you. The statement *"I did it unconsciously"* is not true. You may not be aware of the choice, but you did make it.

Your conscious mind, your waking mind, can access all the power and information contained in the subconscious and unconscious and give it form and direction in the illusion you call reality. Your choices make the illusion real for you. Your choices can also liberate you from it.

Change your choices and decisions, your thoughts and feelings, your beliefs and attitudes, and your life, your story, changes.

There's a call to change, yes. But more so to change from a place where real change happens, that place within you. The call is to discover the more real you. The call is to make different choices, choices sourced in real power: your dreams, your visions, your hopes, your valued imagination, your beauty, truth and goodness, and your truer self.

Keep searching, keep reaching, and pursue the more of you. You'll not fail in your pursuit. Don't give so much weight to cosmetic changes. Stop rearranging the chairs. Replace them.

*"Nothing changes until you do."*

*Be real*

# 77

# Grandmother Seeta's Words of Wisdom

## Suggested Areas of Attention

* Lighten up! Lift your Spirit! Wash behind your ears!
* Change your perception and your perspectives. Start looking for the bigger picture in the crumbling world about you. Ask your Higher Self for help with this.
* Walk the Narrows. Don't get caught up in the whirlwinds, chaos, and upheavals all about you. Don't get stuck in their paradoxes.
* Welcome change and be open to the opportunities change brings with it.
* Your future is calling you. Heed the call.

Lighten up! You're taking things far too seriously.

Amid the dark whirlwind frenzy of the chaos within and about you, find that spark of light. It's the light of hope. It's there. Have the courage to open to it. It's calling you.

Amid the noise and raging, find the stillness; within the stillness, find the hush. It's there. Have the courage to experience it. It's the hush of the eternal. It's the presence of God/Goddess/All That Is. Peace, freedom, and knowing dwell within this stillness. Within the stillness, find the hush. It's calling you.

Between the paradoxes within and about you, there's a slender path. It's called 'the Narrows.' Walk the Narrows. Walk this slender path. Don't be seduced by the frenzy and noise on either side of you. Don't get swept into them. Pay attention to the chaos; don't ignore it, but don't buy into it either. Walk the Narrows. Stay the course. At the other end, you'll discover peace, freedom, and knowing. The paradoxes will not be solved, but they can be resolved. What waits beyond the Narrows calls you.

Chaos always precedes change and opportunity; the more significant the chaos, the more significant the change and opportunity.

Your world is ending; you're ending. Chaos is growing. A new world, a new you, is emerging.

Your past is ending, and you're experiencing the chaos of that ending. Your world and all you've held to be true and sacred are no more. But on the other side of this chaos of ending, in that place beyond the Narrows, a new you and a new world ripe with hope, beauty, enchantment, love, and blessed solitude wait. Oh, and most certainly light and laughter wait. A new 'you' is emerging; a new 'you' is calling.

Change your perception and alter your perspectives. Challenge what you see, what you believe, and all you hold to be true. They're like shadows moving on a cave wall. They're not real.

You don't see the bigger picture yet. But, until you do, keep walking the Narrows and don't heed the fearsome voices. On the other side, your future's calling. Amid the fearsome voices hear your future's call and go to it.

*Oh, and don't forget to wash behind your ears!*

# 78

# Holiest of Holies

## Suggested Areas of Attention

* Lighten up! You're taking yourself much too seriously.
* Do you hold the belief that having the good things in life involves having to earn it? Do you believe that not having such things means you failed? Stop thinking this and learn to receive because you're loved and for no other reason.
* Let go of your investment in entitlement. It's a losing investment.
* Stop trying to be a good boy or a good girl. Grow up and be an adult.

There's a whisper here to pay attention to entitlement.

Entitlement is a lie told by your negative ego. It says that since you're so special, you're entitled to all you desire. Well, you aren't entitled because you aren't special.

The blessings and love of God/Goddess/All That Is are yours for the claiming. All you desire you can freely have, not because you earned them, or because you're owed them, but because it's their grace to bestow them. It's their boundless love that offers them. And the endless love of God/Goddess/All That Is encompasses all without exceptions.

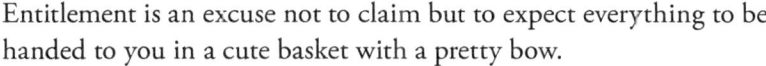

Entitlement is an excuse not to claim but to expect everything to be handed to you in a cute basket with a pretty bow.

*"Why should you claim it?"* says your ego. *"Why claim it when it's owed to you?"* This ego voice is the static that stands in your way of claiming and receiving.

There's also a whisper here to lighten up.

You're taking your life much too seriously, dear one. Stop being the good boy and girl, and from time to time, let the little devil in you out to play. Are you afraid you'll be punished?

Most learn from a very early age that receiving comes from earning, so they desperately struggle at earning and feel a failure if they don't, and of course, they believe that if they fail, they'll be punished.

*"I have to earn the right to be loved."*
*"I need to earn the right to be happy."*
*"To be successful, I'll have to work hard at it."*
*"I'm such a failure; of course I'm being punished."*

Listen to these voices in you. It's your negative ego speaking, it's your parents speaking, it's your teachers speaking, it's your religion speaking, and it's the consensus speaking. They're wrong, they always have been. Stop listening and giving such voices sway over your life.

Life with all its fullness and richness is a gift from God/Goddess/All That Is. All you need to do is receive it; no earning required. All you need do is to learn how to create it and have fun doing so. And since all of life's an illusion, know you can have as much illusion as you desire. Illusions are free! No earning necessary.

Stop putting pressure on yourself. Stop trying to get it right. Stop trying to *'earn'* at the living of life. The earn/reward template is deep within all of us. It will involve paying attention to transcend it. So get started.

The failure/punishment template is also deep within us. Pay attention to that as well.

Life was never supposed to be as hard as we're making it. Stop for a moment. Take a deep breath. Maybe have a beer or two. Then get busy and have some fun. You'll have plenty of playmates if you wish.

*And they'll play with you for free!*

# 79

# Entering the Hall of Eternal Bliss

## Suggested Areas of Attention

* It's time to put an end to your ego's belief in entitlement with its false pursuit of specialness; you're not 'owed' the right to bliss.
* Stop projecting mother and father onto others, instead, mother and father the younger parts of you longing for such parenting.
* Choose to become the spiritual adult you're destined to become.

You're entitled to nothing. You're owed nothing. The Hall of Eternal Bliss is open to all with the courage and maturity to enter. God and Goddess gave you life; they gave you All That Is. You're entitled to no more. There is no *'more'* in All That Is.

Entitlement is your ego's belief that you're owned something for past virtues or perceived wrongs. It's a child's belief in his or her specialness. It's a limiting belief based on anger and hurt and the private war you fight with God and Goddess. You were never wronged, and you were never special, but you were always loved.

Your virtues do not come with an allowance. They're expressions of the virtuous you. Stop making them into a debt owed to you. You're owed nothing. You're the owner of your reality, not an employee.

You will not accept the bounty of your existence as long as you choose to hold out for special treatment. You're like a stubborn child who has a hissy fit if not given what it demands. Instead of being exceptional, you want, instead, to be the exception. God/Goddess/All That Is will not play such games with your negative ego. To do so would enable those games you play, and those lies you think are true. They wait beside you patiently, always patiently, non-judgmental. They wait for you to make a different choice. When you're willing, and only when you're willing, and when you freely choose, the gate to the Hall of Eternal Bliss will open to you. You're an adult becoming a spiritual adult. Stop behaving like a child.

God and Goddess are not your father and mother. Don't treat them as such. When you do you diminish their relationship with you, you deny their realness to you. You're an adult becoming a spiritual adult. You no longer need a father and mother. If the child in you longs for this, then you be the father and mother they seek. Love, nurture, and parent them.

Life's an illusion; you can have as much of an illusion as you like. And life's a gift from God and Goddess, and you're here to learn to receive that gift. When you grow to realize this, when you grow to make this real for yourself, when you learn to accept this gift, then you'll drop your silly ego games and claim your right to bliss, bounty, and freedom.

*Oh, how much fun it is to be a spiritual adult at play in the Hall of Eternal Bliss!*

# 80

# The Gathering

## Suggested Areas of Attention

* Be open to the idea of co-creating with a community of fellow travelers each upon a separate journey of becoming more.
* Be willing to accept the help of others. Be considerate enough to allow their help to matter.
* Stop hiding in your solitary places. Reach out to others.
* It's time for you to stand up, stand out, and step forth. Heal your world with your love and your magic. Let your beauty, truth, and goodness shine.
* Do the work you came to do. Do your 'Great Work' and do it now.

It's time to lift your magic, dear one. Without letting go of your current magic in the crafting of an elegant and magical life, choose to elevate your magical crafting through the incredible power of co-creation. There's greater power and magic in community. Co-creating reality lifts your magic beyond what you can do on your own. Working with a community can elevate your life to wondrous heights.

Choose one or more co-creators to work with; no more than seven. These co-creators may be among your seen friends or your friends unseen. Work from time to time with your seen friends; work meditatively with those unseen.

(Refer to *'Cultivating the Scented Flowers.'* Work with the meditation in the section *'Working With Your Spiritual Family.'*)

In meditation, go to your Safe Place. Then from your Safe Place journey to an ancient place of magic. It will be in nature. Call forth those who wish to participate with you. An Ancient Grandmother (Crone) or Grandfather (Hermit) may come, or a friend in your present reality or fellow magicians from different times and places may answer your call. Your Higher Self and Soul will be there if you wish, maybe a famous or not so famous person from the past or present you admire and whose judgment you respect. No more than seven in total.

Now ask for a reality you wish to create together and listen to their input. Pay attention. Don't dictate what to do. Let the gathering be magical. Don't try to control or manipulate. Work the commerce of magic by discussing amongst yourselves the magic you'll be performing and who will do what. When all are in agreement, work your magic, and they'll work theirs. Together you'll create a synergy much grander than your separate magical workings. Now flow this magic born of synergy into the world. Like rain, let everything and everyone be awash in it.

Meanwhile, beyond your meditative activity, pay attention to your apprehensions and resistances to what it is you're creating. Pay attention to what it is you truly desire and why you desire it. *"What do I really want here?" "Why do I want it?"* Let go of your old self-limiting agendas, uncertainties, and weak resolve; process through them and keep your ego out of the process.

Now is the time to reach beyond your solitary comfort. Now is the time to work with others. Together stand up, stand out, and let your impact matter. And most of all, this is a time to discover, heal, and forgive yourself for why you're resistant to such impact and mattering.

Have the courage to ask for help. You don't have to carry the weight of the world on your shoulders. To do so is to martyr yourself.

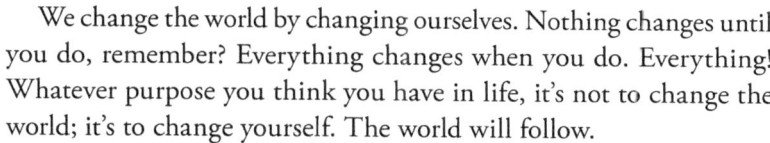

## The Magic of the Scented Flowers

We change the world by changing ourselves. Nothing changes until you do, remember? Everything changes when you do. Everything! Whatever purpose you think you have in life, it's not to change the world; it's to change yourself. The world will follow.

You're not alone. Have the courage and humility to ask for help. Have the courtesy and respect to allow it.

The answer is always "yes," but never when the ego is asking. Pay attention to who's asking.

Lift your magic to the rising star and let its light ignite it. Then behold the light of each magician's magic joined as one in a singularity of power and light. Now send that glorious light of magic into an awaiting world so much in need of magic.

*Be like the Ancients.*
*Work the blessed magic of your heart, dear one.*

# 81

# Tandori Had Two Teachers

## Suggested Areas of Attention

* Lead with the wisdom of your heart, the learning's of your mind will follow. Be at play in the fields of laughter; let lightness be your teacher.
* Pursue your education in the Hallowed Halls of Nature. Which calls to you the loudest; beauty, enchantment, blessed solitude, or love? Go there. Learn all it has to teach you.
* Feel your emotions deeply and feel them cleanly. Stop using them to lash out, to hurt, to control, or to manipulate.
* Honor your body of knowledge and experience by valuing them and using them.
* Stop escaping into your head when fear approaches. Stop trying to deflect it. Bring your fear 'to ground.' There you can release it.

Your '*body of knowledge*' is the totality of all the knowledge you've acquired throughout your life.

Your '*body of experience*' is the totality of all your experiences.

No one has ever had, or ever will have, the body of knowledge and the body of experience you possess. You're unique this way; everyone is. Your body of knowledge and experience is a gift you possess to aide in your growth and expansion. Still, you can avail yourself of grander knowledge and experience by pursuing the wisdom and teachings found in the Hallowed Halls of Nature.

The wisdom gained within these Hallowed Halls will carry you to remarkable heights. Seek beauty, enchantment, blessed solitude, or love. It's from within these Hallowed Halls your Soul speaks to you. It's from within these sacred places God/Goddess/All That Is calls you to Come Home. You may have forgotten many things you've learned from school, teachers, books, and classes, but you'll never forget what you've learned in the Hallowed Halls of Nature.

When in fear, go to ground.

When animals are frightened, they go to ground. When humans are frightened, they escape into the safety of their heads. They try to figure out the danger. They look for answers; they search for solutions. This escaping is a human reaction to fear and perceived threat.

Do as the animals do; go to ground. When you find yourself in fear or perceived threat, feel deeply the emotion you'd otherwise try to run from. When animals feel distressed, their entire being focuses on it. They're totally in the moment with it. In so doing, they feel and release it.

Like the animals, focus entirely on what you're feeling. Be in the moment with it. Go through the feeling to the other side. Don't run from any emotion, dark or light, that surfaces. It surfaces to be felt and attended to. It surfaces because it's ready now to be expressed and healed. If, for example, you're feeling fear or anger, feel it deeply and release it. If, for instance, you're feeling happiness or love, feel it deeply and release it within you and all about you. Let it shine from you like a beacon.

Feeling an emotion without using it to attack, manipulate, blame, harbor, or recycle is called, *'feeling your emotion cleanly.'* You'll experience true emotional freedom when you feel all your emotions this way. You'll go from being captive to emotions to owning them. You'll be able to harness and grow from them.

Pay attention when you find yourself using logic and reason to hide from vulnerability; this, again, is a fear response. Be vulnerable but be grounded in your vulnerability. Ground yourself in your feelings, integrity, principles, character, and strength. Ground yourself in the understanding and acceptance that you're growing and becoming more. Ground yourself in the pursuit of the truth of you. Ground yourself in the realization and acceptance that you're loved and loving. Ground yourself in the awareness and acceptance that you're always protected. And above all, ground yourself in the knowing that you'll not fail in your pursuit. Knowing beyond certainty is your grounding; Knowing beyond certainty is your anchor. And knowing, beyond learning, is your freedom.

Listen to the whispers of your heart. They call you to mystery and to magic. They call you to wisdom and understanding beyond the finite boundaries of logic and reason. They call you to fun, laughter, and adventure. They call you to the 'Knowing.' You can hear these whispers in the Hallowed Halls of Nature; in beauty, enchantment, love, and blessed solitude.

*Seek the Hallows.*
*You'll discover a more real you waiting there.*
*You'll find your wisdom there.*

# 82

# The Child Who Could

## Suggested Areas of Attention

* Find the Magical Child within you and set it free.
* Question your beliefs. Discard the ones that hold you back; expand the ones that free you.
* Awaken fantasia. Let go of childish fantasies.
* Stop limiting your imagination. Expand your imaginings, dreams, visions, and hopes.
* Stop dumping your shame on others. Take it back so you can heal it. Now let go of what you carry by sincerely asking your Higher Self to take it from you.
* Let your life become play. Start enjoying it once again, or perhaps for the first time.

Find the Magical Child within you. Oh, the wonders and magic this blessed child can show you! It lives within you still though deeply hidden. Discover your Magical Child.

It yearns so desperately to play and dance, and to laugh and sing, and to fly to heights unlimited. It will ignite the spark in you again, or perhaps for the first time. This enchanted child will guide you to lost passions. This sacred child will teach you how to enjoy life once again, or perhaps for the first time.

No, you should not pursue lost childhood fantasies. You're an adult now. Such pursuits will not lead you to where you're going for childhood fantasies are for children only; they're not for the adult you are. But when you discover your Magical Child, and when you experience wonder through its eyes, it will show you the doorway to infinite fantasias and rekindle lost dreams and imaginings destined to be. It will guide you to your magical future.

It was the passing of shame to this little one that led to its imprisonment. It was the passing of the deadened hopes and lost dreams of others that silenced its singing and stifled its play. Give back the shame to those who passed it onto you. It's not yours to carry.

As well, take back the shame you dumped on others. Stop punishing others because of your pain and because of your lost innocence. Your 'shame dumping' deprives those you claim to love of their joy and innocence. Grow up and take responsibility for your life. Grow up, be an adult, and heal the shame of your creation by acknowledging it, recognizing it, forgiving it, and releasing it. Then you'll discover this Magical Child once again, or perhaps for the first time.

Question your beliefs. Are they the beliefs of your more real self, or beliefs from your painful past? Are they beliefs that will lead you to magical futures, or beliefs that will keep you locked in endless disappointments and mediocrities? Beliefs are powerful, dear one. It's your beliefs that keep you from your dreams and visions and your imaginings and desires. So question the beliefs you hold. Let go of the ones that hold you back; expand the ones that free you. Choose well, dear one. Choose well.

You're only limited by your imagination. And you limit imagination when you hold so tightly to past disappointments and the pains of shattered dreams. Let go of your disappointments and begin the healing of the pains of your past. Stop wallowing in times long gone and respond to the 'Futures of Light' that call to you.

Dream! Dream! Dream! Imagine futures! Imagine your hopes for a better world! Imagine a new and grander you! Your Magical Child can help you if you take the time to find it; if you take the time to play with it.

*Oh, the fun and adventure that awaits you;*
*you and your Magical Child!*

# 83

# Amil and the Most Beautiful Flower

## Suggested Areas of Attention

* Stop hiding your heart. Let it free to soar, walk on air, and awaken miracles.
* Stop controlling to keep love safe; it can kill the love you're trying to protect.
* Re-awaken your innocence. It will take you to places beyond what your intellect can fathom.
* Devote yourself to goodness, truth, and beauty. Be devoted to your kindness, truth, and beauty.

The wonders of the human heart have no limit! Within its depths, miracles abound, and the impossible becomes possible.

The human heart nurtures the simplest yearnings of an innocent child and gives meaning to the seasoned understandings of the wise. It is infinitely complex, yet amazingly simple. It is fragile and invincible at the same time.

Open your heart. Give it flight. Let it soar upon the air.

## The Magic of the Scented Flowers

Be open to the many faces of love. Love can be painful, all-embracing, exuberant, incomprehensible, demanding, hurtful, liberating, ugly, unbelievably beautiful, frightening, maddening, ephemeral, ever-present, and ever-elusive. Love is so much more than our intellect can ever fathom, but its power, its essence, can be experienced by us more and more through committed practice.

Open your heart. Give it flight. Let it soar upon the air.

Freedom can be found on the path of knowledge; this is true. But freedom can also be found on the path of love and devotion. Knowledge will take freedom only so far. Love and devotion will take it to heights unfathomable. Lead with your heart; your intellect will follow. Take the path of love and devotion, dear one.

Your heart is calling you to venture forth, to venture into unknown and unfamiliar places. It's calling you to trust it and urging you to discover its invincibility.

Your heart calls you to stop hiding in your thinking. It calls you to stop using thoughts as a means to control your fear. As humans, we go to our heads when we're afraid. Animals go to ground. We try to think it out as opposed to feeling it through. When in fear, if you find yourself escaping into your head in search of answers, stop. Slow down. Let yourself feel what you're feeling. If it's fear, feel it. If it's anger, feel it. Whatever the emotion, feel it. Recognize it, acknowledge its presence, forgive yourself, and then release it. Stop thinking about it, stop worrying about it, stop planning solutions, and just pick the damn flower! Magic happens when you learn to trust the invincibility of the human heart.

Open your heart. Give it flight. Let it soar upon the air.

*Oh, and did we mention, "Get out of your head."*

# 84

# The Woman Who Had Everything

## Suggested Areas of Attention

* Live your life in magic and fulfillment.
* Process through your dreams and desires. Filter out those belonging to others. Pursue the ones that are yours and yours alone.
* Stop struggling to fulfill your dreams. Make more elegant choices to accomplish them.
* Lighten the load you're carrying. Have fun. You're making life too complicated.
* Let go of your martyr and your belief in not being good enough or deserving enough.
* Lean on your Higher Self, not to make your successes happen, but to help lift your resistance to them happening.

*"Life's an illusion. You can have as much of an illusion as you like."*
*- Lazaris*

You can have all you desire, dear one. The question you need to ask yourself is who or what is doing the desiring.

Is it your negative ego?

Is it your belief that having certain things is proof of your success, proof that you've arrived?

Is it your lesser selves who believe that having the big house, the fancy car, and the splendid trappings will somehow make their pain go away, that it will give them the vindication they desperately seek, or provide proof of their validation?

Is it consensus thinking that says the bigger and more expensive something is the happier you'll be?

Is it the weight you put on consensus norms such as having a family, having kids, having a home with the white picket fence that still has meaning for you? Maybe you'd be happier without such things? Maybe, maybe not.

Is it your ego's need for competition that spurs you on toward bigger and better?

Is it your parent's dashed hopes and unfulfilled dreams they wish for you to fulfill? Or are you pursuing, out of duty and obligation, the dreams and goals they expect of you? Do you hold such psychic contracts?

Who or what holds your desires; holds your dreams of success and achievement? Who or what sets the goals in the living of your life? And who or what dictates what will truly fulfill you? Yes, you can have anything you desire, as long as it's you doing the desiring.

Process through your dreams and visions; process through the goals and futures you're pursuing. Filter out the dreams and visions of others; pursue the goals and futures that you, and only you, genuinely want. There's nothing beyond your reach if it's what you truly desire. The form may not be as you imagine it, but the desire, in essence, will be fully met and more; since essence is more real than form.

In life, there's no situation you get yourself into that you've not given yourself a means of escape. There's no genuine dream you have that you've not provided the means to fulfill.

Live this life for you, dear one. You'll best serve others by doing so. Pursue your real heart's calling. Flow into your world the fruits of your creating and receiving. The more you do so, the more you'll create and receive. Bask in the radiance of your destined dreams.

Have fun, dear one. Let fun and joy be a higher priority. No, you're not wasting precious time. That's another foolish belief held by consensus thinking. In maintaining fun and joy as a higher priority, you're laying the foundation of all your successes.

Live this life for you, dear one. You'll best serve others by doing so. Pursue your real heart's calling, and flow into your world the fruits of your creating and receiving. In so doing you'll have successes, you'll achieve the fulfillment you seek, you'll be awash in glorious accomplishments, and most of all you'll live a magical, meaningful, and bountiful life.

*Let your work be play, and your play be work.*

# 85

# The Demon Within

## Suggested Areas of Attention

* Stop shutting down, storing, and imprisoning your emotions. Feel you're feelings. Let them have a voice. Set them free.
* Own, express, and integrate your positive emotions. Own, express, and release the negative.
* Undertake the healing of your rage. It's time now to do so.
* Pay attention to the voices and whispers in your life. Always pay attention and respond.

Beyond your anger well-hidden, lies your rage. Like anger, rage is a genuine emotion as it possesses both positive and negative energies and values.

Outrage (positive): a free expression of anger, highly charged, that acts as a motivator of change.

Enrage (negative): deep and intense anger, highly charged, that gnaws at and tears down an individual over time.

We all hold rage within us. It's an emotion we felt as children. Rage was born from the hurts, pains, and shame we experienced growing up. As children, we were unable to process rage or express it for fear of punishment. So we did what we could and stuffed it deep inside us.

Rage grows stronger when unattended, and over time it can and will consume its host. Over time it will kill you. Your 'Rage Beast' lurking in the dark shadows of a prison deep inside you, a prison you've condemned it to, will keep emerging and re-emerge throughout your life. It will demand to be heard. And if ignored, it will become even more enraged and will become even more determined to seek your destruction.

Rage can express itself violently and loudly. It can manifest itself passive-aggressively and quietly. Know your rage, face it, feel its wrath and hatred. Give it your attention by answering its calls for help. To do otherwise will deny true healing, will deny your dreams and visions from manifesting, will deny you a magical life filled with happiness and joy, will deny you freedom, and will prevent your Coming Home. To do otherwise will lead to your becoming consumed by it. Healing rage is not an elective; it's mandatory.

## Meditation

Make an honest and genuine commitment to healing your rage. But do not make this choice from a place of desperation and self-pity.

1. Gently close your eyes. Allow yourself to become quiet and still in whatever way best works for you. When you feel calmer, slowly count down from seven to one. With each count, feel yourself shifting and changing mentally and physically.

2. On the count of one slowly open your mental eyes. Find yourself in your Safe Place. Your Safe Place should be in nature away from the hustle and frenzy of daily activity. It should be outdoors, not in a building of any kind. Let this place be beautiful, enchanting, loving, and filled with blessed solitude. This Safe Place is yours and yours alone. No one can disturb you here. No one can enter this place unless invited.

This place in nature may be a place created in your imagination, a place you select from a movie or picture, or a place of beauty and safety you remember from the past. The important thing is that you feel safe, protected, and at peace in this haven in nature. In each meditation, return to the same place; in each meditation, take the time to explore a little more of this place. Explore each detail. *"Love pays attention to detail."*

3. After you've spent a little time allowing your senses to take in this place, invite your Higher Self to join you. Sit together for a little while and feel your Higher Self's presence and love. You may want to talk about your rage, *"for there's magic in the telling."* When you said what needed to be said, ask your Higher Self to take you to the 'Lear of your Rage Beast.'

4. Close your mental eyes. Your Higher Self will surround you in a radiant cocoon of white light. When fully cocooned, sense yourself lifting gently off the ground and floating through the air. When you reach your destination, the cocoon will float gently to the ground and fade away, leaving you amid a dark and desolate place.

Now open your mental eyes and sense this place around you. Let your five physical senses make this place real for you. Feel the doom and hopelessness here. The more you get emotionally involved, the more you feel the dread, the loneliness, the hurt and pain, the more powerful this meditation will be for you.

5. Notice an opening in the ground before you. Choose to enter there. But know that you can always open your physical eyes and return if you feel the need to do so. You don't have to complete the meditation at this time if you're not ready. But if you are, enter the dark and forbidding opening.

6. Slowly descend a winding stairway into the darkness below. The deeper you go, the more putrid the scent, the more fear you feel.

7. When you reach the chamber at the bottom, all will be dark except for a solitary candle burning at the back of the room. This light will cast ominous shadows.

8. Sense something or someone watching you. Feel its hateful gaze and hear its deep and steady breathing. In time a horrifying beast will very slowly emerge from the shadows and very slowly approach you.

9. Feel its hatred. Feel its rage. Feel its intensity. Feel its loneliness. Feel its helplessness and despair. Feel it because these feelings are yours.

10. Now extend your arm, palm out, and shout;

*"Stop, Stop, Stop! You will not come closer! I forbid it! I am the one who created you! I am the one who gave you birth! And I am the one who imprisoned you in this dark and vile place! And for that, I'm truly sorry! But you shall not harm me! I forbid it!"*

11. The beast will suddenly stop; it glairs at you, peering deep within you.

12. Now gently say to the beast;

*"You are the offspring of my anger. You are the child of my rage and hurt and pain. And I pledge to you that I'll always listen for your voice of pain, and will answer when you call to me. I'll attend to your loneliness, and ease your pain, and give you my love to heal you. But you shall not harm me. I forbid it."*

13. The beast, much conflicted, saddened, and in pain, will slowly retreat to the shadows. It could not harm you; you forbid it.

14. Now close your mental eyes and slowly count from one to five. On the count of five, open your physical eyes and return to your room. Your meditation is now complete, and the magic is undertaken.

Return to this meditation from time to time. Descend the stairs, call forth your rage beast, and feed it your anger, hurt, and shame. It will devour them. Nurture this Rage Beast within you; listen to its wails and pain, and give it love. It's a part of you, dear one. It always will be.

Whenever you feel rage welling up in you, or see its out-picturing in the world around you, it's your Rage Beast calling for your attention. Respond by going into meditation and attending to it.

Remember, rage is a human emotion. Its positive expression as highly charged as it is, can motivate you to change. It will be an important resonance to employ on your journey Coming Home.

It will take time and attention to transform your rage from the negative to the positive. Have patience, dear one. You'll find that

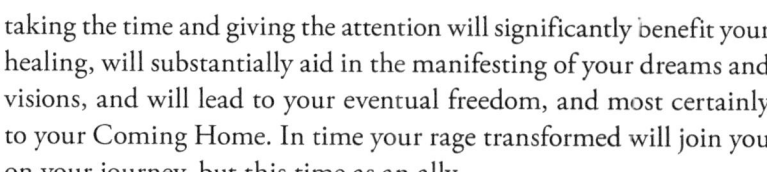

taking the time and giving the attention will significantly benefit your healing, will substantially aid in the manifesting of your dreams and visions, and will lead to your eventual freedom, and most certainly to your Coming Home. In time your rage transformed will join you on your journey, but this time as an ally.

# 86

# The Artist and the Fisherman

## Suggested Areas of Attention

* Don't orchestrate crises. But when they come, welcome them and work with them. There's a grander you that waits on the other side of the crisis.
* Process your need to control. Choose to stop doing it.
* Over time, cultivate the energy of trust. Ask your Higher Self for help in this.
* Attend to the various parts of yourself, especially during times of chaos and crisis.
* During times of crisis, strengthen your hope, exercise the power of gratitude, and trust in the love of your Higher Self and God/Goddess/All That Is.

Chaos always precedes change; the greater the change, the greater the chaos. In physics, chaos is found in a *'phase transition.'* In spirituality, it's sometimes referred to as *'The Dark Night of the Soul.'* In the healing arts, it's called a *'Healing Crisis.'* People fear change because they fear chaos. They fear chaos because they fear the unknown; they fear losing control. This fear is a natural human response. Since change is an integral part of our growing and becoming, chaos is an integral part as well; albeit an unpleasant one.

You're being called now to profound change, called to become more, called to freedom, not just freedom *'from'* something but freedom *'to be'* something. And you're called to Come Home. This profound change will be preceded by chaos and, as such, will be met with great fear.

Don't run from chaos; embrace it, respect it, and know it for what it is. You're not wrong or bad for being in it; you're not failing. The truth is you're succeeding. You're changing and growing. If anything, you should be celebrating this.

A crisis can also occur when you stray too far from your destined journey. Crisis brings you back into compliance. In time you'll be grateful there is such a mechanism.

Don't give your crisis to your negative ego to interpret. It'll always tell you that you're a failure. Remember, your ego always lies.

Give this crisis instead to your Higher Self; it will guide you safely through it and will help you extract its incredible power and healing so necessary for the new 'you' you're becoming. Your Higher Self always tells the truth.

You're guided and protected at all times, dear one. If bad things happen, it's because you've either created or allowed them. The one constant in all the bad things that ever happened to you is that you were there when it happened.

Yes, you're always guided and protected. But you can choose not to allow this guidance and protection. Again this does not make you wrong or bad. But you may want to pay more attention to what you're creating or allowing.

At times of change and transition, it's particularly important to check in with all the various parts of yourself: the lesser and the more (See Appendix One). You're changing, but the less developed parts of you do not understand that change, they cannot calibrate it, and as such, they're terrified by it. During these times of crisis, they're much in need of your attention and support. They need reassurance that they're not going to be abandoned. They need to know that their fears are being heard and that they're loved and protected. Self-awareness involves responding to the calls of all your many selves. And self-awareness is necessary to navigate crises more elegantly and to avail yourself of the power within all chaos.

You're not two-dimensional, dear one; you're three-dimensional evolving into multi-dimensionality. This profound evolutionary change will involve considerable chaos.

The dark times and the light ones are part of your reality, especially during these exciting times of transition. Accept this, understand this, work with this, and ask for help.

A brighter day lies just beyond the darkness of chaos. Keep moving elegantly through it. You're not alone. You never were.

*You're where you're supposed to be, dear one.*
*You're going to be just fine.*

# 87

# The Compassionate Thing to Do

## Suggested Areas of Attention

* Stop controlling and manipulating the choices of others, stop interfering with the choices they're making, and stop making choices for them even if you believe it's in their best interest.
* Process the intentions that motivate the choices you're making.
* Although others have a right to their choices, they do not have a right to harm you or others by them. Take action. Remember, you're stopping the harm to you and others, not their right to choose. Yes, there's a paradox here. Resolve the paradox by walking the narrow space between the opposites.
* Stop holding onto your need to be special. Stop buying into your ego's lies.

'Virtue Signaling' is the need to show others how virtuous you are in order to feel special.

As the saying goes, *"The road to Hell is paved with good intentions."* But are those intentions really good and noble? Maybe they're not.

If intentions come from the negative ego, the result will always have negative consequences.

The pursuit of specialness is a trap set by the ego to hold you back from growing. Such pursuits are certainly not paved with good intentions.

It's not a virtue to control or interfere with another's choice regardless of how destructive that choice may be for the person and others. God and Goddess gave us all a single gift - choice. If God and Goddess will not interfere with one's choice, then who are we to do so? To do so displays our arrogance.

You can encourage better choices, inspire better choices, even help another see the destructive nature of the choices he or she is making, but it's none of your business what he or she eventually chooses. People who manipulate others despite so-called *'good intentions'* do so to satisfy their ego or do so out their own self-interest. It's never about doing the right thing.

If the choice a person makes affects you and others in a harmful way, then you have a right and obligation to yourself and others to take action to correct the situation. You have the right to stop them, not the right to manipulate their act of choosing. The offending person has a right to their choices, but they don't have a right to harm you or others with them.

Children and adolescents are a different matter. It's the responsibility of adults to set boundaries for the young. But in time, the young will need to set boundaries for themselves, be they constructive or destructive. It's essential for the path they're on. Guide them but don't manipulate or control them; this is a hard lesson to put into play, but an essential one to their growth. They'll crash, or they'll fly, it's up to them.

Be aware of the real intentions underlying what you do. Are they coming from a place of higher understanding, or are they coming from your negative ego?

You're not responsible for the choices of others, only your own. How other people travel the path they're on is for them to learn and grow. Their choices and decisions may make their journey harder and more painful, but this is how they're choosing to play it right now. God and Goddess are infinitely patient and forgiving. Can you be?

You're only responsible for the path you're on. Choose wisely.

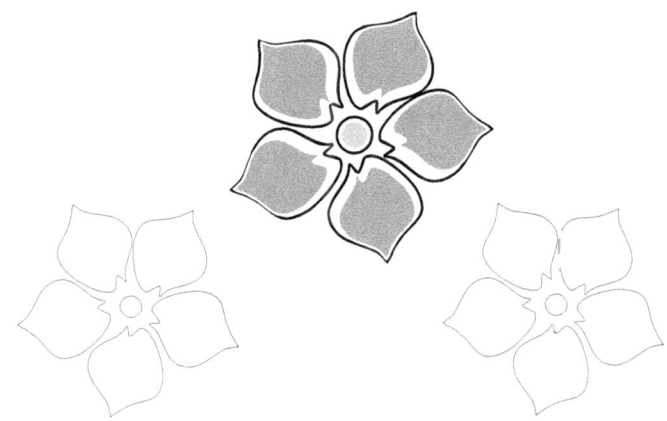

# 88

# Knowing

## Suggested Areas of Attention

* Pay attention to your need to control. It will signal the presence of fear in you. Attend to the parts of yourself that hold the fear. Their healing and yours requires you to feel it.
* Elevate your learning. Grow in wisdom beyond your learning and ground your wisdom in the certainty of *'knowing without certainty.'*
* Seek the wonder in all things; *'Knowing'* is there. Seek always the Hallows of beauty, enchantment, blessed solitude, and love. There's *'knowing'* there that will lift you beyond the prison of certainty.
* Allow the growing of trust. Take your time and never trust blindly.

'Knowing' is more than just a state of being informed. One can know based on verifiable information and personal experience that's true, but knowing also involves awareness; the higher one's awareness, the greater the depth and range of knowing. Awareness elevates 'knowing' to a state of being, a state of being *'Knowing.'* The highest expression of knowing is the state of *'knowing without certainty.'*

"How do you know?"
"I don't know. I just know."

Knowing without certainty can be fearful to many. There can be a fear of being wrong, a fear of being ridiculed, a fear of chaos, a fear of loss of control, and a fear of being vulnerable and unsafe. This fear, like any fear, leads to the need for control.

We often hear it said that a person is smart because he or she knows a lot of stuff. But without awareness, without the willingness or ability to elevate knowledge into originality, action, or heightened perception, a person is not smart just knowledgeable.

There's a whisper here to look to your fear. Your need for answers, your need to figure things out, is a form of control. And we always control to keep ourselves safe from fear.

Recognize your fear, acknowledge it by feeling it, forgive yourself, and let go of it. Beyond your need to control freedom waits, also the knowing that you're safe and loved and the magnificently liberating *'knowing without certainty.'*

You'll find liberation from the prison of mental control, the fear-based need to figure things out, by letting yourself be seduced by the lure of beauty, or becoming enveloped in the mystical mists of enchantment. You'll find your liberation in the eternal embrace of love, or nurtured in the blessed womb of solitude.

Your freedom, your knowing, resides in wonder. Wonder transcends all need to know.

*There's knowing in the wonder,*
*and wonder in the knowing.*

## 89

# Some Things Are Just Worth Saving

### Suggested Areas of Attention

* Process through all the 'stuff' you're still holding onto from the past. Discover, heal, forgive, and release what needs releasing. It's time to clean house.
* Stop blaming the past for your present failures.
* Be the refuge for your wounded selves that haunt you still. Be the home that you have for lifetimes sought.
* Make space for your future's dreams, loves, memories, and hopes for you.
* Respond to your futures call, and never ignore the cries of your past.

The past is over, yet you're still holding onto it. Why? Isn't it time now to forgive your past and embrace your future? What in your past is so valuable that you'd deny your happiness, freedom, and future to keep it? This is not a rhetorical question.

There's no power in things long past unless you give power to it. What you're becoming is where the real power lies. What you're becoming is what is real. The things of the past no longer have reality unless to make it so. Let go of the shackles of the past by responding to the voices still imprisoned there. You're their future. You have the power to love and comfort them. You're the savior they so desperately search to find. You're the one more real. Your realness is the realness they seek.

As a child and adolescent, you did not possess the tools and maturity capable of handling the pains and hurts and the shames of growing. You discovered, much to your credit, ways and means to cope and survive. What you couldn't handle you stuffed deep inside to be addressed another day and another time when you'd best be able to tend to them.

The day is here. The time is now. Hear the voices from your wounded past. Respond and lift the many burdens they sadly carry. Hear their shouts and whispers as they call out to you in the tumult of your current crisis, in the hollow emptiness of your stalled dreams and aspirations, and within the dark places of your present anger, fear, hurt, loneliness, despair, helplessness, and shame.

Choose to recognize and answer their calling. Choose to acknowledge their pain and terror. Choose to forgive yourself for ignoring their desperate wailings and panicked shouting. Choose to love and nurture them. Reassure them that you'll hear their cries and respond, and remind them they'll be forever a part of your journey Home. Reassure them that you'll never leave them behind, like God and Goddess will never leave you behind. Now together with your many parts of self, move forward.

The value that these savings of the past possess is in the energy and power they carry. Reclaim this energy, restore this power, let go of these savings, and move on. With energy claimed and power restored, you'll no longer need these relics. They have no place where you're going. But you'll still need all the many parts of you as you go nowhere without them. You're going nowhere without the totality of you; this is what *'wholeness'* means.

There are so many amazing experiences, precious memories, miraculous adventures, and wonderous miracles that lie ahead of you. Let go of the past, not those who in their time and space reside there still. Forgive your past, and love and value the 'you' still living there.

And make time and space for the love that's yet to come. Make time and space for the life that awaits your coming. And make a home in you for the many parts of you both dark and light, past and future.

*You are ready now, dear one.*
*Oh, you are most certainly ready!*

# 90

# The Ministers of Kushtan

## Suggested Areas of Attention

* Stop giving your peace of mind and your power to other people, or life's circumstances, or anything outside yourself.
* Be the author of your reality. Don't put others in that position.
* Face the neediness in you; stop being and doing it.
* Accept the fact that nothing changes until you do.

Stop giving your power away. Stop giving your happiness and peace of mind to political leaders, spiritual guides or gurus, therapists, family members, antagonists real or imagined, your need for consensus validation, and the countless other persons or things you give it to. You create your reality. Don't let others create it for you. Re-claim the authorship of your life. If you don't, others will author it for you.

When you find yourself blaming others for your misery and unhappiness, you're giving your power to them. They have no power over you unless you give it to them.

When you find yourself needing and searching for mothering or fathering, you're giving your power to those from whom you seek such things. You're an adult. You don't need a mother or father now.

When you search for others to lead you, or save you, or make you whole, you're giving your power to them. Such a waste of attention and power! They can never provide what deep inside you seek!

When you expect others to lead you and make you safe and secure, you're giving your power to them. You're already safe and secure. But you won't realize it if you expect others to accomplish this for you.

When you expect others to provide you with prosperity and success, you're giving your power to them. Prosperity and success are yours to create freely. They're not blessings that others can bestow on you.

When the world about you is in the throes of chaos and insanity, and you find yourself caught up in its madness, you're giving your power to the chaos and insanity. You cannot author a different world when you're spinning in the whirlwind of the current one.

Don't look for your peace, freedom, prosperity, and happiness in anything outside you. It's not there you'll find it. Your outer world is an illusion. It's an out-picturing of your inner world. The peace, freedom, prosperity, and happiness you seek are within you. It's there you'll find it. Search within, not outside. Nothing changes until you do, nothing.

Look within and face your neediness. Look within and attend to those in search of saviors and leaders. Love them, feel their fear and terror, respond to their cries for help, and reassure them that they're safe and secure in you. You're their guardian. You're their Moses. With compassion, patience, and love guide them forward. You're going nowhere without them.

Take your power back from the people or things you give it. Claim your right to peace, freedom, prosperity, and happiness. Yes, they're always available for the claiming. Take back your power and claim your authority. It's what you're in this lifetime to do.

You be the author of your reality. You be the leader you seek. Step outside the consensus and author a new world. It's what you're in this lifetime to do, dear one. Remember?

# 91

# A Gift of Laughter

## Suggested Areas of Attention

* Discover, awaken, and accept your beauty, truth, and goodness; what a wonderful gift to yourself.
* Be genuine and authentic. You have nothing to prove to anyone.
* Have the strength to ask for help; have the courage to allow it.
* Feel all your emotions deeply, both dark and light.
* Lighten up and let yourself shine. Shine so the world can see it; laugh so the world can hear it. What a wonderful gift that would be.

Discover, awaken, and accept your beauty, truth, and goodness; you'll not discover them in their entirety because they're always growing, expanding, and becoming more, even so, never stop the pursuit to discover them more. Oh, don't fret you won't find them, they're there just beyond your resistance.

You're so much more than you let yourself believe, dear one. Admit who you are, trust who you are, lean on who you are and let the beauty, truth, and goodness of who you are guide you through those dark times when you must journey the Dark Wood of your fears and dread to discover the Light of you. Let your beauty, truth, and goodness guide you through the mazes and swamps of your doubts, uncertainties, and confusion. Let them guide you upon your sacred quest for the *'Light of the Truer You'* waiting on the other side.

Let your beauty, truth, and goodness unravel and release all your resistances and apprehensions. Let your beauty, truth, and goodness nurture and comfort your younger selves who cry out to be heard and loved. Let your beauty, truth, and goodness guide you into the waiting arms of God/Goddess/All That Is who know only your beauty, truth, and goodness.

Always look to the more real of you. Your destiny asks you to do so. Your world needs you to do so. You'll discover your realness in the beauty, truth, and goodness all about you. Open your eyes and open your heart and see it.

Lighten the load you carry. Ask your Higher Self and Soul to lift it from you. They'll happily do so. Don't fear; they'll not be tainted by the dark lies, the destructive patterns, and the old fear-based templates you give them for they have no investment in such things. And, dear one, they know how to dispose of them. They'll gladly do so.

Don't make a mood of lightness and laughter. Stop pretending. Stop mood-making. Honor your feelings by feeling them all both dark and light. When you're honest with your emotions and genuinely feel them, you can own them; you can release them. Honor your feelings for to do otherwise is to lie to yourself and deny your fullness. Without honoring your feelings, you become a shadow of a false you. When you hide what you feel and perform shallow emotions, you conceal your authenticity, and you hide your beauty, truth, and goodness from yourself and others, which is the point of such hiding.

Lighten up and laugh. Dance in the sun. Weep during those times of weeping. Get angry at those times of anger, but do so honestly and from a place of self-awareness and integrity. Give and be given. Love and be loved. Flow your kindness, compassion, and hope to others and celebrate the kindness, compassion, and hope others share with you. Embrace the kindness, compassion, and hope that God/Goddess/All That Is has for you and your world.

The more beauty, truth, and goodness you flow into your world, the more beauty, truth, and goodness there is for you to flow; this is a Divine Law. The more laughter you allow yourself, the more amusing the world becomes to you; this is a Divine Principle.

You're in this world to shine; you're in this world to lighten others. You're in this world to make a difference; you're in this world to love and be loved. You're in this world to work the magic of your heart; you're in this world to unfold the more real you. You're in this world to discover more of the beauty, truth, and goodness of you. And above all, you're in this world to have fun and to laugh. Accept this precious gift of laughter and let in the following truth.

*'You're in the right place at the right time, dear heart.*
*And you're doing just fine.'*

*So, it's ok for you to laugh now!*

# Appendix One

Working With Your Many Selves

Imagine all your many lifetimes past and future living their separate realities at this very moment, although not at the same time and space. Now imagine the entire myriad 'you' of the past and future of this current lifetime, likewise living out their separate realities at this present moment, again not at the same time and space. Now imagine being able to influence and change these many lifetimes of the past, and imagine being influenced and changed by future lifetimes more evolved and more real than the 'you' you are today. And imagine being able to heal and transform the myriad of 'you' throughout this current life. Can you imagine the possibilities of such a reality? Can you imagine the opportunities for healing, growth, and wholeness such a reality could provide? Well, according to science, such a thing is not only possible; it's how everything works. Science has discovered that all existence past and future exist simultaneously. And all forms come into being and are changed by the simple act of 'attention.' Attention turns waves into particles, resonance into form, thoughts into manifestation.

## A Straight Line or a Spiral?

As humans, we love to make our reality linear. We love to view everything from the perspective of a straight line. This perspective sees pasts and futures playing out on a line from a beginning to an end. History starts at point A and goes to point Z. We begin as a soft, delicate infant and end up a wrinkly old curmudgeon. Along this straight line, we create a sense of time and space to compartmentalize and manage our life. Time and space are illusions each of us makes real to help navigate this straight line.

But as our perceptions and perspectives evolve, as our measuring devices change, we observe reality differently; we experience our existence differently. With our evolving, we grow to experience more and more of the true nature of creation. And we're in the midst of a change in perception now. Chaos always precedes significant change, and chaos is what we're experiencing within and around us today. Very much so!

All of existence, in truth, functions as a spiral with pasts and futures existing concurrently in an ever progressing movement upward. Our many selves past and future are playing out their separate realities upon that evolutionary spiral at this very moment in their own time and space. Everything exists in a singular moment of continual expansion and elevation. And we're slowly beginning to experience this.

## Resonance Causation

Resonance is a wave, a frequency of vibration.

Creation does not fundamentally happen by Newtonian particle or impact causation as commonly believed because existence is not composed of particles. Everything is, at its essence, waves. Reality is created and influenced by what is called *'resonance causation.'* Resonance causation, simply stated, occurs when two or more waves meet, leading to the emergence of an independent wave called a *'standing wave.'* The other waves do not create this separate wave; it emerges from their interaction. Synergy is an example of resonance causation.

This independent, or standing wave, is also called a *'grand attractor'* as it attracts other waves to it.

In the meeting of two or more waves, the higher wave will lower, or the lower will lift, or they'll meet somewhere in between. For example, when you engage with the resonance of martyr (when you're in martyr), you'll lower your resonance to the resonance of martyr, or you'll elevate and transform the martyr, or you'll compromise with it. The result will attract resonances (realities) that reflect and enable your lowered frequency, or reflect and enable your elevated frequency, or reflect and maintain a state of compromise between you and the resonance of martyr. In other words, you'll attract a martyred life, a magical life, or a compromised life with martyrhood. There's only one acceptable outcome here, and that's to lift your martyr; to change its resonance, not yours.

When you're in a relationship with your Higher Self, or your Soul and Spirit, or God/Goddess/All That Is, they will never lower their resonance but will lift yours instead. There's no compromise. This 'lifting' is inherent in an elevated spirituality; your relationship with 'that which is more than you.' The relationship always lifts you. You always become more by it.

All the various selves of the 'you' you once were, in their different times and spaces, are influenced by your resonance, your frequency, this standing wave of you. You're the grand attractor at this time and in this space. And likewise, all your future selves both dark and light align with you according to the resonance, lowered or heightened, you're holding today. You being a higher resonance can elevate your lesser selves. Those future selves that contain a higher frequency will be attracted to you by the elevated attraction you carry.

You, at this moment, are the grand attractor for all your pasts and futures. The choices and decisions, thoughts and feelings, and beliefs and attitudes you hold and make can lift your younger selves and can align you with more awakened futures, or it can lower or compromise if those raw materials are limited and dull. It's up to you. Your future can become a nightmare, a radiant state of light and joy, or somewhere in between. It's your call. It's your choice. It's your resonance.

Choosing to work with your various selves by giving them attention and providing them with nurturing and support is a wise choice to make on your journey of growing and become more. It will prove to be a valuable step in your total healing and the lifting of your resonance.

## Elevating Your Lesser Selves

Your lesser selves are not your inferior selves. They're the parts of you who possess less awareness, have fewer resources, and have less understanding and maturity. The 'you' you were at age 5 or 16 are not as evolved, not as aware, and not as resourceful as the person you are today. Likewise, the parts of you that are more, your future selves, possess more conscious awareness, have more resources, have keener insight, and are more evolved than you.

Like you, your younger selves have a broad array of possible futures, you being one of them. Like you, they'll align with those futures that resonate with the choices and decisions, thoughts and feelings, and beliefs and attitudes they hold and make in their time and space. When you attend to them, when you give them your love, healing, understanding, and patience, you become aligned. You elevate their resonance, you inspire in them new choices and decisions, more elevated thoughts and feelings, and more productive beliefs and attitudes, and you awaken more of a sense of wholeness in you. You rise to a state where you genuinely love the totality of yourself and the grander 'you' you're becoming.

Since you also have a broad array of possible futures, the choices and decisions, thoughts and feelings, beliefs and attitudes you hold and make in this present time and space will align with those futures dark or light that resonates most with them. By questioning and elevating your choices and decisions, by monitoring your thoughts and feelings, by challenging your beliefs and attitudes, you lift your resonance to align with the more real you, those futures that resonate more with the 'you' you're destined to become.

By attending to your younger selves and by leaning on the 'you' more real, the more magical, more evolved, and more consciously aware you'll become. And the more powerful will be the realities you, the grand attractor, will draw to you. You'll embark on a journey more magnificent than anything you can yet fathom. You'll become that grander you beyond the limits of what you currently imagine, you'll more elegantly and gracefully travel your destined journey of Coming Home, and you'll do so by way of fun, magic, and bountiful adventure rather than through the rigors and struggles of others.

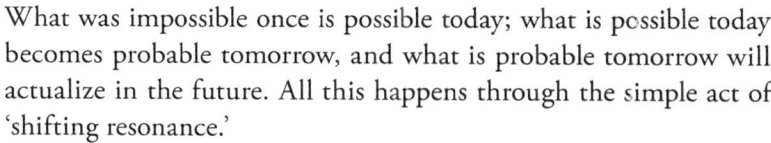

What was impossible once is possible today; what is possible today becomes probable tomorrow, and what is probable tomorrow will actualize in the future. All this happens through the simple act of 'shifting resonance.'

Although your younger selves are not aware of 'you' their future, they are influenced by you. What you believe, the attitudes you have, what you feel and think, and what choices and decisions you make will affect them. It resonates to them since you all share the same moment with different frequencies. Change and hone these raw materials and you'll lift their resonances and elevate their frequencies.

You are likewise not aware of your future selves, but like your younger selves, you too are influenced by their higher resonances and elevated frequencies. They can lift your resonance and elevate your frequency if you're in alignment with them.

Again, you're the singular representative of all the many parts of yourself, past and future. The resonance you hold aligns you and your past with futures dark or light. Your future comes into alignment with you, the grand attractor. And since all your thoughts and feelings, choices and decisions, and beliefs and attitudes contribute to the synergy that is your resonance, elevating these raw materials aligns you with elevated futures and lifts the resonances of your younger developing selves. You cannot change the details of your past, but you can alter the outcomes, and the effects they have on you today. You cannot know what your future holds, but you can be lifted by it, assuming you're aligning with futures more real and more luminous.

Being attentive and nurturing to your lesser selves, and being willing to be attended to and nurtured by the more real you, are wise choices to make. They'll ensure a more elegant journey to 'becoming more.'

*"What lies within the unconscious will in time become conscious*
*In the form of fate" - Lazaris*

You can navigate more elegantly through life by attending to your lesser selves who reside within your unconscious. You can evolve more gracefully by choosing to respond to their whispers instead of reacting to their many shouts.

Use the following meditation regularly to respond to the whispers of your less developed selves and to those we call 'the dark counselors.' And pay particular attention to the suggestions outlined in the section 'Important Points to Consider.'

Following these suggestions, and doing the meditation, will change your resonance. You'll experience magic unfolding. You'll awaken more profound healings. You'll experience true wholeness. And you'll discover the luminous love you genuinely have for yourself.

## The Dark Counselors

In addition to your younger biological selves, there are resonances you formed alliances with, energies to help you handle the many pains and terrors of childhood and adolescence. These resonances are parts of you now, and like your biological selves must be given attention. They should never be dismissed or neglected. Everyone engages these resonances to a greater or lesser degree. It was to your credit that you made such alliances; without them, you may not have survived the rigors of growing up. Although these resonances are harmful and destructive, they fulfilled their function in keeping you safe and able to cope. But now that you're an adult, these energies, having grown much more potent, will impede and destroy you over time.

The following are some of the main resonances you engage, and to whom you give your power.

a) Negative Ego  
b) Control (Dominator)  
c) Martyr  
d) Shame  
e) Rage  
f) Inner Terrorist  
g) Chauvinist (men and women both are plagued by this)

There are more, but these are the more dominant. Of these energies, your negative ego is the strongest and most troublesome.

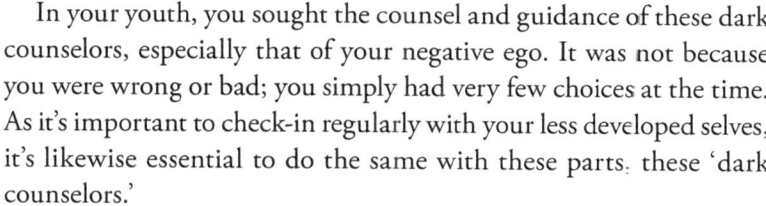

## The Magic of the Scented Flowers

In your youth, you sought the counsel and guidance of these dark counselors, especially that of your negative ego. It was not because you were wrong or bad; you simply had very few choices at the time. As it's important to check-in regularly with your less developed selves, it's likewise essential to do the same with these parts, these 'dark counselors.'

We call these non-biological parts 'counselors' because they serve you in this capacity. To them, their very existence and survival require they maintain this role in your present and future life. But your growth and healing require that you no longer allow this. To use a metaphor, *"You and only you must drive the car. To let them do it will most certainly result in a crash."*

The more you grow and change, the more they'll fight and resist you. These parts of you experience your growing and evolving with dread. In your growing and changing, they see their very existence in jeopardy. They'll fight very hard and will use every means available to hold you back. In truth, they're not dying but instead transforming into higher resonances. But they will not see it this way. They're going to be desperate and terrified of your growth.

Once you engage with and sustain a resonance, in this case, your dark counselors, it becomes a part of you; it seeks to grow and survive. As such, you must attend to it with patience, love, and acceptance. Never accept what they are and do, but always recognize them as parts of yourself. Since you gave them attention, and thus life, you're responsible for their healing and eventual transformation.

What they are today will not be the same in your future. As you evolve and become more, they'll likewise evolve with your changing resonance. Remember, when two waves meet, the higher wave (you) will lower, the lower wave (dark counselors) will lift, or they'll meet somewhere in-between. When you lift their resonance, in time, they'll transform to become your *'light counselors,'* but not without a struggle.

The higher resonance of the negative ego is the 'positive ego.' The higher resonance of martyr is 'magic.' The higher resonance of rage is 'outrage.' The higher resonance of shame is 'self-acceptance.' The higher resonance of control is 'love.' The higher resonance of chauvinism is the 'awakened feminine energy within you,' be you male or female. As they evolve, they'll eventually die to their darker side and transform into their lighter, like a phoenix emerging from its ashes. These higher resonances, now a part of you, will elevate your growing beyond what you can yet fathom.

By listening to their calls, by attending to their fears and dreads, by patiently being present with their raging and panic, you transform them; you help them evolve. The result will be a state of true self-love and true self-acceptance.

*"if you can love the least of you,
you'll most certainly love the whole of you."*

Let your dark counselors take a personified form when working with them meditatively. It would be interesting to see how they appear to you. Remember, you're not trying to change them. Change must be organic. It must be in its own time and in its own way. You're there to listen, love, and reassure them. You attend to them meditatively so you won't have to deal with their rage and fear in the form of life's many crises and whirlwinds. They'll get your attention one way or another. I recommend giving them your attention meditatively.

Your outer reality is an out-picturing of your inner reality. Attend meditatively to the whispers and shouts of your many biological selves, and the fears and wailings of your dark counselors, and you won't have to deal with them in your outer experiences. It's much easier that way.

## Important Points to Consider

When attending to your younger selves and dark counselors, be mindful that there are ways you should approach your work with them. Success will depend on how you respond to them and by knowing what your intentions are in engaging them. Some of your parts will be unpleasant, some less so. Engage them not as a scornful parent but as a loving and patient friend and guardian. There are things you should do and things you should not do to aide in their healing and growth. There are ways to work and behaviors you must avoid.

* Don't become angry or impatient with your younger selves or dark counselors. Be understanding and forgiving at all times.

* Always be loving and attentive no matter how angry or enraged they are with you. Learn to listen. Cultivate empathy.

* Don't rush or expect them to change at your pace; they must always be allowed to grow and evolve at the pace that's most comfortable for them. Working with your lesser developing selves is a lifelong process; rushing them and being hard on them is rushing and being hard on yourself. Always avoid this. Remember, these parts are you!

* Listen to them; don't lecture them.

* Catch yourself when you're becoming angry or annoyed with them; they'll feel your resonance; they'll feel cut off and abandoned by you their future. You are alienating these parts by your negative feelings toward them. You're there to respond to their fears and fits of anger. You're there to reassure them that they're going to be protected by you. You're there to offer them love and support. Don't abuse them. Remind them with sincerity that they're loved and supported. Assure them that you'll respond whenever they call out to you. Be the loving and supportive future that you desire for yourself. When you do this, you'll awaken self-love, and everything will change for all of you.

* Always be sensitive to their feelings. Let yourself feel what they're feeling. Never forget that these younger selves are you. You're going nowhere without them. Their healing is your healing; their growth is your growth.

\* The happier you become, the more successful you become, the more awakened you become, and the more elegantly your life unfolds, the more fearful and angry the various parts of you will be. Remember, in their time and space, such feelings and elevated experiences are unknown or calibrated differently. As such, these experiences are terrifying to them.

For example, your experience of greater love resulting from your growing and maturing is different from what they believe love to be from their limiting and often painful experiences. For some, love may equate with sacrifice or loss. For some, love may equate with pain and abandonment. For some, it may be akin to violence and abuse. As you awaken more love in your life, your younger selves will feel a sense of sacrifice or loss, or pain or abandonment, or violence and abuse, etc. They experience the higher resonance of love, but it's calibrating through their limited receptors of dark and painful experiences. They'll need more attention and more patience. They'll need reassuring that they're not going to be abandoned. They'll need time to grow their receptors.

\* When times are going well, take time to pause to let your younger selves catch-up, when times are not going well check-in and give them attention.

\* Stop believing that your less developed selves are holding you back. Stop blaming them because your life's not unfolding as quickly or as elegantly as you'd like. You're all journeying together, though in different times and spaces, and at different resonances. You must never allow yourself to race too far ahead of them. You'll need to pause and wait for them to catch up; this is self-pacing. Self-pacing is essential on any journey.

\* Promise that you'll always be there when they need you, and always keep your promise. Listen and respond to their many whispers and shouts.

\* Cultivate in you the patience of your more developed self. It will be a valuable aid in your work of healing and attending to the lesser of you. Think how patient your Higher Self and God and Goddess are with you.

\* Your dark counselors are not creative, but they're very persistent. They use the same methods of holding you back over and over again. Learn to identify their patterns and routines. Watch for them in your reality, and when discovered, do not allow them to be at play.

\* Respond meditatively to your younger selves and dark counselors. Respond when you feel in the doldrums, and when unpleasant emotions surface. Respond when your life becomes chaotic and when you're in a crisis. Respond when you feel overwhelmed. And respond when your life is racing so fast that it requires you to slow down to let the less developed parts catch-up. Even when times are good, and success and happiness abound, go into meditation and check-in; your lesser selves need time to integrate these positive times. As instructions for cold relief medication tell you *'Take at the first sign of a cold,'* meditate at the first sign that something is not right in your reality. Learn to catch the whispers.

\* Your Higher Self is not physical, it's also not male or female, but it will take a physical form to interact with you in meditation. The form it takes may be of your gender or not. It will be about your age or slightly older. And it will not look like you. Whatever personified form it chooses, it will be for your comfort and ease of interaction. No, it will not take the form of a rabbit (as one of my clients wanted to make it.) Your Higher Self is not Roger the Rabbit, or Jiminy Cricket, or the Mad Hatter, or Princess Leia, or any other such nonsense. This foolishness is the minimizing work of your negative ego. Let your Higher Self take whatever form it takes and let it be consistent.

\* If you're younger selves are fearful, they'll do whatever it takes to get your attention. Don't worry that you'll be unable to work with them. They're desperate to get your attention. They want you to hear and to respond to them. They're calling out to you always. It's better to address their fears proactively than to have your reality force your attention.

## Meditation

1. Gently close your eyes. Allow yourself to become quiet and still in whatever way you feel comfortable. When you feel calmer, slowly count from seven to one. With each count, feel yourself shifting and changing, both physically and mentally.

2. On the count of one slowly open your mental eyes. Imagine yourself in your Safe Place. Your Safe Place should be outdoors in nature, far from the hustle and frenzy of daily activity. Let it be beautiful, enchanting, loving, and filled with blessed solitude. This Safe Place is yours and yours alone. No one can disturb you here. No one can enter this place unless invited.

This place may be a creation of your imagination, a place you'd like to use from a movie or a picture, or a place of beauty and safety you remember from your past. It should not be a building, house, fortress, or castle as these images send the wrong message to your subconscious. The important thing is that you feel safe, protected, and at peace in this haven in nature. Return to the same Safe Place in every meditation. In each meditation, explore a little more of this space; explore each detail. *"Love pays attention to detail."*

3. After you've spent time allowing your senses of sight, sound, touch, taste, and hearing drink in this place, invite your Higher Self to join you. Sit together for a little awhile. Feel your Higher Self's presence and love. Talk about what's troubling you. Talk about your desire to attend to your developing selves. *"There's magic in the telling."*

4. Now invite your younger selves or dark counselors or both to come and join you. Those most in need of your attention will appear. Maybe many will come to join you, perhaps only one or two.

5. Who wants to speak with you? Ask. One or two will step forward to talk with you. They may express in words. They may

communicate by lashing out at you in anger, rage, fear, or through other emotions. They may communicate by way of memories from your past. They may express themselves through the feelings you're having. In whatever way they interact with you, listen, and give them your full attention.

Don't debate with them. Don't argue with them. Just be patient and listen. Let them lash out at you. Let them rage at you. Let them cry and weep. Let them express in whatever way is important to them. Your Higher Self is with you. You're safe. They cannot and will not hurt you. All they want is for someone to hear their anguish. Isn't that what you want?

6. When they've expressed themselves, let them know that everything is going to be ok and that no one is going to be left behind. Assure them that you're changing and growing does not mean you're moving away or that they're being abandoned and forgotten. Commit to them that you'll heed their calls and respond to their fears. Give them your love; envelop them in your light. It's the desire of your Light and Love that you listen and respond to them, that you love them, not try to fix or correct them. They must heal and grow in their own time and way. All they ask is that you listen and hear their pain, fear, and mournful cries.

Your dark counselors, on the other hand, will try to obstruct and hold you back. They'll use whatever means they can to keep you from your growing. Listen patiently but do not heed their counsel. You drive your car, not them. You author your life, not them. Be patient, forgiving, understanding, and loving. But don't heed their counsel.

7. When you're younger selves and dark counselors finish, thank them for expressing their concerns. Promise them you'll continue responding when needed and reassure them once again that you're not abandoning them. They will then withdraw from your Safe Place.

8. Now let your Higher Self hold you. You may want to cry, get angry, or express other emotions. Do so. Whatever feelings surface,

let them come up. When you're ready, and only when you're ready, thank your Higher Self, close your mental eyes, and slowly count from one to five. On the count of five, open your physical eyes and return to your room. Your meditation is now complete; the magic is now undertaken.

Writing down your experiences could be very beneficial, but only if you want to.

# Appendix Two

Questions and Answers

Question: *I've been working on my martyr and shame for years now. They still keep coming up in my life. When will I finally be done with them?*

Never. As humans, we love to view reality as a straight line. As such, we think of healing as a straight line with a beginning, middle, and end. Healing doesn't work that way. Healing is a spiral, not a straight line. And it always spirals upward. It always comes back around but never in the same place. Healing elevates, it does not extend. The more you work with such things as martyr and shame, the less control they have over you. Martyr and shame will always be present though not in the same place on the spiral.

Think of it this way. Let's say you've successfully stopped smoking. You haven't had a cigarette in a long time. But now and then, you sneak out behind the shed to light up. OK! No big deal! No, you didn't fail. No, you're not a failure. No, you're not backsliding. You had your quick fix, now go on with your life and continue smoke-free. And if now and then you sneak behind the shed, no big deal. The point is that even though you healed your smoking habit, the urge to smoke will always be there. The difference is you're controlling it, not it controlling you. You've transcended the urge. You're the author of your reality, not the cigarette. Martyr and shame will always be there. And from time to time, you may slip into them. Don't worry. Catch yourself when you slip up, brush yourself off, and get on with living your life; this is healing.

Question: *I've been trying to get my husband to work with the book, but he keeps resisting. Do you have any suggestions?*

Yes, leave him alone.

Question: ***I would like to get my children to work with this book, any suggestions?***

This work is not for children or adolescents. They're not yet at the point where they possess the consciousness and the adult level of responsibility necessary for this work to be most effective. Most grown-ups are not adult enough to respond to this work. This work is suited more for *'spiritual adults.'* It would, however, be most beneficial for children and adolescents just to read and re-read the stories in *The Scented Flowers of Sinjin-Ka*. If you feel as if they'd respond positively, you may suggest they write commentaries on the stories; this would be an excellent exercise for them. But do not push them to do so.

Question: ***I've been working with my younger selves for years, but they still keep coming up in my life. What do I need to do to fix them?***

Stop trying to fix them! Stop blaming them! They're a part of you; they are you. They must evolve in their own time and at their own pace. Just keep responding to them and loving them. As God/Goddess/All That Is are infinitely patient with you, be patient with them. Be patient with yourself.

Question: ***What is the 'Inner Terrorist?'***

Say your life's moving along wonderfully then, without warning, something disastrous happens. Something happens that turns everything upside down. This something is the work of your Inner Terrorist.

This Terrorist, brought into being during your younger years, was meant to halt you. Its function was to prevent you from moving too far beyond control. Its purpose was to 'blow up' your reality and to instill fear so you won't relax your guard. The terrorism we see in the world is a shout and an out-picturing from each person's Inner Terrorist.

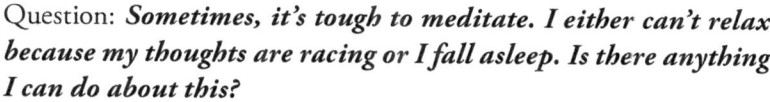

Question: ***Sometimes, it's tough to meditate. I either can't relax because my thoughts are racing or I fall asleep. Is there anything I can do about this?***

What you're describing are symptoms of fear. Ask your Higher Self to help you with this. Work with the fear stories and commentaries listed in the *'Cross-Reference Chart.'* But there are some things you can do in the meantime.

Sleeping: Try meditating at a time when you're less likely to be sleepy. Meditating at night before you go to bed may not be a good idea. Also, don't meditate lying down. Sit up when meditating.

Too Many Thoughts: Trying to push away the thoughts or fighting against them will just make the matter worse. Don't force the meditation. Stop trying and come back another time when you feel less tense. Try *'Freewriting'* to open a dialogue with the frightened parts of yourself (Refer to the section on *Freewriting in 'Cultivating the Scented Flowers.'*) *Freewriting* can also help bring to the surface your fear so you can feel and lift it. You may find *Freewriting* to be more beneficial for you right now. Later, when you feel less frightened, you can return to meditating.

Question: ***I randomly selected numbers on many occasions and read their commentaries. Nothing relates to me. Nothing works for me. Am I missing something?***

You may want to go to the *'Cross Reference Chart'* and read the stories and commentaries on Specialness, Martyr, and Negative Ego.

Question: ***I don't have the time to meditate or do much of the work you suggest. My time is limited. What else can I do that won't take up much time?***

Time's an illusion. You can have as much time or as little time as you want. It's always your call. If you're too busy to process and meditate, you're too busy. Before you proceed further, I would suggest looking honestly at your priorities. If you find that you're growing is not on the top of the list, read the commentaries on martyr, struggle, and authorship.

**Question: *Since using your book and working on myself, a lot of unpleasant emotions have surfaced, and I'm experiencing a lot of resistance. Is this normal?***

Yep! You're succeeding. There will always be resistance to this work. The more you move forward, the more resistance you'll experience. But you'll find that as you grow, your resistances will be better processed by you. Don't forget to pace yourself. Remember, there'll be times when you'll need to move forward, and times when you'll need to pause and integrate. There'll be times when some of your younger selves will need attention. Don't force your process. Slow down to allow your less develop selves to catch up. You're not in a race here.

Think of your lesser selves as young children hiking with you on a long mountain trail. There'll be many times when you must pause and wait for them. The worst thing you can do is to run wildly ahead. In your exuberance to reach your goal, don't forget the little ones that follow. You're going nowhere without them. Unpleasant emotions surfacing and resistances occurring is a message for you to slow down, pause, and attend to the various parts of yourself who are feeling abandoned. Pacing is everything on your journey. Responding and always attending to your lesser selves is of the utmost importance.

**Question: *Much of what you talk about does not fit into my religious beliefs. Can you help me with this?***

Religion will not fit into where you're ultimately going. In time you'll need to expand your spirituality beyond the confines of religion. Becoming a spiritual adult supersedes and surpasses being a religious one. Remember, although you can find spirituality in religion, you'll never find religion in spirituality. Ultimately your relationship with God/Goddess/All That Is must stand as a personal relationship unfettered by dogma, collective belief, or shared rituals. It must shine in its uniqueness and individuality. You're Coming Home to your *'Oneness,'* not your *'group-ness.'*

Question: ***I'm a therapist and would like to use these books for my sessions with clients. Would this be OK?***

Absolutely! As I had written in the *Introduction,* this is what I did with much success after writing the stories. Let the client pick a number from one to ninety-one. Have the client read the story. Now have the client read the commentary on that story. Have the client identify what in the story and commentary he or she finds relevant to present circumstances. Have a discussion. Also, make sure the client works with the *'Suggested Areas of Attention'* section of the commentary. As always, honesty is essential in this work. Have fun with the process.

Question: ***What if I want to invite others who come from different perspectives and approaches to be a part of my Healing Community? Would that work?***

Not really. Each person must be on the same page here, or it can turn into a mish-mash of differing views and agendas. Better to invite those who are comfortable and focused on this path. You can always organize other groups to serve different purposes. Your Healing Community should contain people who can focus their attention on this work, and this work only.

Question: ***This book has been so helpful for me! People need this. How can we get more people interested?***

First of all, thank you for allowing the book to touch you. Secondly, no one needs this book. And thirdly, this approach to personal growth and awakening is not for everyone. Very few will appreciate it because this work is not everyone's "cup of tea." It's an esoteric path not suited for most people.

I wrote this book for me. If others, such as yourself, grow and evolve with its help, it's because you've created or allowed it to assist you. You're the author of your life, not a book or a set of beliefs.

You make of your life what you will, and you'll create the means to get you to where you're going. So I guess it was you who created or allowed this book, or it wouldn't be in your reality (but I still get to keep the royalty).

It's proclaimed in the Veda, *"The knowledge of the book remains in the book."* It's you who lift the knowledge out of the book. It's you who give it meaning. And it's you who give it life in you.

Thank you for inviting me to be a part of your journey.

# Appendix Three

Cross-Reference Chart

**Anger/Rage**   Page
- 17: Nilla's Dearest Friend — 71
- 44: An Abandoned Garden — 140
- 73: The Sweet Taste of Vindication — 214
- 77: Grandmother Seeta's Words of Wisdom — 226
- 85: The Demon Within — 247

**Authority/Empowerment**
- 08: Standing Before the Judge — 43
- 11: The Testing of Amit Don — 52
- 13: The Saint Who Could Not Be Harmed — 58
- 16: The Man Who Said, "Thank You" — 68
- 20: The Tale of the Chuckling Saint — 79
- 22: The Path Maker — 85
- 29: What a Rare and Special Child! — 102
- 30: The Secret Teaching — 105
- 31: Kotia and the Bawdy Woman — 107
- 34: Three Old Women — 114
- 36: The Actor Assumes His Role — 119
- 38: Thirty Days in the Infinite — 125
- 40: The King of Beasts — 130
- 48: Rathgar Gets His Name — 151
- 50: The Way of the Dreamer — 156
- 57: Manju Among the Saints — 173
- 66: Sinji's One and Only Tale — 196
- 70: The Sweet Old Couple — 206
- 71: A Most Unconventional Master — 209
- 90: The Ministers of Kushtan — 263

## Beauty, Truth, and Goodness

| | | |
|---|---|---|
| 16: | The Man Who Said, "Thank You" | 68 |
| 21: | Two Healings | 82 |
| 31: | Kotia and the Bawdy Woman | 107 |
| 32: | Bindu at the End of the World | 109 |
| 40: | The King of Beasts | 130 |
| 47: | The Poet's Skill at Fishing | 148 |
| 51: | The Laughing Fool of Binduvan | 159 |
| 63: | Mother Seagull and the Ocean | 187 |
| 64: | The Man Who Talked With Trees | 189 |
| 66: | Sinji's One and Only Tale | 196 |
| 88: | Knowing | 258 |
| 91: | A Gift of Laughter | 265 |

## Blame

| | | |
|---|---|---|
| 23: | Mohan at the Gate of Bliss | 87 |
| 38: | Thirty Days in the Infinite | 125 |
| 46: | The Passing of the Torch | 145 |
| 48: | Rathgar Gets His Name | 151 |
| 58: | The Selfishly Generous Woman | 175 |
| 63: | Mother Seagull and the Ocean | 187 |

## Co-Creating

| | | |
|---|---|---|
| 01: | The Fool and the Apple | 23 |
| 32: | Bindu at the End of the World | 109 |
| 37: | The Greatest Gift | 122 |
| 61: | Where the Two Worlds Meet | 182 |
| 63: | Mother Seagull and the Ocean | 187 |
| 69: | Sumitra and Her Friends | 204 |
| 80: | The Gathering | 233 |

## Coming Home

| | | |
|---|---|---|
| 01: | The Fool and the Apple | 23 |
| 03: | Where the Animals Went to Die | 29 |

| | | |
|---|---|---:|
| 12: | The Man Who Walked Backward | 55 |
| 13: | The Saint Who Could Not Be Harmed | 58 |
| 14: | What Danila Learned of Love | 61 |
| 15: | How the Master Found Enlightenment | 65 |
| 19: | The River | 76 |
| 22: | The Path Maker | 85 |
| 27: | The Answer is Always, "Yes" | 97 |
| 30: | The Secret Teaching | 105 |
| 34: | Three Old Women | 114 |
| 37: | The Greatest Gift | 122 |
| 49: | The Counting of the Stars | 154 |
| 52: | The Thousand Coats of Suma Ti | 161 |
| 59: | The Master's Perfect Imperfection | 178 |
| 62: | My Life Has Never Been So Bad | 184 |
| 68: | Coming Home | 201 |
| 72: | The Secret of Sima Sen | 209 |
| 75: | Galen's Glimpse of Hell | 220 |
| 89: | Some Things Are Just Worth Saving | 260 |

## Community

| | | |
|---|---|---:|
| 52: | The Thousand Coats of Suma Ti | 161 |
| 57: | Manju Among the Saints | 173 |
| 61: | Where the Two Worlds Meet | 182 |
| 63: | Mother Seagull and the Ocean | 187 |
| 69: | Sumitra and Her Friends | 204 |
| 80: | The Gathering | 233 |

## Competition and Winning

| | | |
|---|---|---:|
| 09: | The Love of Winning | 45 |
| 84: | The Woman Who Had Everything | 244 |

## The Consensus

| | | |
|---|---|---:|
| 01: | The Fool and the Apple | 23 |
| 09: | The Love of Winning | 45 |

| 12: | The Man Who Walked Backward | 55 |
| 13: | The Saint Who Could Not Be Harmed | 58 |
| 22: | The Path Maker | 85 |
| 25: | The Saint Who Loved Science | 92 |
| 30: | The Secret Teaching | 105 |
| 31: | Kotia and the Bawdy Woman | 107 |
| 42: | A Tale of Two Villages | 134 |
| 45: | The Purpose of Life | 142 |
| 49: | The Counting of the Stars | 154 |
| 50: | The Way of the Dreamer | 156 |
| 53: | In the Valley of the Singing Stones | 163 |
| 54: | Just Imagine | 165 |
| 69: | Sumitra and Her Friends | 204 |
| 71: | A Most Unconventional Master | 209 |

## Control

| 87: | The Compassionate Thing to Do | 255 |
| 88: | Knowing | 258 |

## Creativity

| 10: | Gobi's Tiny Seeds | 48 |
| 16: | The Man Who Said, "Thank You" | 68 |
| 28: | In the Fire of the Muse | 99 |
| 32: | Bindu at the End of the World | 109 |
| 47: | The Poet's Skill at Fishing | 148 |
| 54: | Just Imagine | 165 |
| 64: | The Man Who Talked With Trees | 189 |
| 66: | Sinji's One and Only Tale | 196 |

## Death and Dying

| 03: | Where the Animals Went to Die | 29 |
| 05: | A Gift from a Squished Squirrel | 35 |
| 13: | The Saint Who Could Not Be Harmed | 58 |

| 21: | Two Healings | 82 |
| 24: | Rumesh Pays Respect | 90 |
| 32: | Bindu at the End of the World | 109 |
| 34: | Three Old Women | 114 |
| 56: | The Eternal Companion | 170 |
| 77: | Grandmother Seeta's Words of Wisdom | 226 |
| 86: | The Artist and the Fisherman | 252 |

## Dreams and Desires

| 06: | The Doll Maker's Helper | 37 |
| 10: | Gobi's Tiny Seeds | 48 |
| 12: | The Man Who Walked Backward | 55 |
| 27: | The Answer is Always, "Yes" | 97 |
| 50: | The Way of the Dreamer | 156 |
| 54: | Just Imagine | 165 |
| 60: | King or Seeker | 180 |
| 65: | Mukta and the Magic Purse | 192 |
| 74: | What Kamila Learned From a Chipmunk | 217 |
| 76: | Being Real | 223 |
| 78: | Holiest of Holies | 228 |
| 80: | The Gathering | 233 |
| 82: | The Child Who Could | 239 |
| 84: | The Woman Who Had Everything | 244 |

## Elegance

| 01: | The Fool and the Apple | 23 |
| 11: | The Testing of Amit Don | 52 |
| 16: | The Man Who Said, "Thank You" | 68 |
| 20: | The Tale of the Chuckling Saint | 79 |
| 22: | The Path Maker | 85 |
| 30: | The Secret Teaching | 105 |
| 36: | The Actor Assumes His Role | 119 |
| 39: | Sundeep and the Simple Life | 128 |

| 42: | A Tale of Two Villages | 134 |
| 62: | My Life Has Never Been So Bad | 184 |

## Emotional Healing

| 03: | Where the Animals Went to Die | 29 |
| 05: | A Gift from a Squished Squirrel | 35 |
| 07: | The Witch of the Darkened Wood | 40 |
| 17: | Nilla's Dearest Friend | 71 |
| 21: | Two Healings | 82 |
| 23: | Mohan at the Gate of Bliss | 87 |
| 24: | Rumesh Pays Respect | 90 |
| 29: | What a Rare and Special Child! | 102 |
| 39: | Sundeep and the Simple Life | 128 |
| 41: | A Legitimate Profession | 132 |
| 44: | An Abandoned Garden | 140 |
| 46: | The Passing of the Torch | 145 |
| 53: | In the Valley of the Singing Stones | 163 |
| 56: | The Eternal Companion | 170 |
| 72: | The Secret of Sima Sen | 211 |
| 85: | The Demon Within | 247 |
| 86: | The Artist and the Fisherman | 252 |
| 91: | A Gift of Laughter | 265 |

## Entitlement

| 78: | Holiest of Holies | 228 |
| 79: | Entering the Hall of Eternal Bliss | 231 |

## Fear

| 07: | The Witch of the Darkened Wood | 40 |
| 10: | Gobi's Tiny Seeds | 48 |
| 30: | The Secret Teaching | 105 |
| 32: | Bindu at the End of the World | 109 |
| 39: | Sundeep and the Simple Life | 128 |

| 45: | The Purpose of Life | 142 |
| 49: | The Counting of the Stars | 154 |
| 51: | The Laughing Fool of Binduvan | 159 |
| 53: | In the Valley of the Singing Stones | 163 |
| 72: | The Secret of Sima Sen | 211 |
| 75: | Galen's Glimpse of Hell | 220 |
| 77: | Grandmother Seeta's Words of Wisdom | 226 |
| 81: | Tandori Had Two Teachers | 236 |
| 83: | Amil and the Most Beautiful Flower | 242 |
| 86: | The Artist and the Fisherman | 252 |
| 88: | Knowing | 258 |
| 91: | A Gift of Laughter | 265 |

**Forgiveness**

| 08: | Standing Before the Judge | 43 |
| 23: | Mohan at the Gate of Bliss | 87 |
| 52: | The Thousand Coats of Suma Ti | 161 |
| 68: | Coming Home | 201 |
| 72: | The Secret of Sima Sen | 211 |
| 73: | The Sweet Taste of Vindication | 214 |
| 75: | Galen's Glimpse of Hell | 220 |

**Freedom**

| 20: | The Tale of the Chuckling Saint | 79 |
| 27: | The Answer is Always, "Yes" | 97 |
| 29: | What a Rare and Special Child! | 102 |
| 31: | Kotia and the Bawdy Woman | 107 |
| 35: | Gopol Talks to God | 117 |
| 44: | An Abandoned Garden | 140 |
| 46: | The Passing of the Torch | 145 |
| 49: | The Counting of the Stars | 154 |
| 51: | The Laughing Fool of Binduvan | 159 |
| 57: | Manju Among the Saints | 173 |

| | | |
|---|---|---|
| 72: | The Secret of Sima Sen | 211 |
| 74: | What Kamila Learned From a Chipmunk | 217 |
| 82: | The Child Who Could | 239 |
| 88: | Knowing | 258 |
| 89: | Some Things Are Just Worth Saving | 260 |
| 90: | The Ministers of Kushtan | 263 |

## Fun

| | | |
|---|---|---|
| 04: | The Disciple and the Idiot | 32 |
| 11: | The Testing of Amit Don | 52 |
| 16: | The Man Who Said, "Thank You" | 68 |
| 20: | The Tale of the Chuckling Saint | 79 |
| 30: | The Secret Teaching | 105 |
| 37: | The Greatest Gift | 122 |
| 42: | A Tale of Two Villages | 134 |
| 45: | The Purpose of Life | 142 |
| 69: | Sumitra and Her Friends | 204 |
| 74: | What Kamila Learned From a Chipmunk | 217 |
| 77: | Grandmother Seeta's Words of Wisdom | 226 |
| 78: | Holiest of Holies | 228 |
| 81: | Tandori Had Two Teachers | 236 |
| 82: | The Child Who Could | 239 |
| 84: | The Woman Who Had Everything | 244 |
| 91: | A Gift of Laughter | 265 |

## God/Goddess/All That Is

| | | |
|---|---|---|
| 01: | The Fool and the Apple | 23 |
| 06: | The Doll Maker's Helper | 37 |
| 11: | The Testing of Amit Don | 52 |
| 16: | The Man Who Said, "Thank You" | 68 |
| 19: | The River | 76 |
| 23: | Mohan at the Gate of Bliss | 87 |
| 27: | The Answer is Always, "Yes" | 97 |

| | | |
|---|---|---|
| 30: | The Secret Teaching | 105 |
| 32: | Bindu at the End of the World | 109 |
| 34: | Three Old Women | 114 |
| 35: | Gopol Talks to God | 117 |
| 37: | The Greatest Gift | 122 |
| 63: | Mother Seagull and the Ocean | 187 |
| 68: | Coming Home | 201 |
| 75: | Galen's Glimpse of Hell | 220 |
| 79: | Entering the Hall of Eternal Bliss | 231 |
| 91: | A Gift of Laughter | 265 |

## Gratitude
| | | |
|---|---|---|
| 16: | The Man Who Said, "Thank You" | 68 |
| 86: | The Artist and the Fisherman | 252 |

## Grief
| | | |
|---|---|---|
| 03: | Where the Animals Went to Die | 29 |
| 05: | A Gift from a Squished Squirrel | 35 |
| 24: | Rumesh Pays Respect | 90 |
| 51: | The Laughing Fool of Binduvan | 159 |
| 56: | The Eternal Companion | 170 |
| 86: | The Artist and the Fisherman | 252 |

## The Hallows
| | | |
|---|---|---|
| 42: | A Tale of Two Villages | 134 |
| 43: | The Captain and the Sea | 137 |
| 64: | The Man Who Talked With Trees | 189 |
| 81: | Tandori Had Two Teachers | 236 |
| 88: | Knowing | 258 |

## Healing
| | | |
|---|---|---|
| 05: | A Gift from a Squished Squirrel | 35 |
| 07: | The Witch of the Darkened Wood | 40 |

| | | |
|---|---|---|
| 10: | Gobi's Tiny Seeds | 48 |
| 12: | The Man Who Walked Backward | 55 |
| 13: | The Saint Who Could Not Be Harmed | 58 |
| 16: | The Man Who Said, "Thank You" | 68 |
| 17: | Nilla's Dearest Friend | 72 |
| 21: | Two Healings | 82 |
| 23: | Mohan at the Gate of Bliss | 87 |
| 36: | The Actor Assumes His Role | 119 |
| 41: | A Legitimate Profession | 132 |
| 44: | An Abandoned Garden | 140 |
| 46: | The Passing of the Torch | 145 |
| 52: | The Thousand Coats of Suma Ti | 161 |
| 53: | In the Valley of the Singing Stones | 163 |
| 55: | A Marriage Made in Heaven | 168 |
| 64: | The Man Who Talked With Trees | 189 |
| 72: | The Secret of Sima Sen | 211 |
| 85: | The Demon Within | 247 |
| 89: | Some Things Are Just Worth Saving | 260 |

## Higher Self

| | | |
|---|---|---|
| 09: | The Love of Winning | 45 |
| 14: | What Danila Learned of Love | 61 |
| 17: | Nilla's Dearest Friend | 71 |
| 20: | The Tale of the Chuckling Saint | 79 |
| 23: | Mohan at the Gate of Bliss | 87 |
| 27: | The Answer is Always, "Yes" | 97 |
| 37: | The Greatest Gift | 122 |
| 44: | An Abandoned Garden | 140 |
| 48: | Rathgar Gets His Name | 151 |
| 53: | In the Valley of the Singing Stones | 163 |
| 65: | Mukta and the Magic Purse | 192 |
| 75: | Galen's Glimpse of Hell | 220 |
| 86: | The Artist and the Fisherman | 252 |

## Hope
| | | |
|---|---|---|
| 10: | Gobi's Tiny Seeds | 48 |
| 12: | The Man Who Walked Backward | 55 |
| 32: | Bindu at the End of the World | 109 |
| 44: | An Abandoned Garden | 140 |
| 51: | The Laughing Fool of Binduvan | 159 |
| 53: | In the Valley of the Singing Stones | 163 |
| 62: | My Life Has Never Been So Bad | 184 |
| 63: | Mother Seagull and the Ocean | 187 |
| 67: | A Simple Tale of Hope | 199 |
| 77: | Grandmother Seeta's Words of Wisdom | 226 |

## Imagination
| | | |
|---|---|---|
| 54: | Just Imagine | 165 |
| 69: | Sumitra and Her Friends | 204 |
| 76: | Being Real | 223 |
| 82: | The Child Who Could | 239 |

## Judgment
| | | |
|---|---|---|
| 04: | The Disciple and the Idiot | 32 |
| 08: | Standing Before the Judge | 43 |
| 11: | The Testing of Amit Don | 52 |
| 13: | The Saint Who Could Not Be Harmed | 58 |
| 75: | Galen's Glimpse of Hell | 220 |
| 78: | Holiest of Holies | 228 |
| 87: | The Compassionate Thing to Do | 255 |

## Love
| | | |
|---|---|---|
| 03: | Where the Animals Went to Die | 29 |
| 14: | What Danila Learned of Love | 61 |
| 19: | The River | 76 |
| 23: | Mohan at the Gate of Bliss | 87 |
| 24: | Rumesh Pays Respect | 90 |

| | | |
|---|---|---|
| 26: | The Two Lovers Who Never Met | 95 |
| 31: | Kotia and the Bawdy Woman | 107 |
| 37: | The Greatest Gift | 122 |
| 44: | An Abandoned Garden | 140 |
| 51: | The Laughing Fool of Binduvan | 159 |
| 56: | The Eternal Companion | 170 |
| 58: | The Selfishly Generous Woman | 175 |
| 61: | Where the Two Worlds Meet | 182 |
| 63: | Mother Seagull and the Ocean | 187 |
| 68: | Coming Home | 201 |
| 75: | Galen's Glimpse of Hell | 220 |
| 83: | Amil and the Most Beautiful Flower | 242 |
| 91: | A Gift of Laughter | 265 |

## Magic

| | | |
|---|---|---|
| 01: | The Fool and the Apple | 23 |
| 07: | The Witch of the Darkened Wood | 40 |
| 10: | Gobi's Tiny Seeds | 48 |
| 15: | How the Master Found Enlightenment | 65 |
| 16: | The Man Who Said, "Thank You" | 68 |
| 20: | The Tale of the Chuckling Saint | 79 |
| 33: | Martyr's Many Lifetimes | 112 |
| 53: | In the Valley of the Singing Stones | 163 |
| 61: | Where the Two Worlds Meet | 182 |
| 63: | Mother Seagull and the Ocean | 187 |
| 65: | Mukta and the Magic Purse | 192 |
| 69: | Sumitra and Her Friends | 204 |
| 80: | The Gathering | 233 |
| 83: | Amil and the Most Beautiful Flower | 242 |

## Manifesting

| | | |
|---|---|---|
| 01: | The Fool and the Apple | 23 |
| 02: | Not Enough Enough | 26 |

| | | |
|---|---|---|
| 06: | The Doll Maker's Helper | 37 |
| 07: | The Witch of the Darkened Wood | 40 |
| 08: | Standing Before the Judge | 43 |
| 10: | Gobi's Tiny Seeds | 48 |
| 55: | A Marriage Made in Heaven | 168 |
| 60: | King or Seeker | 180 |
| 61: | Where the Two Worlds Meet | 182 |
| 65: | Mukta and the Magic Purse | 192 |
| 70: | The Sweet Old Couple | 206 |
| 76: | Being Real | 223 |
| 78: | Holiest of Holies | 228 |
| 80: | The Gathering | 233 |

## Martyr

| | | |
|---|---|---|
| 14: | What Danila Learned of Love | 61 |
| 33: | Martyr's Many Lifetimes | 112 |
| 58: | The Selfishly Generous Woman | 175 |

## Negative Ego

| | | |
|---|---|---|
| 09: | The Love of Winning | 45 |
| 15: | How the Master Found Enlightenment | 65 |
| 18: | A Lesson on Believing You're Special | 74 |
| 20: | The Tale of the Chuckling Saint | 79 |
| 23: | Mohan at the Gate of Bliss | 87 |
| 27: | The Answer is Always, "Yes" | 97 |
| 28: | In the Fire of the Muse | 99 |
| 36: | The Actor Assumes His Role | 119 |
| 48: | Rathgar Gets His Name | 151 |
| 65: | Mukta and the Magic Purse | 192 |
| 79: | Entering the Hall of Eternal Bliss | 231 |
| 87: | The Compassionate Thing to Do | 255 |

## Negative Self-Image

| | | |
|---|---|---|
| 13: | The Saint Who Could Not Be Harmed | 58 |
| 29: | What a Rare and Special Child! | 102 |
| 36: | The Actor Assumes His Role | 119 |
| 55: | A Marriage Made in Heaven | 168 |
| 70: | The Sweet Old Couple | 206 |
| 76: | Being Real | 223 |

## Pain

| | | |
|---|---|---|
| 03: | Where the Animals Went to Die | 29 |
| 05: | A Gift from a Squished Squirrel | 35 |
| 10: | Gobi's Tiny Seeds | 48 |
| 24: | Rumesh Pays Respect | 90 |
| 38: | Thirty Days in the Infinite | 125 |
| 41: | A Legitimate Profession | 132 |
| 44: | An Abandoned Garden | 140 |
| 51: | The Laughing Fool of Binduvan | 159 |
| 53: | In the Valley of the Singing Stones | 161 |
| 56: | The Eternal Companion | 170 |
| 58: | The Selfishly Generous Woman | 175 |
| 72: | The Secret of Sima Sen | 211 |
| 73: | The Sweet Taste of Vindication | 214 |
| 85: | The Demon Within | 247 |

## Parts of Self

| | | |
|---|---|---|
| 08: | Standing Before the Judge | 43 |
| 23: | Mohan at the Gate of Bliss | 87 |
| 26: | The Two Lovers Who Never Met | 95 |
| 29: | What a Rare and Special Child! | 102 |
| 30: | The Secret Teaching | 105 |
| 31: | Kotia and the Bawdy Woman | 107 |
| 32: | Bindu at the End of the World | 109 |
| 38: | Thirty Days in the Infinite | 125 |

| | | |
|---|---|---|
| 43: | The Captain and the Sea | 137 |
| 48: | Rathgar Gets His Name | 151 |
| 52: | The Thousand Coats of Suma Ti | 161 |
| 53: | In the Valley of the Singing Stones | 163 |
| 58: | The Selfishly Generous Woman | 175 |
| 65: | Mukta and the Magic Purse | 192 |
| 71: | A Most Unconventional Master | 209 |
| 72: | The Secret of Sima Sen | 211 |
| 73: | The Sweet Taste of Vindication | 214 |
| 79: | Entering the Hall of Eternal Bliss | 231 |
| 82: | The Child Who Could | 239 |
| 86: | The Artist and the Fisherman | 252 |
| 89: | Some Things Are Just Worth Saving | 260 |
| 90: | The Ministers of Kushtan | 263 |
| | Appendix 1: Working With Your Lesser Parts of Self | 271 |

## Patience

| | | |
|---|---|---|
| 11: | The Testing of Amit Don | 52 |
| 29: | What a Rare and Special Child | 102 |
| 31: | Kotia and the Bawdy Woman | 107 |
| 47: | The Poet's Skill at Fishing | 148 |
| 48: | Rathgar Gets His Name | 151 |
| 51: | The Laughing Fool of Binduvan | 159 |
| 62: | My Life Has Never Been So Bad | 184 |
| 63: | Mother Seagull and the Ocean | 187 |
| 72: | The Secret of Sima Sen | 211 |

## Punishment

| | | |
|---|---|---|
| 13: | The Saint Who Could Not Be Harmed | 58 |
| 17: | Nilla's Dearest Friend | 71 |
| 29: | What a Rare and Special Child! | 102 |
| 60: | King or Seeker | 180 |
| 62: | My Life Has Never Been So Bad | 184 |

| 75: | Galen's Glimpse of Hell | 220 |
| 78: | Holiest of Holies | 228 |

## Relationships
| 02: | Not Enough Enough | 26 |
| 03: | Where the Animals Went to Die | 29 |
| 14: | What Danila Learned of Love | 61 |
| 19: | The River | 76 |
| 29: | What a Rare and Special Child! | 102 |
| 35: | Gopol Talks to God | 117 |
| 56: | The Eternal Companion | 170 |
| 58: | The Selfishly Generous Woman | 175 |
| 87: | The Compassionate Thing to Do | 255 |

## Self-Awareness
| 04: | The Disciple and the Idiot | 32 |
| 06: | The Doll Maker's Helper | 37 |
| 13: | The Saint Who Could Not Be Harmed | 58 |
| 18: | A Lesson on Believing You're Special | 74 |
| 20: | The Tale of the Chuckling Saint | 79 |
| 22: | The Path Maker | 85 |
| 25: | The Saint Who Loved Science | 92 |
| 31: | Kotia and the Bawdy Woman | 107 |
| 37: | The Greatest Gift | 122 |
| 41: | A Legitimate Profession | 132 |
| 49: | The Counting of the Stars | 154 |
| 55: | A Marriage Made in Heaven | 168 |
| 64: | The Man Who Talked With Trees | 189 |
| 66: | Sinji's One and Only Tale | 196 |
| 70: | The Sweet Old Couple | 206 |
| 72: | The Secret of Sima Sen | 211 |
| 76: | Being Real | 233 |
| 81: | Tandori Had Two Teachers | 236 |

| | | |
|---|---|---|
| 86: | The Artist and the Fisherman | 252 |
| 89: | Some Things Are Just Worth Saving | 260 |
| 91: | A Gift of Laughter | 265 |

## Self-Worth

| | | |
|---|---|---|
| 20: | The Tale of the Chuckling Saint | 79 |
| 29: | What a Rare and Special Child! | 102 |
| 31: | Kotia and the Bawdy Woman | 107 |

## Shame

| | | |
|---|---|---|
| 02: | Not Enough Enough | 26 |
| 03: | Where the Animals Went to Die | 29 |
| 18: | A Lesson on Believing You're Special | 74 |
| 20: | The Tale of the Chuckling Saint | 79 |
| 29: | What a Rare and Special Child! | 102 |
| 31: | Kotia and the Bawdy Woman | 107 |
| 46: | The Passing of the Torch | 145 |
| 55: | A Marriage Made in Heaven | 168 |
| 73: | The Sweet Taste of Vindication | 214 |
| 78: | Holiest of Holies | 228 |
| 82: | The Child Who Could | 239 |
| 85: | The Demon Within | 247 |

## Specialness

| | | |
|---|---|---|
| 02: | Not Enough Enough | 26 |
| 04: | The Disciple and the Idiot | 32 |
| 07: | The Witch of the Darkened Wood | 40 |
| 15: | How the Master Found Enlightenment | 65 |
| 18: | A Lesson on Believing You're Special | 74 |
| 20: | The Tale of the Chuckling Saint | 79 |
| 28: | In the Fire of the Muse | 99 |
| 29: | What a Rare and Special Child! | 102 |
| 31: | Kotia and the Bawdy Woman | 107 |

| | | |
|---|---|---|
| 48: | Rathgar Gets His Name | 151 |
| 59: | The Master's Perfect Imperfection | 178 |
| 78: | Holiest of Holies | 228 |
| 79: | Entering the Hall of Eternal Bliss | 231 |

## Spirituality

| | | |
|---|---|---|
| 25: | The Saint Who Loved Science | 92 |
| 34: | Three Old Women | 114 |
| 35: | Gopol Talks to God | 117 |
| 37: | The Greatest Gift | 122 |
| 60: | King or Seeker | 180 |

## Struggle

| | | |
|---|---|---|
| 01: | The Fool and the Apple | 23 |
| 11: | The Testing of Amit Don | 52 |
| 39: | Sundeep and the Simple Life | 128 |
| 42: | A Tale of Two Villages | 134 |
| 51: | The Laughing Fool of Binduvan | 159 |
| 58: | The Selfishly Generous Woman | 175 |
| 62: | My Life Has Never Been So Bad | 184 |
| 65: | Mukta and the Magic Purse | 192 |
| 67: | A Simple Tale of Hope | 199 |
| 78: | Holiest of Holies | 228 |

## Success

| | | |
|---|---|---|
| 02: | Not Enough Enough | 26 |
| 06: | The Doll Maker's Helper | 37 |
| 08: | Standing Before the Judge | 43 |
| 09: | The Love of Winning | 45 |
| 16: | The Man Who Said, "Thank You" | 68 |
| 36: | The Actor Assumes His Role | 119 |
| 60: | King or Seeker | 180 |
| 78: | Holiest of Holies | 228 |
| 84: | The Woman Who Had Everything | 244 |

## Techniques
| | | |
|---|---|---|
| 10: | Gobi's Tiny Seeds | 48 |
| 36: | The Actor Assumes His Role | 119 |
| 46: | The Passing of the Torch | 145 |
| 73: | The Sweet Taste of Vindication | 214 |
| 80: | The Gathering | 233 |
| 85: | The Demon Within | 247 |
| | Appendix 1: Working With Your Lesser Parts of Self | 271 |
| | Cultivating the Scented Flowers (Spiritual Family) | 16 |

## Vindication and Validation
| | | |
|---|---|---|
| 73: | The Sweet Taste of Vindication | 214 |
| 84: | The Woman Who Had Everything | 244 |

## Wholeness
| | | |
|---|---|---|
| 19: | The River | 76 |
| 26: | The Two Lovers Who Never Met | 95 |
| 27: | The Answer is Always, "Yes" | 97 |
| 37: | The Greatest Gift | 122 |
| 43: | The Captain and the Sea | 137 |
| 52: | The Thousand Coats of Suma Ti | 161 |
| 64: | The Man Who Talked With Trees | 189 |
| 72: | The Secret of Sima Sen | 211 |
| 85: | The Demon Within | 247 |
| 89: | Some Things Are Just Worth Saving | 260 |
| 91: | A Gift of Laughter | 265 |
| | Appendix 1: Working With Your Lesser Parts of Self | 271 |

# Appendix Four

Glossary

**Ancient Ones:** The ancient grandmothers (Crones) and grandfathers (Hermits) of times long past. They're highly evolved and are distinguished by having overcome death. Though they still offer guidance and healing through their counsel and love, they no longer walk among us. Yet, if you call upon them with sincerity, integrity, and maturity, they'll respond.

**Archetypal Energy:** Primal, first cause energy.

**Arrogance:** The belief that you're better or less than others. It's a means some adopt to mask feelings of shame and insignificance.

**Becoming more:** The never-ending, ever-evolving process of growing and expanding to become more of 'who' and 'what' you are.

**Blame:** Placing on oneself or others the source or cause of discomfort as a means to avoid taking responsibility.

**Chauvinism:** Distorted perceptions and beliefs caused by the overpredominance of masculine energy. Masculine energy is not male energy, as feminine energy is not female energy. Chauvinism negatively affects both men and women. Because of chauvinism, men fear feminine energy; women mistrust it. One of its many voices is the devaluation of imagination (feminine energy) and the overreliance on logic and reason (masculine energy). *"Fire's hot. Water's wet. What you see is what you get."*

**The Chauvinist:** One of the dark counselors. It kept you safe by denying or minimizing the power of feminine energy. This distorting energy castrates masculine energy in men and devalues the power of feminine energy in women.

**Coming Home:** An ineffable state of being where we fully realize our goodness, truth, and beauty, and awaken to our oneness with ourselves, our Higher Self, our Soul, and God/Goddess/All That Is.

**Consensus:** The accepted and acceptable views, beliefs, and attitudes held by the vast majority of people.

**Constructive Emotion:** Any emotion, positive or negative, you allow yourself to feel: with positive emotions to feel them fully and to integrate, with negative emotions to feel them fully and to release.

**Control:** The panic-driven need and action to keep love safe.

**Cowardice:** The refusal to tell oneself the truth.

**Crisis:** Chaos that forces compliance and change.

**Dark Counselors:** See Appendix One.

**Denied Dreams and Futures:** The refusal to allow yourself a sense of future, goals, dreams, or visions.

**Destructive Emotions:** Any emotion, positive or negative, you'll not allow yourself to feel.

**The Dominator:** One of the dark counselors. It was born during your youth as a protector to keep you safe from fear. When you felt frightened and out of control, it encouraged more control and domination.

**Dread:** The highest frequency of fear. It's the fear that your very being, your very existence, is in jeopardy.

**Efforting:** The effort you put into challenging, fulfilling, and internally rewarding work and activity. It can leave you gloriously tired.

**Elegance:** The ease and effortless flow in the living of life and the fulfillment of desires. It's an evolving process to a state of action where one does less and accomplishes more, and where over time, one does nothing and accomplishes everything.

**Entitlement:** The erroneous belief you're owed special treatment because of your pains, hurts, and disappointments.

**Fantasias:** Dreams, hopes, desires that are meant to happen.

**Fantasies:** Dreams, hopes, desires that were never meant to happen.

**Free will vs. Determinism:** You have free will and free choice in the direction and pacing of your life. What is determined is that you'll someday remember your promise to Come Home, and you'll choose to keep that promise.

**Gratitude:** A powerful generating energy that elevates one beyond thankfulness and appreciation. Gratitude can lift us to virtuous action and can inspire us to awaken our goodness, truth, and beauty.

**Guilt:** A non-emotion resulting from self-judgment over feeling an emotion you believe you've no right to feel.

**Higher Self:** Between you and your Soul is your Higher Self. As the name says, it's the higher you. You're a part of your Higher Self, and your Higher Self is a part of you. Your Higher Self is not, and never was, physical. It will, however, take on a physical form to interact with you meditatively. It was your Higher Self who created you and all your many lifetimes. Your Higher Self walks with you always as a guide and companion on your journey Coming Home. And your Higher Self always tells you the truth.

**Higher Senses:** The senses beyond the five familiar senses: the sense of voice, presence, movement, light, balance.

**Hope:** An expectation for a desired outcome. Hope inspires inspiration and is a crucial necessity for dreaming and visioning.

**Judgment**: A fear attempt to distance oneself from the object of judgment.

**Lesser Selves:** Your younger less developed, less conscious selves (See Appendix One)

**Magic:** Changing reality in accordance with one's will, preference, and love.

**Manipulation:** The act of and panic-driven need to get others to do what you want.

**Martyr:** One of the dark counselors. They're the silent sufferers who need an audience to witness their melodrama of being unloved, unappreciated, or overworked.

**More Real Selves:** Your higher, more conscious selves; your future selves. (See Appendix One)

**Negative Ego:** That part of yourself that entered with you at birth. Its function was simply to provide information for your interpretation. But time and time again, it was expected to do the interpreting, a task it was doomed to fail. Over time it came to hate you for this, and now it seeks to destroy you. Your negative ego always lies to you.

**Noblization:** Blaming past occurrences for your current actions. "Because I was hurt so badly in the past, I cannot trust anybody now."

**Parts of Self:** Those parts of yourself, past or future, that comprise the totality of you. Though they reside in different times and spaces, they are greatly influenced by your resonance: by your choices and decisions, thoughts and feelings, and beliefs and attitudes. You go nowhere in becoming more without attending to them. You're no more evolved than the least of you. (See Appendix One)

**Passion:** Focused attention.

**Passive Aggression:** Doing things in such a way as to cause others to become angry at you so you can retreat into self-righteousness.

**Principles and Character:** Principles are the fundamental truths that serve as the foundation of your belief and behavior. Character is the choice and the act of living your principles.

**Projections:** Placing onto others your inner images or needs (i.e., projecting father and mother onto other people).

**Psychic Contract:** An unconscious bond that ties one person to another living or dead. For example, because your father struggled his whole life "to make ends meet," out of love and honor, you'll unconsciously not allow success to be easy for you. You'll struggle "to make ends meet." Or, because your father expected you to be successful, and because you hated your father, you won't become successful. These bonds are either forged out of love or forged out of hate. All psychic contracts need to be relinquished or re-written.

**Rage:** The highest frequency of anger. As a natural human emotion, it has opposing values: Enrage (negative) - a fit of deep and intense anger, highly charged, that gnaws at and tears down an individual over time. Outrage (positive) – an expression of anger, highly charged, that can motivate one to change.

**Raw Materials:** Beliefs and attitudes, thoughts and feelings, choices and decisions.

**Resonance:** A quantum wave. All existence, at its essence, functions as a quantum mechanical wave of energy. When two or more waves meet, an independent wave emerges that acts as an attractor. Synergy is an example of wave functioning. A resonance when interacting with other resonances can elevate, lower, or compromise its frequency.

**Retribution:** The erroneous belief in karmic or divine punishment for evil deeds or sins committed, real or imagined.

**Sacred Hallows:** A place of peace, healing, and renewal found in beauty, enchantment, blessed solitude, and love.

**Self-Image:** Who and what you hold yourself to be.

**Self-Pity:** A non-emotion designed to numb a real emotion.

**Shame**: The feeling and belief that you're flawed, defective, broken, or unworthy.

**Specialness:** An ego trap that holds the belief of being better than, or worse than others. It's a form of arrogance.

**Spirituality:** One's personal relationship with that which is more than oneself. This relationship includes your Future Self, your Higher Self, your Soul and Spirit, and God/Goddess/All That Is.

**The Terrorist:** One of the dark counselors. During your youth, you tasked it with halting yourself from stepping too far beyond control. Its function was to 'blow-up' your reality and to instill fear so you won't relax your guard. The terrorism we see in the world is an out-picturing of each person's inner terrorist.

**Tools of Manifestation:** Desire, imagination, and expectancy.

**Trust:** Having confidence, faith, or hope in someone or something. Trust should never be given blindly.

**Validation:** The desperate need to prove you're valid, that you belong.

**Victim:** The vocal sufferer who needs an audience to tell his or her dark story.

**Vindication:** The desperate need to correct the wrongs done to you in the past, real or otherwise.

**Wholeness:** The synergy of all parts of one's self, and their integration into a state of oneness with God/Goddess/All That Is.

**Wise Fool:** An archetypal energy and state of being achieved by very few in their later years. You will find it in those who glow with a mature fire, radiate profound wisdom, and enjoy a life of fullness. They're the 'realized ones.' They know that all life is both an illusion and the play of the Divine. They're the ones foolish enough, and wise enough, to pursue the power of the Unknown.

# About the Author

**Martin Hart** is author of the book, *The Scented Flowers of Sinjin-Ka* (ASAT Press) and co-author, along with Skye Alexander, of the book, *The Best Meditations on the Planet: 100 techniques to Beat Stress, Improve Health, and Create Happiness in Just Minutes a Day* (Fair Winds Press).

Martin is the founder and president of the American Society of Alternative Therapists (ASAT™) and has been in private counseling and alternative health education for more than forty years. Since 1978, Martin has conducted workshops and lectures throughout the United States and internationally on alternative healing and other life-enhancing subjects. He has taught at some of the largest corporations in India, as well as top colleges and research facilities. In the late 1980s, Martin combined a series of remarkably effective modalities with his unique and highly successful counseling approach producing an innovative healing system called *'ASAT™ C.O.R.E. Counseling.'*

*"Through the efficacy of ASAT™ C.O.R.E. Counseling, my students and I have witnessed the lives of thousands of our clients' blossom and grow in remarkable ways. They're crafting exceptional lives that are fun, empowering, and magical. Where struggle and conflict once existed, adventure and elegance now thrive and flourish. And all this happens for them in a remarkably short time. Our clients report being happier, healthier, more successful, more productive, and their lives are magically flowing with remarkable synchronicities."*

As a result of the success of his approach, Martin started training ASAT™ C.O.R.E. Counselors in 1990 to meet the growing number of people seeking this road to greater self-awareness and healing. His training courses are conducted through both home-study and live session formats. There are now more than 1,700 certified ASAT™ C.O.R.E. Counselors world-wide.

Martin still travels the United States and internationally conducting his training courses as well as related lectures and workshops. His classes and seminars have been featured in the Wall Street Journal, The Boston Globe, The London Sunday Telegraph, and other publications. He has also appeared on popular national and international talk radio programs discussing his unique work.

To contact him for more information regarding his courses and workshops, visit ASAT's website at www.asat.org.